Alone in a Crowd

Women in the Trades Tell Their Stories

In the series
Women in the Political Economy,
edited by Ronnie J. Steinberg

Jean Reith Schroedel

Alone in a Crowd

Women in the Trades Tell Their Stories

Temple University Press   Philadelphia

Temple University Press, Philadelphia 19122
© 1985 by Temple University. All rights reserved
Published 1985
Printed in the United States of America

Library of Congress Cataloging in Publication Data

Schroedel, Jean Reith.

Alone in a crowd.

(Women in the political economy)

Includes index.

1. Sex discrimination in employment—Washington (State)
—Seattle Region—Case studies. 2. Sex discrimination
against women—Washington (State)—Seattle Region—Case
studies. I. Title. II. Series.

HD6060.5.U52S437   1985   331.4′133′09797   84-16159
ISBN 0-87722-378-5

To my parents,
Genevieve and Robert Schroedel

Contents

CONTENTS

Preface

At eleven, I decided to become a paper boy. They made two cents for every newspaper they delivered, and I was making only thirty-five cents an hour babysitting. No wonder the boys could afford shiny headlights for their three-speed bicycles. I was stuck with fat balloon tires on my baby one-speed bike without a headlight. My path was clear until someone told me, "I'm sorry. We have a policy that girls cannot become paper boys."

At seventeen, I became one of the first female boxboys in the state. The pay beat waiting tables or the old standby, babysitting. With great pride I dressed in my dark shoes, black slacks, white shirt, black bow tie, and red vest—the company uniform for "courtesy clerks," as we were called. That first day of work I discovered one of the economic realities of life. The employer will pit worker against worker if he can get away with it. All of the male boxboys had been called to a meeting the day before and informed that, if they didn't work harder, they would all be replaced by girls. Needless to say, my welcome to the grocery business was less than pleasant.

At twenty-three, I decided I had to find a job that paid better than sewing cuffs on ski parkas in a garment plant or typing forms for an insurance company. The help-wanted section of the newspaper was full of ads for machinists at twice the pay I was making. With no idea about what a machinist did, I enrolled in machine-shop classes at the local vocational-technical school. Being the first woman in the program, I discovered only one bathroom in the shop and it was marked MEN. "No, you cannot tack a sign saying WOMEN on the door when you need to go," I was told. I either had to hold it or find another bathroom.

After a year of holding it, having my tools stolen, and learning the intricacies of chip-control and backmilling, I was ready to practice the trade. But all that those straight As in trade school got me was "Sorry, we don't hire girls," or "Sure, I love to hire girls for sweeping floors." I had applied at over seventy firms before being hired as an apprentice at a local truck manufacturer. After completing my apprenticeship, I moved on to practice my trade at an aerospace subcontractor, but was fired from that job for union organizing. I then returned to the University of Washington on a union scholarship.

I found it impossible, though, to leave the factory behind. In English classes I wrote essays about blue-collar workers and demanded to know where the working-class women were in literature. In political science classes I wrote essays like "The Implications of a Declining Trade Union Movement on Democracy in America." I sat through economics classes where questions of cost-benefit analysis and economic efficiency were thinly veiled attacks on workplace safety and the minimum wage. The graphs and charts could not hide the images of my friends with chopped-off fingers and crushed vertabrae.

Finally one of my professors, Alex Gottfried, became curious and asked me about my background. In May 1981, after two hours of my stories about life on the assembly line, he told me that someone should write the stories of women in nontraditional blue-collar work. I laughed and told him that nobody gave a damn about people like us. Three days later I decided to collect those stories.

Objectively, I knew writing a book was a totally crazy thing for me to commit myself to doing. Here I was, a twenty-nine-year-old single parent trying to get a college education while working a part-time shit job to keep food on the table. I knew absolutely nothing about writing a book, much less about getting one published. But I am a very stubborn person and once I make up my mind to do something, that's all there is to it. I would do things one step at a time.

Preface

The first thing I did was tell a lot of people about my decision. That way, even if I lost my nerve, I'd be afraid to back out for fear of losing face. Then I began reading collections of oral histories to get some sense of how they were done. After deciding I had learned enough to keep from embarrassing myself, I met with Ginny NiCarthy, who was completing work on a collection of oral histories about battered women. NiCarthy spent two afternoons patiently explaining the nuts and bolts of being an oral historian—from the wording of publication releases, to asking probing questions without being offensive. "Don't just ask people what happened in their lives, ask how it made them feel."

Keeping NiCarthy's advice in mind, I then turned my attention to the interview questions. I wanted them to serve both as a way to get the women talking and as a guide to provide a unifying structure for all the interviews. The initial questions were fairly straightforward, dealing with the individual's background and motivations for entering a trade. With these questions I hoped to discover if there was any specific type of woman, say a tomboy for example, who was most attracted to non-traditional blue-collar work. (There wasn't.) The next group of questions was designed to find out about the woman's on-the-job experiences—training, finding a job, physical surroundings, using tools, health hazards, unions, socializing with co-workers, discrimination, and so forth. The final series of questions dealt with some of the more complex emotional issues of how non-traditional work affected the woman's family and self-perceptions.

Once these preparations were completed, I took on the task of finding a cross section of women performing non-traditional work. I shamelessly exploited every contact I had ever made. Friends, acquaintances, union officials, and co-workers were all used as means of meeting women.

I jokingly referred to the time when I was interviewing as my "have tape recorder, will travel" period. I went to whatever place the women preferred for the interviews—homes, restaurants, parks, and even once to a sailboat. Even though the entire two- to five-hour conversations were being recorded, most of the women forgot about the machine after a few minutes and were quite candid in discussing their lives. In some instances, I had to edit out highly personal sections.

After transcribing the tapes, my questions were edited out and portions of each interview were woven together into a unified story. What essentially remains is the woman telling her life story in her own voice. I only had to add a few phrases to ease transition between parts. I tried to keep this interference to an absolute minimum because I believe the women are far more eloquent than I could ever be.

To further ensure accuracy, every edited story was sent to the woman interviewed for her approval. She was also given a choice as to whether she wanted her own name or a pseudonym used. In most cases, the woman chose to use her own name. In the seven cases where another name was chosen, the woman felt that either her job or her personal life would be jeopardized if her identity were known. I think those concerns deserve our respect.

The twenty-five women whose stories appear in this collection are a remarkably diverse group. They are employed in some of the Pacific Northwest's most important industries, such as aerospace, shipbuilding, maritime, and forestry; no two are in the same trade. They range in ages from twenty-four to sixty-nine. They are white, black, Asian, Chicana, and native American. They are straight and gay, married and single, and divorced. Some are parents and some are not. For some, being successful in a trade means upward social mobility from minimum-wage jobs and welfare. For others, it was seen as moving down the social scale from a profession. In short, these women are very much like other women, except for the way they choose to earn a living.

Preface

They all come from the Seattle area, but that does not negate the importance of their experiences to people living elsewhere. As several of the women commented, Seattle provides, if anything, a more favorable climate for women entering non-traditional work than many other parts of the country. In general, the Pacific Northwest has a liberal, open social climate with few constraints on personal behavior. In the early 1970s, women's access to the trades was facilitated by Mechanica, an employment referral service specializing in placing women in non-traditional blue-collar work. Later, some of these functions were taken over by the YWCA and the city's Office of Women's Rights. Emotional support and practical advice can be obtained through Women in Trades, a group organized by and for women working in traditional male blue-collar jobs. In addition, both the city and county have affirmative action guidelines for the employment of women on construction projects and in permanent trade positions. Yet I do not mean to imply that craftswomen in Seattle have an easy time of it. Knowing the difficulties encountered by women in this comparatively supportive region, I can only shudder and wonder, "Oh my God, how do women in the rest of the country survive?"

The purpose of this book is threefold. The first function is to help bridge the isolation experienced by women in non-traditional work; often they have almost no contact with each other. This isolation can lead to self-doubts, especially when male co-workers and families are not supportive. I want to let these women know that they are not alone out there. Second, I want to create a real picture for women considering non-traditional blue-collar occupations. Neither horror stories nor romanticism creates an accurate image of this kind of work. Finally, I want to help overcome what my favorite writer, Tillie Olsen, calls "women's silences of centuries." Accounts of women's lives, in particular working-class women's lives, have not been viewed as worth recording. I believe the opposite is true, the thoughts and feelings of these women are of the utmost importance to all of us; everyone can learn from the courage of these women, leavened with human frailty.

This book is organized into five sections: Feminism, Occupational Safety and Health, Race, Unions, and Family. The placement of stories into the different sections is somewhat arbitrary. Each of the selections is far too rich in themes to fit neatly within any single category. I did, however, try to organize them according to themes which they especially emphasized. The stories in the Feminism section explore the complex, often ambiguous relationship that women working in non-traditional blue-collar work have with the contemporary women's movement. In the section on Safety and Health, the physical toll this work has taken on many is starkly contrasted with the sense of being supremely fit. The stories in the Race section chronicle what it is like, both as a woman and a member of a racial minority, to be discriminated against. In the Union section, the women talk about how unions can be either a vehicle for bettering their lives or just another male-dominated organization. It is a truism of modern life that the family is undergoing great change, and the stories in the Family section capture what happens to those already transitional families when the woman ventures out into the male world of blue-collar work.

There are two other common themes that appear frequently: the emotional devastation experienced by some is contrasted to the confidence gained by others; the frequently expressed discovery that men's familiarity, ease, and comfort with tools is a great advantage they begin acquiring as toddlers. Probably the most positive theme is the belief that for the first time in their lives, the women *can* provide for themselves and their families.

The sense of alienation felt by all the women in this collection was so great that it provided one of the main purposes for gathering these stories, and ultimately gave rise to the title of this book. Finally, there is one theme which is so universal, so pervasive, that it cuts across all accounts and could not be isolated into one specific section. That is the theme of sex discrimination in its multitude of forms. Supervisors, co-workers, families, and the woman's own individual response all play a part in lessening or increasing the discrimination.

One last note—while writing this book, I supported myself by doing non-traditional work, bus driving.

Acknowledgments

I wish to thank the many people who liberally gave their assistance over the last three years. I owe a great debt to Alex Gottfried, Sydney Kaplan, and Carolynn Allen of the University of Washington for behaving like it was the most natural thing in the world for an undergraduate to write a book. That support gave me the self-confidence necessary to tackle this project. In a like manner, M.I.T. professors Suzanne Berger and Deborah Stone encouraged me to continue the effort while in graduate school. Ginny NiCarthy's practical how-to-do-it advice helped me bridge the gap between reading about oral histories and actually collecting them. Christine Suksdorf, Dee Clapp, Donna Burgess, and Caroline Clarke have been marvelous about transcribing tapes, a truly onerous task. At this point, I must single out Trucia Tureman for special thanks. Trucia has been an integral part of this project from the very beginning— part-time typist, editor, critic, sounding board, and full-time friend. Sometimes I feel this book bears as much of her imprint as mine.

Finally, last but obviously not least, are the women who have generously shared their lives with us. Thank you.

Alone in a Crowd

Women in the Trades Tell Their Stories

Feminism

The struggle by women for equality in employment is deeply bound up with their achievement of political equality. The periods when women were accorded the greatest citizenship rights were also the periods when women had the most employment opportunities. Surprisingly for those of us who think women's rights are a relatively new phenomena, immigrant women during the colonial period had the same rights as men to own land, enter occupations, marry whomever they wished, and vote if they met the property qualifications. This egalitarianism has been attributed to the short supply of women and labor in general during those years. None of these rights applied to indentured servants and slaves, who were considered less than full citizens.

The theory of the British legal scholar Blackstone, that husband and wife are one person and that the woman has no legal existence whatsoever, gained credence on this side of the Atlantic during the Revolutionary War period. By the time the Constitution was ratified in 1788, women had been denied the franchise in Georgia, South Carolina, Pennsylvania, and Delaware. Within twenty years only white men could vote in any part of the United States. Women were also beginning to be excluded from professions, such as law and medicine, which they had previously practiced. This trend culminated in an 1873 Supreme Court decision upholding the right of a state to exclude women from the legal profession because "the natural and proper timidity and delicacy which belongs to the female sex evidently unfits it for many of the occupations of civil life."*

But factory work, which we currently think of as an almost entirely male enclave, was viewed as a proper domain for these same delicate women. In fact, surplus female farm labor provided most of the workforce in the first American factories, namely the New England textile mills. At the same time, however, it had become a mark of status for a man to have enough wealth to maintain a wife who conformed to the Victorian model of femininity. Working-class and slave women continued to labor up to sixteen hours a day in factories or on plantations while middle- and upper-class women either led lives of enforced idleness in the home or were restricted to the role of supervising servants. Many of the later tensions in the women's movement can be traced back to this fundamental division between lower- and upper-class women.

There have been two important waves of the women's liberation movement in this country. The first, with its roots in the abolition and temperance movements, can claim the Married Women's Property Acts of the 1860s as its first success. These acts once again gave women a legal status. Middle- and upper-class women then turned their attention to gaining the vote, while working-class women were left to struggle for labor rights. When the Nineteenth Amendment, granting women suffrage, was passed in 1920, the women's movement died out as an organized political force.

The next major change in women's status occurred during World War II, another period of labor scarcity, when the number of women workers increased 57 percent. Women employed in heavy industry rose from 340,000 to over two million during the course of the war. This need for labor changed the way women viewed their role in life. In 1942, 20 percent of

*Beadwell v. Illinois, 83 U.S. (16 Wall) 130121 L. Ed 442 (1873).

the women working in industry wanted to continued working after the war. In 1945, that figure rose to 80 percent. At the end of the war, however, 2,800 out of 3,102 child-care centers closed when federal funds were withdrawn. This, coupled with a massive number of women workers being fired, left blue-collar work firmly in male hands again.

The second wave of the women's liberation movement began in the early 1960s. The women activists of this period honed many of their political skills in the civil rights and anti-Vietnam War movements. But a major boost to the women's liberation movement was provided by the passage of the Civil Rights Act of 1964, which made sex and race discrimination illegal. It is one of history's little ironies that sex discrimination was included in this landmark law. Southern segregationists, in an attempt to halt the law's passage, added sex discrimination to the bill thinking that Northern liberals can tolerate race equality, but absolutely no one favored equality between the sexes. Thanks to this political miscalculation, women were included in this major anti-discrimination law. Without this and subsequent laws, affirmative action, which allowed women to gain entry into non-traditional blue-collar work, would never have come into existence, and few of the women who tell their stories here could have obtained these jobs.

A few of the women in this book, such as Mary Rathke, explicitly give credit to affirmative action for their jobs. Teresa Selfe talks about the importance of women's groups in making non-traditional work accessible to women. Laura Pfandler and Geraldine Walker, in very different ways, strive to make sure women following them have it a bit easier, and Elaine Canfield is reaping the benefits of the pathbreakers in her field, carpentry.

Other women have much more mixed feelings about feminism. For these women there is a tenuous relationship between their struggle for lives of dignity and any organized women's

movement. Feminism for them is associated with media carica-
tures and pampered upper-class women, not with the lives of
women like them. They might complain about discrimination
they personally feel, but blame other women for the difficulties
they experience. Provocative clothing, female laziness, and the
ERA are blamed for their problems. The women are also of two
minds about traditional and non-traditional women's roles.
Nora Quealey speaks for many when she expressed a preference
for traditional women's work, but finds the pay too low.
Although Irene Hull's political affiliations are atypical, her belief that feminism harms both working men and women is very
common.

But the truth of the matter is that these women are part of the
women's movement—a struggle for a decent living and better
working conditions for all women. What else can we call Irene
Hull's battle to preserve a child-care center for working women
after the Second World War? Or how about Laura Sarvis, who
opposes the ERA? Her anger at the discriminatory treatment of
women workers led her to lead a union drive. Or Nora Quealey's
plea for assembly line workers to be treated as human beings,
rather than animals? In many ways, the women like Irene Hull,
Laura Sarvis, and Nora Quealey represent the women's movement's greatest challenge and hope—challenge in how to win
them over to feminism, and hope because they are women of
boundless strength and courage.

Steel Hauler

MARY RATHKE

She appeared far too young to have seventeen- and fifteen-year-old sons. An unexpected pregnancy at thirty-seven led to a leave from her job hauling steel.

My mom wanted me to go into the medical profession some-how, as a nurse or as a technician in the lab. And that's what I started out to do when I went to Seattle University. But I wasn't interested in physiology, biology, all that stuff. I could do it, but you know, I wasn't that interested in it. I was doing what my *mother* wanted me to do, not what *I* wanted to do. In nineteen sixty-three I dropped out of school. I didn't have any money so I had to work full time for a while. I went to work at a big insurance company and, believe me, working with an office full of women is the most God-awful way to spend eight hours, especially if it's a closed office, like if you don't have the public as a buffer. Women are so bitchy, they're cliquey; they go on and on and on about who's got the most paper clips—it's disgusting. I have never worked in such a horrible situation in all my life, and I never will again, I don't think. After nine months my attendance record got so bad, they called me into the personnel office and said, "You seem to be having a problem."

And I said, "Yes, yes, I'll come on time. I'll be here every day—blah, blah, blah." I finally had to quit the job. It was futile.

Then I met the man of my dreams and got married and had a couple of babies. I did some part-time waitressing work and went back to work full time in nineteen sixty-seven. That was at one of the libraries at the U. I liked working at the library because I like books. Once in a while you did get into the office baloney, but mostly you didn't because there was the public to deal with. They take your mind off the baloney. Then I stayed home for a year or two before going to work in the pre-school my youngest son attended. I liked the kids. I can get into their fantasy games, play with them real easily.

Eventually I got a full-time job with the county library. It must have been seventy-two because both of my kids were in school. I started out as a shipping clerk for minimum wage and worked my way up to the supervisor of the shipping department at the Service Center. The Center provided all the books and stuff for all the branches—Bothell, Burien, Bellevue, all of them. I had eleven people working for me and made a fat three dollars and fifty cents an hour. All the headaches that go with a supervisory position. I discovered after six months that I'm no good at telling people what to do. I can't do it. I'd come home with a stomach ache. Meanwhile, I was sick of working for peanuts, you know, just nothing. And my husband said one day that he saw a girl driving a cement truck, the first one in Seattle. Shoot, I had been driving relief for the library when I had to. So he said, "If you're going to drive a truck and fool around, why don't you drive a big one and make some decent money, like that girl is doing?" This was in nineteen seventy-four and I made the connection in my head; this was when equal rights was beginning to be talked about, and I knew that people with federal contracts had to start hiring minorities. The blacks were beginning to yell a lot about not being hired to work on the Kingdome [Seattle's domed stadium]. With all the federal money on this project, they were discriminating still. And the same was true of women.

So I went down to a sand and gravel company that I knew had the Kingdome contract and also Freeway Park. That's two federally funded things, and I knew they needed a woman. So I walked in and said, "I'd like to learn to drive."

Mary Rathke, steel hauler

They said, "Yeah, fine, on your own time." So I took a week's vacation from the library and they taught me to drive. I was real nervous that first week while getting taught. They told me that one of the hardest things to convince me of was that I had to keep the throttle, the accelerator, down all the time. I didn't understand that with a truck, once you've got the momentum going, you don't lose it, no matter what. You keep the pedal on the floor the whole time. And I was trying to drive it like a car where you can back off the throttle. They had the hardest time convincing me of that.

I learned on a five-and-four conventional transmission, which means you've got two sticks. It's a bit more complicated than a thirteen-speed; that's real easy to shift. There, you don't have to deal with two sticks and double clutch all of the time. Maybe I had better start over with the basics. On a conventional truck there are two transmissions, a main one and an auxiliary one right behind it. In the main transmission you've got five forward gears and in the little auxiliary you've got another four. I wasn't understanding that at all. The guys would say, "Now you need to be in second-over," or "second-under," or "second-direct," and I would do it, but not understand what was going on.

Finally, what made it click was he said, "Now you need to be in second overdrive." Overdrive! Overdrive! Now I understand what this extra box is about! It was a half-gear under third gear, or a half-gear over, or straight third gear. It just clicked when he said that. So you have a second stick for each transmission. The way it works is you don't start out in first gear. That's too low. You start out in second gear and under, then you go to direct, and then you go to over—all on the auxiliary transmission. Then you shift the main box to third, then under, direct, and over in the auxiliary again. I spent four days learning this and on the fifth day they sent me out by myself. I worked for pay that day and made sixty bucks. It would take me a week at the library to make the same money. So why was I fooling around at the library? I mulled this over in my mind for a couple months, quit my job, and told the sand and gravel outfit to put me on their call list.

They needed *me* as a minority, so I worked maybe one or two days a week all winter. Still, in a month I brought home more than I did working full time at the library. Plus, when I wasn't working I could pick up unemployment. And then in the spring and summer—it's seasonal work, you know—things really picked up. I got a lot of hours in.

The dispatcher was a real chauvinist and made suggestive remarks all the time. Once in awhile I felt like I had to sort of play along with him. Otherwise he wasn't going to call me into work. Since I wasn't on the seniority list, he didn't have to call me if he didn't feel like it. I didn't get involved with him or anything, but I couldn't just say, "Knock it off, you idiot." I felt like it sometimes. But I found, like for me, you have to walk on a fence, you have to be willing to put up with a certain amount of teasing and carrying on, and joking. You can't just be straight-arrow rigid. You gotta be willing to be teased, to flirt back. You gotta be willing to just get along. You can't be offended by it. Here you are, the only woman in this man's world, and you'd better get along or get out. But that didn't mean to me that I had to go to bed with anybody or risk my marriage or anything like that.

In general I was treated a lot nicer than the guys were, because I got sent to the easy jobs a lot. Part of that was due to the quota thing. I got to go to the Kingdome and Freeway Park, which were easy jobs because you deliver to a pump and aren't fooling around in somebody's muddy back yard. I actually saw a federal chart for the Kingdome pour with the date, how many loads of concrete were delivered, the names of the drivers, and the races, so I know that one of the reasons I got easy jobs was to satisfy government quotas.

Mary Rathke, steel hauler

I did get thrown off one job because the contractor didn't want a woman. I could see he thought I was going to be incapable the moment I got to the site. Most contractors are real patient, explaining exactly what they want. Not this guy! He was short and didn't explain what he wanted, and then started hollering and screaming and swearing at me. I just got more and more upset and nervous about the pour. Then the dispatcher called me on the radio and said, "How come you got thrown off the job?"

I said, "What?" Then he told me the contractor had called him, wanting me off the site. And I said, "Thank God for small favors." The thing about concrete drivers is all the other drivers can hear all this baloney going on. They're sitting in their trucks waiting for a load and listening to this on the radio. They told me later they all laughed. It was funny. You should be upset getting thrown off a job, but I was glad.

Another time I ruined an entire load of concrete. It was probably the worst day I had on that job. It was the first winter I worked, and it had gotten icy and was freezing out. The water tanks on the truck have to be drained at night or they'll freeze. Well, I didn't know that. There's a valve that you open to drain the water tank so the water goes into the drum where the cement is. So I got this load to take to the Kingdome, and it turned out this valve had been opened the night before, and I didn't know how to check it. By the time I got to the Kingdome I was spilling concrete out the back of the truck and it was all watery. I called the dispatcher up to see what kind of awful mix he had given me. It dawned on the dispatcher what had happened and that I should bring it back. It was so embarrassing!

Cement-truck drivers are members of Teamsters Local 174. In the sand and gravel division of the Teamsters Union, at that time, if you worked four hundred hours in six months, the company had to give you seniority. Well, they would work me three hundred and eighty hours and send me down the road to another company, so they wouldn't have to put me on the seniority list. So I'd go work for the second company for the next six months until I had too many hours, and they would send me back to the first one, right?—so they didn't have to put me on the seniority list. The *third* time that happened to me I lost my temper, and I stomped upstairs and I said to the boss, "You either want to have me work for you or you don't. I'm either a good employee or I'm not. I want you to stop doing this. I've been hanging around for almost two years. Are you going to put me on the seniority list or not?" And he was really mad at my attitude, because I don't usually say anything until I'm in a rage, I can't control it any longer. So I lost it and he got really mad at me and said, "We'll see, blah, blah, blah." The company did have to pay vacation hours, and I thought with my vacation hours I was going to have enough to get over the four hundred hours required for seniority. So I went in and demanded my vacation pay and thought I would be on their list, whether they liked it or not. Right? Well, they had two plants. One's in Tacoma and I had worked in the Tacoma plant and hadn't counted on those hours not counting towards my seniority. So when they gave me my vacation pay and added up my hours, I came up a half an hour short. So that was my big coup, and I didn't pull it off. So by that time they were so mad at me that they never wanted to see my face again. So I said, "Fine, I never want to see your face again either." After that I couldn't get on at any of the cement companies because I didn't cooperate. The fact that I had cooperated for a year and a half didn't matter.

So I went down to Mechanica, a job placement service for women doing non-traditional work, and got referred to a steel manufacturer. That was in April of seventy-seven. I got through the interview and then got sent out on a road test with a mechanic to see if I could drive or not. So what they were going to have me drive was a semi, you know, that pulls a forty-foot trailer. I'd never done that. I'd just driven concrete trucks. The

Mary Rathke, steel hauler

truck they had me drive was completely different from anything I'd ever touched. It had a Detroit engine, which is a lot different from a Mack, and had a Road Ranger transmission. A Road Ranger transmission is almost like an automatic. It's just one stick with a button on it. And a Detroit engine, as opposed to a Cummins engine, operates in a much smaller r.p.m. range. You've only got two or three hundred r.p.m.'s in which to move. With a Cummins it is six or seven hundred. You've got a long way to go before you have to shift again. In a Detroit, you just have to keep it all together. You can't be so loose. First, they tested me with just the tractor, and then I had to do it with the trailer hooked up. Going ahead wasn't bad, but backing up was something else. I knew I had to do everything exactly opposite with the trailer, but I had all these patterns from backing up with the concrete trucks. Anyway, I survived the trailer test, and they said to come to work on the next Monday. So I started there, not knowing anything about driving this equipment, without any training and I just had to teach myself, which is what I did. I faked it when I had to, and the rest of the time hoped nobody was looking. I was their first woman driver so it was all real new for them.

They have two plants. At the one in Kent, which is where the big furnaces are, they melt the scrap down into steel, and in Ballard they roll the steel into rebar [steel reinforcing for construction]. The core of the driving job is hauling the steel from Kent to Ballard. It was a forty-five-minute trip. I could do four loads a day. Loading and unloading is done with an electro-magnetic crane. There are crane operators, but you have to land the steel on the bed of the truck and chain it down. The thing that dawned on me was that construction was a whole new world. One of the real glaring differences was that men help each other and cooperate. Without saying words, like "Let's lift this thing," they automatically do it. Women don't operate that way. I have never seen women in an office operate like that.

Men automatically work together. I don't know if they've been taught that from childhood or what, but they do. The other thing that dawned on me was that the bigger the job you have to do, the less physically demanding it is, because you have equipment to do it for you. You don't depend on your own muscles. Now if you're hauling twenty-five-pound parcels around all day, you're going to be more tired than if you're hauling five-thousand-pound ingots of steel 'cause the equipment does the lifting for you. So what you want to do is get into a big job where they're working with big stuff—I'm not kidding you—'cause then you're relying on equipment and not your back.

When I wasn't hauling steel between the two plants, I was hauling it to construction sites. In a lot of ways that is easier than hauling cement to the same sites, because concrete can't wait. Steel can wait all day if it has to. So you sit and read, have pop or whatever, while you're waiting. On the big jobs there are ironworkers to unload the stuff for you so all you have to do is take the cables and binders off, and then the ironworkers hook the steel up and get it off. I've delivered steel all over the state. For a while we were delivering to the Chief Joseph Dam. Leave the plant at three o'clock in the morning, get to the dam about nine or nine-thirty, and get back at around three-thirty or four o'clock in the afternoon. Those were fourteen-hour days, real hard days.

Most of the time I really love my job. You're given a job to do and you're expected to go do it, and I like that. One of the neatest things is to have a song that I like come on the radio in my truck, and it's a sunny day, I'm way up high, traffic is fine, no hassles, and I haven't got a load to be nervous about and check all of the time. That is the greatest feeling in the world—the music, the sun, and wheeling along the freeway. I really love it. I like being on the road where you haven't got somebody looking over your shoulder, bitching all the time.

Mary Rathke, steel hauler

Sometimes driving's a little scary. Mostly I'm pretty cautious. If I've got a real shaky-looking load, usually I'll say, "I don't like the looks of this load, and if part comes off on the highway, you buy the ticket 'cause I'm telling you right now I don't like the way it looks." Our contract says if something looks unsafe, you can say, "I'm not going to drive it." But sometimes you have to just go, and you cross your fingers and hope that you don't lose it. There have been some real scary times when I've driven up and down the road crying because I've been so scared.

One time a guy got hurt and I cried all the rest of the day. I was going to park the truck and go home, but my boss wouldn't let me. He did the right thing, because if I had parked it, I never would have gotten back on a truck again. I didn't run over anybody, but at a job site a guy walked under a chute I was lowering, hit his head, and cut his forehead open pretty good. They had to send him to the hospital. I take that kind of stuff seriously. And driving in the snow. Sometimes when you've lost it, when the trailer starts coming around on you, that's frightening. Then you wonder, "Why couldn't you be satisfied with staying in your kitchen? What are you doing in the middle of a snowstorm?" But then there are the sunny days with the radio, and it all balances out.

I'm not working right now. I took a six-month maternity leave, and when I was supposed to go back, the Steelworkers were on strike, and at that point drivers weren't crossing the picket line. Since then the Teamsters have decided to go back, but I haven't been called back. I'm glad I haven't been involved. The strikers were throwing rocks and things. One guy got his face cut and they had to have the cops down there for a few days. I guess they still do. I'm glad I'm not there. I don't know why we're crossing the picket line. The Teamsters usually have honored the strikes of the Steelworkers. I don't think the reverse would be true 'cause there's only half a dozen drivers. There are over a hundred and fifty steelworkers, and that's a lot of people to be out over six people's rights.

I heard the company used scabs to drive the trucks at first, and they don't seem to be making any effort to settle with the Steelworkers, so maybe they don't want to deal with unions any more. I don't know. The drivers' position is real weak. The two senior drivers are in their late fifties and don't want to switch jobs. And since there's so few of us, we don't have the power to do anything. If we're offered anything reasonable, we'll go for it. And the Teamsters in the past have always encouraged settlement. They haven't backed strikes at all.

Anyhow, like I was saying, I got pregnant and that really changed things. I lost my temper a few times. Mostly it was chemical and hormonal more than anything else, but I was a whole lot harder to get along with. I was really feeling sorry for myself and throwing temper tantrums right and left. I used my pregnancy to vent my emotions. My attitude got to be, "I don't give a damn! I'm a person, too; I can get mad"—that was my attitude while pregnant.

One job we do requires putting rain tarps on the truck. Now a rain tarp for a forty-foot trailer weighs about one hundred pounds, and we had to have two of them, one for the front half and one for the back half of the trailer. That's probably our crummiest job. It's a bitch, and you have to do it in the rain. You get soaking wet; it's heavy work, and you come home beat. Anyway, it was wintertime and I had just discovered I was pregnant, and I was already four months along and feeling very sorry for myself, when my boss sent me out on that job. And I stomped upstairs, up to the big boss, and I said, "Well, I'm not doing that job anymore, blah, blah, blah, because I'm pregnant. And if I lose this baby it's gonna be your fault!" You know, on and on about it, and he was real nice about it, you know. I'm sure

Mary Rathke, steel hauler

that after I walked out, he was just shakin' his head like I'm some kind of crazy lady.

If I continue that way, I'm sure they'll fire me. The thing of it was that I was so angry all of the time. My husband was unemployed, and I felt so sorry for myself because I had to do this very, very hard job in my condition. I took it out on the guys at work and they were real good about it. They should have told me a long time ago, "Stuff it, Mary. We don't want to hear it."

But they didn't. In fact, they practiced reverse discrimination and put me on an easier job than I had been doing. They didn't create the job for me. Hauling scrap, which is a bit easier, had to be done anyway. And nobody got bent out of shape about my doing it steadily. The guy I bumped from the job didn't care. They're all nice guys, real understanding. They did tease me about working so far into my pregnancy. I worked up until six weeks before delivery, and towards the end I was getting really big. I was really tired all of the time, my mood was really crummy, and I was getting to be a drag to be around. The guys kept asking me when I was going to quit, and when I finally did come in and say, "Two weeks from now is my last day," you know, my boss said, "God, I thought you were never gonna go!" Everybody had that reaction. "Jeez, we thought you were gonna go on forever!" In fact they were making jokes that "pretty soon we'll have to deliver it here. In the sleeper, no less—jokes like that. And I didn't know that was the attitude until I let people know that my last day was coming up.

Okay, I had intended to be working until I was vested in the union. I think that'll take another three or four years. With ten years you get retirement, not full retirement, but something. This baby has thrown a monkey wrench into the works. I don't like the idea of working full time with a baby, so I don't know what I'm going to do. Maybe I'll open a day-care center. I've been looking for day care for him and what's available is just pathetic.

There's a need for good day care and that's the other thing I like to do—take care of kids. I don't know why those two things are attractive to me—taking care of kids and driving truck. I could do day care for a few years and then go back to driving truck if I haven't fallen apart by that time. I'll be pretty old. I always thought that once I approached forty, I'd look pretty ridiculous in a semi. But the closer I get to forty, the more I think I'll change that to fifty.

Pipefitter

LAURA PFANDLER

A former school teacher, she took on the task of educating her fellow pipefitters on how their language was degrading to women. It has not been an easy endeavor.

My parents thought I would make a good teacher. They kinda did that to all of their children. They picked out a career for everyone. There were three older girls and they had definite careers for all of us, and each one of us did these careers.

I got a master's in elementary education and taught kindergarten through sixth grade in an alternative school. It was a private non-accredited school in eastern Washington. The public school system over there wasn't the best, so parents who were unhappy with the school system put together their own school in nineteen seventy-six. The only thing I really loved was working with the children, the relationship between you and the children. What I disliked was the pay, which was eighty dollars a month and room, and having to deal with the parents. Parents are real difficult to deal with. It was hard making ends meet. There were some breaks. People did bring money and food, but I don't think I bought a stitch of clothing for the two years I was there.

When I left the school I thought it was just for the summer. I was gonna go to Seattle and make some money before I came back. I knew I didn't want a teaching job. I needed a rest and ended up at this women's employment service which is no longer in existence. Turned out the gas company was hiring, and

19

all it took was one call. I started out at five dollars and six cents an hour as a helper. Now, two years later, as a fitter I earn ten twenty-two.

I had a lot of fears about being a woman with so many men. The scariest thing was the sense of being alone. It was real obvious to me, like the first or second day that I was there, that the men weren't overjoyed about my being there. Their general attitude was that women are hired by the gas company, but aren't worked. They were surprised to find that I was really willing to do the work. For a while I was in the tool room and then I was put out on the street. The men just pretty much ignored me until I started talking up. I started telling them I didn't like the way they referred to women as bitches and cunts. That led to me getting the nickname of Hothead. It meant they couldn't tease me in that way and that I'd call them on a lot of their shit.

As a helper you don't have a whole lot of power, but some things have to be dealt with. I used to try and explain how abusive dirty magazines were to women. Finally one day we were workin' out in the middle of Rainier Avenue and this young man, who had been hassling me ever since I started, was standing around with the other guys looking at a dirty magazine. I think it might have been *Playboy* because it had a center foldout. They were all giggling and brought it over to me. I said, "I've had enough of this shit," and pulled the centerfold out of the magazine and burnt it up with a cigarette lighter. That kind of stopped them, and as new people would come in they would get the story, so I didn't have to deal with a lot of that afterwards.

For a long time I wasn't allowed to do certain types of jobs. I had to fight for that. Some of the men would take the tools out of my hands. You see it is just very hard for them to work with me because they're really into proving their masculinity and being tough. And when a woman comes on a job that can work, get something done as fast and efficiently, as well, as they can, it

Laura Pfandler, pipefitter

really affects them. Somehow if a woman can do it, it ain't that masculine, not that tough.

There was a long time when all they would allow me to do was dig. That's not good because when you're a helper you're supposed to be out there getting trained, getting hands-on experience. Some of it I put down to my own personality because I kept holding back from pushing "the man." And what you gotta do is as soon as the pipe gets uncovered, you gotta jump down into the hole. The first person in the hole does all the work. The only thing helpers can't do is weld. But even when I jumped down in the hole, I sometimes had problems. I've had men take me out of the hole. It has to be because I'm a woman.

I got promoted to fitter eight months ago. At first it was terrible. I was real insecure about being able to do the job, still am. They transferred me from Seattle to the Totem Lake area. I didn't know the supervisor, and they had a somewhat different system over there, so I didn't even know the system. There was different pipe and the area was developed differently, so I felt like I didn't know anything. On top of that I hadn't done any welding in six months so my welding skills were real low. But I did okay and gained a lot of confidence in the last months. I feel fairly competent and on top of it now.

There's a lot involved in fitting. The gas company has it set up so a fitter, a helper, and a truck are sent out on a job. The jobs entail either maintenance, which is taking care of the pipe that's already in the ground, or installing new pipe. All the mains are out in the street and are usually buried three to four feet deep. All the service piping from the main to the house is buried, too. If you have to run a new service, what you have to do is dig up the main. In Seattle you have blacktop and concrete so you have to use a ninety-pound breaker. That's a kind of jack-hammer. Pretty much I would say the most demanding thing for a woman to do on the job is to use the breaker, because it usually takes, depending on the concrete and blacktop, from a half-hour up to three or four hours. Fortunately, they don't run away from you. It's just heavy physical labor.

What does run away is the tamper, which tamps down the earth. It makes a hole solid in the back. The machines had a big, round, four-foot heavy disc type of thing on the bottom. It's run by air and pounds down the dirt. But it'll run away on you and is hard on the lower back. You gotta be fairly strong to even be able to lift it. I did a lot of swimming when I was younger so I've always been fairly broad and didn't have a lot of problems with physically controlling it. I've also gotten a lot stronger since I started working.

But anyhow, after breaking the concrete you either dig by hand or have a backhoe crew come in and do it, depending upon what's happening elsewhere. Once it is dug up, there's different ways to get the pipe in the ground. There's a machine called a holehog which is real popular right now. It's this long five-foot machine that just kind of bangs its way through the earth. With a holehog there's not a whole lot of physical labor. I've spent two, three days digging with it all day long. That's not bad.

As a fitter I do gas welding, which is different from tig or arc welding. Gas welding is where you use oxygen and acetylene, where with tig or arc it is done with electricity. Gas welding is a lot harder and slower because you're actually melting pipe with heat. It's hot and slow. At first it was hard for me to control the puddle of liquid metal. It's a matter of learning how to angle the tip of the welding rod. That controls the way the puddle moves. You have to be fairly confident and the work must be steady. There's different size pipes and you put different size pipes on the other size pipes. And that has, you know, a tendency of one melting faster than the other. All together it's a fairly complicated skill.

I don't think I've ever done anything really dangerous to prove myself, but this job *could* be dangerous. It isn't too much if you follow the set pattern and all the safety precautions. You always

Laura Pfandler, pipefitter

have to remember, though, you're dealing with live gas. You weld on live gas, which can catch on fire. If you have a tendency to weld through the main you can have a gas fire on your hands. Also gas takes up the oxygen in the air so, if there's gas blowing in the hole, you could end up passing out from no oxygen. Those are probably the two most dangerous things as far as work is concerned. To protect yourself, you just follow the standards. When welding on gas have someone there with a fire bottle to put any fire out. *Whenever* there's live gas you should have someone with a fire bottle there to watch it. As far as using the tools and stuff, there's a correct way and an incorrect way. As long as you use them the correct way and listen to what your body's telling you, it's okay. I watch myself real close.

When I first made fitter, the helpers were really pissed and angry that they were going to have to work with me. There was a lot of talk about having to work for a woman, to take orders from a woman. Some of them came right out in saying I didn't know what I was doing. One guy said, "You can't tell me 'cause you don't know what you're doing." I was told they didn't wanna take orders from a woman. And there was one man marching around telling everybody that he wasn't gonna have to work with me because he was too important to have to work for a woman. At the beginning I used my supervisor to back me up with the helpers. Depending on my mood, I sometimes told 'em it was too bad if they didn't wanna work with a woman because I didn't want to work with them either. Others I told to sit in the truck while I did the job.

When you go out on a job, and this still happens, you have to deal with somebody at the house. Usually it's a man, but sometimes a woman—the customers will immediately go to the male helper to talk the situation over. The helper, he won't hold back. They just walk right in the door. When things like this keep happening, I just get more and more angry.

My regular supervisor, like I said earlier, has been real good about backing me up. One time when he was off for a day I learned what it would be like working for someone who didn't back you up. The field rep, who is underneath the supervisor, was put in charge. He got into doing a lot of loud, disrespectful girl talk with the helper that I had. I asked him to change the subject, so he changed it to talking about some gay man who worked in an office over in Bellevue and why don't I go date him, he'd be a real good one for you. I kinda left it at that, but the field rep told the supervisor the next day that I'd gotten hysterical. That I was doing a lot of ranting and raving and screaming and yelling. How am I supposed to get respect out of my helpers when management can do that? And what came out of this was that this man, the field rep, was maybe disrespectful to me because I used bad language. I was told there were standards in language, that I could not say the word "fuck." That's kinda what was told to me.

When I worked in Seattle as a helper there were other women working in that area for the gas company, so there was some support. On the east side, at Totem Lake, where I went as a fitter, there were no other women. I went into therapy to work on building my self-confidence. The counselor was really difficult to find because I wanted a woman who had done work with women in trades. But she has helped me a lot. That and the support I've gotten from my friends has been really good.

Although in some ways this job has put a bit of a strain on friendships. I spend a lot of energy at work and don't have a lot of it for other things. I don't get out as much as I'd like, to the movies or whatever. My friends have had to start accepting that is the way it is. For a while I was playing the flute, but I stopped doing that. I spend my energy at work.

Other than that the biggest difference is I do a lot more consuming than I did before because I have the money for it and enjoy it. I mean I have a good car, you know, and lots of extra clothes and a stereo and a tape . . . .

Fire Fighter

DIANA CLARKE

While visiting her parents on a rare trip out of her beloved woods, Diana Clarke met with me. Pacing the room, ironing clothes and laying out a blouse pattern, she seemed to have far too much energy for mere talking.

We lived in the country when I was growing up, so I played outside a lot. I had one girl friend, but she lived a ways away, and her mother wouldn't let her play with me, so I played with my brothers and boys from the neighborhood. At the same time I was fantasizing about becoming a nun. That's what every Catholic girl wanted to be. That's the best thing you could do—become a nun or a missionary. Later I grew away from religion.

I spent a long time, most of my college years, becoming an artist. In college I studied graphic arts. At home I became a person who made things.

My work history has been rather varied. I've had about twenty-five jobs—a lab assistant, switchboard operator, graphic artist, and seamstress. I've worked in nursing homes, been a governess, waitress, truck driver, bartender, and cook. During college I found out about fire fighting. It contained all the qualities I wanted and it offered a chance to live in a remote area. It was good pay, and it was a non-traditional job which would allow me to live and work in the mountains. It sounded so exciting! It was exactly what I wanted to do, and I haven't changed my mind yet. I've been doing it since seventy-seven.

To get hired you must pass a physical fitness test, and since I had not been leading an active life it took me a few days to pass. It's called a step test. You have to step up and down on a step of approximately eighteen inches for five minutes, and then if your heart rate doesn't return to normal within fifteen seconds you don't pass. Some people don't get hired because they don't pass the step test. The accuracy of the test is a controversial issue, but I am basically in favor of it; I don't want heart attack material out there with me on a wildfire.

They gave us a week-long training program, the field work being mostly on the job. They taught us a little bit about weather behavior, radio communications, how to use a compass and read a map, how to use, sharpen, and carry hand tools—a shovel, hazel hoe, and pulaski, a type of axe. Those are the basic tools that a fire fighter uses. Then there is the chainsaw. I was apprehensive using the chainsaw, mostly about cutting off a foot or making a fool out of myself trying to learn how to use it. And I didn't know if I was strong enough. Yes, learning to run a chainsaw was probably the hardest thing that I had to do as far as training was concerned. Actually, they're very easy to run, though. I have my own chainsaw now and I get all my own firewood. I learned to fall snags from my men friends in the town I live in. I start looking for firewood after work on summer days and bring it home a load at a time. I need about five loads to get through winter comfortably.

When we completed training, we separated into various crews and went out and stacked sticks, which is what you do while waiting for a fire call when you're on a fire crew in the summer. On the crew that I work on, you pile logging slash. What you basically do is treat the slash the loggers leave behind. You either broadcast burn or hand pile it, and cover it with plastic and burn it when the snow flies.

Last year we stacked sticks all summer and went on only three fires. Each year it's different. When St. Helen erupted we

Diana Clarke, fire fighter

didn't go anywhere at all. I much prefer fighting fires to stacking sticks; every fire fighter feels the same way. You'd spend all your time digging hot line if you could; the rest of the time you just wait for the big one. Digging hot line is the initial attack on the fire. You're digging a trench one to eight feet wide, depending on where you are. In California they have to be very wide. If you're in the woods on the west side in the Pacific Northwest, they are narrower and deeper because of rotten wood called duff. It all depends on what fuel type and terrain you are working with.

Fire fighting is very structured. There's an organization to fire fighting and that's what my job is about now. I'm a crew boss and train crews in digging lines, brushing out, and handline construction principles. The number of people working under me always varies, but it's usually around seven to ten, unless I'm on a big fire; then there's up to nineteen.

Anybody who said they weren't ever afraid of fires would be lying. However, I like being right there next to the fire. The only thing that concerns me is someone who doesn't have information on what the fire weather is. You can observe a certain amount about a fire, but you just don't know what the weather is going to be like. When you know the expected fire weather, you can base your strategy on that information. That's the thing that frightens me—being around people that *don't* know what's going on. Wildfire is dangerous, and I want everybody to know what's going on in those situations. I don't want to die in a fire. And I don't want anybody that works with me to die or get hurt. That's my job, taking care of my crew. I make sure they have food, rest, enough sleep, and they get their time recorded accurately.

It sounds dangerous, but after awhile you learn how to read what a fire's going to do and you always plan an escape route and safety zone. That's a bare spot where there's very little fuel, or it's a place you can run back into that's already burned or a rock slide or a lake. It's a place you can go to if the fire closes in and you're not going to be in a fuel-concentrated area. If you are forced to retreat from the fire, you reanalyze the situation and start once more to contain, then control it.

Sometimes we do backburning, which is when you light off an area before the fire gets to it so when it reaches your burnout, it doesn't have fuel concentration. You control what it does and it's actually good strategy, if you have people who know what they're doing. One time in California some people got burned while backburning, and the fire boss forty miles away called up and said, "No more backburning," which meant we were in a very bad area without an escape. There was no place to go. We had a catline to lay in. A catline is a very wide area that's made by a bulldozer, a cat. It gives you some protection. My crew leader kept saying, "Am I nervous? Do I look nervous? Can you tell I'm nervous?" I didn't know he was nervous until he started asking me that. I was his assistant and knew things were very tense, but he kept us all very calm and finally we backburned anyways. It was either that or get burned over.

I've had some burns, but they've all been due to my own foolishness, because I didn't wear my gloves and picked up burning things. If you get burned or cut when you're not wearing your safety gear, you're responsible for that yourself. You have the gear and have been instructed in how to use it. If you don't, that's your problem, your prerogative. You certainly can't collect money because you hurt yourself when you've been instructed in the proper procedure. You've got gloves, hard hat, fire-retardant clothing, fire shelter, safety goggles, and ear plugs. You have to buy your own boots. They have to be eight inches high with Vibram soles.

It's required that you wear the ear and eye protection. However, I don't like to wear ear plugs because, if someone's shouting, it lessens my chance of being able to hear them. When I'm wearing eye protection, the goggles that we wear have a little lip right below the eye so you can't look down to your legs; also they tend to fog up. I wear sunglasses, which are acceptable. When I first started out, I wouldn't wear gloves. I like to get my hands callused. But there are times when your work is slowed down a great deal if you don't wear gloves. Then I require the crew to wear gloves.

When you get to a fire, there's certain rules you have to follow. You always wear a hard hat no matter where you are. You have to wear fire-retardant clothing. You have to have your gloves *with* you, because if you are in a fire situation where you have to get into a fire shelter, which is an aluminum tent, you only have a couple seconds. You pop it out of this little bag that you wear on your waist at all times during fires, and you unfold it and snap it open and fall down with it and get air in it. When the fire spreads, it'll protect you a certain degree more than just being there by yourself, but they're not foolproof. You have to have your gloves so that you can hold down the edges of the shelter. That way the fire just goes around you. I was on a fire where a man died because he wasn't able to hold down the edge of his shelter, and another person, who did have gloves, made it through.

I've never been burned over, but I know people who have been and they were uncomfortable, but safe. It keeps the exceptional amount of heat away from you. I don't have the exact information on how high the heat can get before you're well done, but the shelters protect you from the smoke, which is what would kill you first in a fire. You'd suffocate. You are uncomfortable in a shelter, but you can get through.

The story is, though, that you should *never* have been in a situation where you would have to use your shelter, and if you are required to use your shelter, chances are you will lose your job because you put that crew in a dangerous situation. You will be thoroughly investigated. Why didn't you know where the fire was going to be? Why didn't you have communications? So that's the last thing in the world you want to do, if you want to keep your job and your respect.

You're only supposed to work sixteen-hour shifts now. They feel it is unsafe to work over sixteen hours. I agree. However, it's sort of an ideal. You're only supposed to be in the smoke ten minutes and then you're required to be out ten minutes, which is a big joke. That is impossible. Usually you're in for five hours and out for ten minutes. If you're in a smoke situation, that's the way it's going to be. You're where the danger is. That's why we're there. I'd say the average shift on a fire is twelve to eighteen hours. If your relief doesn't show up, your shift is twenty-five hours. I have put in a fifty-two-hour shift. They wanted us to work another shift, and I got angry. I told the sector boss that there was no way that we could work another shift as we hadn't had any food for two days and people were very tired and punchy. People were making stupid decisions because they were so tired. We were finally relieved. They do the best they can. However, if you're in a very tense spot you're going to have to go with the punches and remember it's in your job description.

When I first started, the guys on the crew felt uncomfortable because they weren't used to a woman and thought they would have to stop swearing and roughhousing. That lasted about five minutes—until I started swearing. I think they were afraid they would have to pull my weight. And I will say now there *are* women whose weight they do have to pull, and that annoys the hell out of me. However, there are men who can't make it as fire fighters either. If they're on my crew, I won't put up with it.

The whole thing about fire fighting is there's a lot of time to lay around, but there's other times when you get very hungry, very hot, thirsty, very tired, and very cold and very uncomfortable. You have to remember this is the job you signed up for and be tough about it—it takes nerve to do this job—and not complain about it and wish you were home and dry and clean.

Diana Clarke, fire fighter

If someone runs around bitching all the time, the crew usually runs them off. We make their life so miserable they
quit.

My first crew boss was not used to working with women. He
did not like the idea, but he did an about-face and changed his
opinion when he saw I was completely capable of doing the job.
He had just come from an environment where women were not
on crews. It didn't matter *why* they weren't. That is the basic
attitude of the men on the interregional crews, which are the big
hot-shot crews. But the thing that is funny is that when they are
forced to hire women, some of them want to do all the things for
them that they were afraid they were going to *have* to do. They
want to carry your hand tool or they take a little extra care of
you. It's difficult for both sides. You have to say, "Thank you, I
appreciate it, but I can do it for myself." My crew boss and crew
did not resent my being a woman. I think they were kind of
proud of it.

Washington, Oregon, and California are good for women fire
fighters. You go to Idaho, you're going to have it much harder,
from what I experienced in nineteen seventy-nine. First time I
was on a fire in Idaho I was with my crew boss. I was his
assistant at that time. When we were walking down the line, I
heard the bosses saying, "You've got a gal on the crew. How do
the guys like working with her? Is that kind of a problem?"

And the crew boss says, "Well, she's my assistant and there's
never been any problem at all." The guys could not believe that
not only was I a woman on the crew, but I was the assistant!

When I'm on a fire and the men come up to me and want to
know where my boss is, I say, "You're looking at her." They do
kind of a double take and are thrown off and say, "Right, no big
deal," but they watch me constantly to see if I screw up. "Oh,
no! It's a woman and she doesn't know what she's doing."
Fortunately, after about one day or a couple hours of just being
around me they know I *do* know what I am doing and they

lighten up a lot. I'll be glad when it's just accepted for women supervisors on the fire line.

You work wherever there's a fire. I'm based in Washington state, have been for six years. But when there's a fire, they'll send you, if needed; it doesn't matter where it is. I've been sent to Idaho, California, and Oregon, and not been sent to Arizona and New Mexico, just by pure chance. Crews go there every summer. We get crews up in Washington from Florida, the Carolinas, the New England states, and the Midwest. We *can* go anywhere in the United States. It's pretty funny when you get a crew in the Idaho wilderness area from Florida, because they've never seen a mountain and they're expected to scurry up this mountain and it's more than some of them can bear. It's simply like stage fright and they can't do it. I've seen crews really terrified. I don't know what our crew would be like down there in the swamps with the alligators and snakes and bugs, but it's exciting. It's great to travel all over.

People think it's great that I have this job. They also think I'm nuts. A lot depends on who they are. A businessperson, who lives in the city, can't believe it at all. A logger, who works in the woods, can't believe it either. Loggers are very old-fashioned; if they see me run a chainsaw, cut down a tree, or dig handline, they become competitive. From what I've seen, loggers don't like women working in the woods. I think it's just fine to show people you can do the job. I have no qualms about picking up a chainsaw and dropping a tree to show someone I am capable of doing my job. I think people should be required to do that more often, because if you can't do it, what are you doing there? If you are going to play with the boys, you are going to have to be tested right along with the boys. I can handle the competition.

Becoming as good or better than some men can lead to some resentment. I would say the most difficult part of my job was putting up with the men who initially trained me for the position I'm now in. It was one thing when I was a grunt on the job and I was doing what they asked me to do. It was another thing when I came into a supervisory position, required to make decisions for myself, and no longer had to ask them what was going on. They resented that a whole lot. Trying to deal with men's fragile egos is something I have a very difficult time with. But I guess you have to deal with men as they exist and I'm not going to win any rounds by being impatient, so I *try* to be calm, stay cool about it.

When I'm in a fire camp I look around and try to find a woman who's forty years old or thirty-five or fifty, like all the men I see. I want to see a woman who's walking around not just in a fire camp, but on the fire line. I've never seen her. And that really *bothers* me because I *want* to see her. I realize the role model has to be myself. *I'm* going to be the role model for other people, and that's one of the reasons why, even when my job was less than I wanted, I decided to stick it out. I want to be that woman on the fire line.

I would climb the ladder in fire management if it weren't for being an artist. A full-time life fighting fire leaves no time for creating, so I only work part time in the woods and devote my winters to creating objects that express my feeling about life.

Carpenter

ELAINE CANFIELD

Elaine Canfield's steel-toed work boots by the front door were in sharp contrast to the art prints and classical music that set the tone of her apartment.

As a girl I loved making Christmas ornaments and dyeing Easter eggs, all crafts I guess. I really enjoyed working with my hands. I had fantasies of some type of small cottage industry, not really a big career woman, but having meaningful work with a husband who was the breadwinner. As I got older I played the flute, mostly jazz. That suited my parents fine. They never steered me in the direction of a profession. They sort of hoped I would have a traditional marriage and be the woman behind the great man. As such, they never got around to telling me that one day, when I got out of school, I was gonna have to support myself. And somehow *I* never got around to thinking about that while I was in college, where I studied archeology, English, and anthropology. I didn't want to be forced into taking a lot of prerequisites, so I designed my own college major and took only the classes I wanted to take.

When I graduated from college in seventy-five, I got a part-time secretarial job at Bard College. Since I didn't like secretarial work, I started looking into the possibilities of repairing woodwind instruments. A professor in school had told me that I was good in music and good with my hands, so I should look into this. I took a short, four-week course at one of the colleges and discovered I liked doing mechanical work and set up an

Elaine Canfield, carpenter

apprenticeship with a man in Kingston, New York. I would take the clarinets home and work on them, and then once a week bring them back to his repair shop. I was paid ten dollars a clarinet for doing what we call an overhaul, which is when you replace the pads, joints, and springs. I didn't make more than eighty dollars a week at the most. But I was living with a man at that time who supported me, so there wasn't much pressure for money.

Then in the summer of seventy-seven I came out to Seattle and tried to continue my apprenticeship out here. I couldn't find anything and ended up doing secretarial work at the University of Washington. I hated my work and started looking for something else. I didn't start thinking about non-traditional work until I heard the carpenters were looking for women. I didn't know anything about carpentry. Didn't know how to use a hammer, how to use a saw, nothing. But as soon as the possibility was mentioned, my imagination went with it. I could have pursued another type of trade, like electrical, but to me carpentry is the most creative, most applicable to your daily life. Plumbing and electrical work have limitations. There's only so much you can do. It's valuable, it's neat, but it doesn't get a house built. And I liked the idea of working with wood. There's also a lot of independence in a trade. You work from job to job, not necessarily full time. Of course, the money is excellent. That definitely was there, a carrot in front of my nose. Besides I was all gung-ho, into being a torchbearer for women's rights. I wanted to get right out in front. That lasted until I realized there was a lot of danger in being a carpenter and had to deal with that on a day-to-day basis. A lot of tradespeople, when they start talking about the rate of fatal accidents, will say you take just as many chances driving to and from work each day. But they don't tell you that you're exposed to that danger level eight hours a day as opposed to an hour a day commuting. I still worry about fatal injuries and try to choose jobs where it's not high work and work for companies with good reputations for safety. I also worry about losing an arm or a hand or having something explode in my face, losing my eyesight.

I was lucky to get accepted into a CETA program run in conjunction with Local 131 of the Carpenters Union. In the six-week program they taught us to use the basic tools—hammer, handsaw, tri-square, crowbars, and skillsaw. I was amazed at how much there was to be learned just at carpentry. I had always been told that carpenters were people that worked with their hands. They did that because they did not have the intelligence to do white-collar-type work. And when I ventured into carpentry, it just blew me away—just what is involved. The mechanics, the math—really, it's pretty intellectual-type work. You're always having to visualize what you're going to be building. You have to know how you're going to connect things, why you're cutting wood in certain dimensions, mechanics, leverage, how things work for you, and how to do it the fastest way possible. That's an awful lot to know at one time.

The other really good thing about the course was they taught you just how to go about surviving in the trade. They said to go out and look for your own work and not wait for the union to call. They never do. This is how you go look for jobs. This is how you dress. Wear your work clothes. Look ready for work and always have your tools in your car. Try to engage the foreman in a conversation, don't just take no for an answer. Tell the foreman you're in the union and ask if he's hiring. And on the two or three jobs where they tell you to come back, you keep coming back, and eventually they'll hire you.

Even after the CETA training program, I still had a very romantic image of what carpenters do—sort of interior, fine woodworking. Even the concrete form work was more small-scale (in my mind) than what it was actually about. And on my first job, I didn't even use a hammer for about a month and a half. I was on a steel form crew where you cut and strip concrete

Elaine Canfield, carpenter

forms, leaving an instant column. Once it's disassembled the crane picks it up and puts it on the ground, and you have an electrical impact wrench and go around tightening nuts and bolts. I did that for a month and a half. Didn't even really get a chance to use my head. That blew me away. I thought, "God, this is carpentry? Where's the wood? Where's the nails?" And I found out that's quite often what commercial construction is about. You're a mechanic doing what's most efficient for things to work. I was disappointed in a sense, because I couldn't see myself doing that for the rest of my life. But the other carpenters assured me there would be other phases to the building. The disappointment was offset by the newness of the job. Being a carpenter, being outside, big machinery, cranes, a lot of stuff going on all at once.

I've never worked on a big building downtown. Usually I work in a big pit that's probably a quarter of a city block long and twenty to thirty feet below street level. It's the foundations of buildings, so you're working in a sub-ground area with a lot of dirt which turns into a lot of mud when it rains. On other jobs, like the Port of Seattle, I've done remodeling. The building had been gutted out and we were building new walls. But new construction or remodeling, my working conditions are always dirty and exposed to the elements. If it's snowing and thirty degrees out, you work outside. If the wind is blowing forty miles an hour, you work outside. Really, the elements are the hardest thing to contend with. But there are other times when it is the best thing going. On a beautiful day, I look at other people in their offices, their factories, and wouldn't trade with them for the world.

As a first-year apprentice, you're pretty much a "gofer." You get the tools needed to do the job. You get out the skillsaws, plug things in, set up the work areas, get the sawhorses, just assist them the best you can. You pick up the mechanical know-how while doing other things, and by the time you're a third-year you've got quite a lot of responsibility. There's always a journeyman telling you what to do and how to do it, but you do it yourself. And by the time you're fourth-year you're pretty much doing what the journeymen are doing, but you don't make the final decision. I'm a fourth-year now and do a lot of the form work and work on my own. I pretty much function on the journey level, but I still have the freedom to ask questions if I need to get advice. Most journeymen carpenters will fake it through somehow, but I still ask questions. I want to continue doing that, because there's so much of what I call "herd" mentality—sheep in a herd, everyone just follows without question. There's not very good communication in the trade. People are not explicit. They don't verbalize things. They just grunt. You're supposed to fake your way through it, get the job done with as little problem as possible. I'm not that kind of worker.

For a woman to survive in the trades, you really have to know how to psych out men, know what's behind their thinking, why they react, why they're prejudiced, be somewhat sympathetic, yet stand your own ground. You have to be tactful, not be hostile, not alienate people. You really have to learn professional survival skills, because men's masculinity is threatened by you being there. Society recognizes construction workers as being very macho and virile. When a woman comes along who's five foot three and a hundred and twenty pounds and can get in there and do their type of work, it's a blow to their ego, a real shock. So the men are threatened by it.

The men show that in different ways. If a foreman comes up to a group, he'll look at everyone except you. He'll delegate jobs to everyone but you, and then you have to go up and ask him. It's sort of uncomfortable things like that. Or the carpenters will pair up and you're the one left out. Or men you're working with just won't talk to you. I used to not push in those situations, but lately I've felt more self-confident, and sometimes I play games with those people. Like, for example, today on the job site there

Elaine Canfield, *carpenter*

is another fourth-year apprentice who is sort of the foreman's pet. He just came over and picked up some wood and started doing some form work on top of the footing another carpenter and I had built. And I yelled at him, "What's going on?" Not in a hostile way, just curious. We'd finished that footing, and I wanted to know what changes had been ordered. He wouldn't answer, so I got a bit flustered and asked again. He still wouldn't answer. I kept probing, and he kept not answering. Finally I said, "I'm talking to you. I want a response." I was just very aggressive, which I'd never been before. But I've gotten to the point where I'm tired of not getting recognition. Finally he answered me and explained there was a change in plans, not any mistake. I could see he was a little taken aback and I felt so good. I had won something. What was more interesting was the reaction of the other man. Right in the middle of all this he looked up at me and smiled.

The crew I'm working with now—it's never been better. I'm accepted. They kid me like one of the guys. They pay me compliments. They treat me like an equal. It has been a real breakthrough. I've had other crews that have been really nice, but I know enough now so that I can talk business as well as pleasure. Not only am I compatible, but I feel they recognize me as a fairly good carpenter. I haven't had that recognition before. Like if a carpenter I've been working with is talking with another man about something we built, he'll mention my name, say, "Elaine and I were working on this . . ." Even a week ago working with someone I wouldn't have gotten that recognition. So they include me, acknowledge me.

Last year I had a difficult time with both the crews I worked on. In one case I worked on a big job site—probably a crew of twelve men—and three of the men were under thirty. It's been my experience with that age group that they are very threatened by a woman doing a man's job. They're just virility and ego and macho and they can't handle it. They gave me a lot of bullshit like, "Here's a mistake. Elaine must have done it." Anything to piss me off. Or they'd make dirty jokes about women. Or the typical things like sighing, burping, farting, and looking to see if they'd gotten a reaction from me. Or if I wouldn't play that game, they'd try to make me look foolish in front of the foreman.

After that, I worked for a small company that had never had a woman before. It went okay for the first three months because one journeyman thought I was very smart. We worked together, ate lunch alone, and had a lot of fun. The rest of the crew ignored us. But when the journeyman left, it was clear I was on my own. The men never talked with me, and laid me off in an uncomfortable way when I couldn't do high work. That left me pretty depressed, wondering if carpentry was gonna turn out to be increasing hostility, alienation, and resentment. I took a few months off in the summer and this year has worked out real well. Now I can see that I happened to hit two bad jobs last year. Not necessarily would I have to deal with that all the time.

Off the job, people in general are threatened by the type of work I do. Even the women I meet for the first time just cannot put the picture together. They just sort of stand back and say, "Oh, isn't that nice." Then they change the conversation really fast. They can't relate to you. They don't know where to begin. They may be threatened. I'm not sure. So in a social sense, you usually just get the silent treatment. They don't want to ask you too much more. They usually let it go at that.

I belong to a group called Women in the Trades and the reason I belong is because I need their support. I need that sympathy, that understanding, and to share the feelings of accomplishment. But mostly the support.

Shipwright / Bindery Worker

IRENE HULL

*From Depression in the 1930's to Recession in the 1980's,
Irene Hull has seen it all.*

I always wanted to go to college. It never dawned on me that I wouldn't be able to, in spite of the fact that we were Depression people. We were always drastically poor. We lost our service station for taxes and my father went over to my aunt's place to help run her orange orchard. Her husband had been injured working on the street cars in Los Angeles. My mother, father, and brother raised and sold chickens to help support us during the Depression.

I got a loan from the Daughters of the American Revolution and some money from my sister and brother-in-law to go to college. I graduated in nineteen thirty-four from UCLA with a bachelor's in education. I was not a brilliant student and almost didn't graduate. That was awful, because my family had sacrificed so much to send me to college. Always in the back of my mind was that I should make something of myself. My mother had instilled that in me.

But I never was a good teacher. I wasn't well organized. I didn't plan my lessons well. It didn't matter a whole lot in nineteen thirty-four because there were no jobs. This was the Depression. We were the best-educated service-station operators, dishwashers, and waitresses. It was really terrible. My folks were on relief. I finally got a playground job through what they called the National Youth Administration. It was a government job. They had been forced to act. There were marches on Washington, D.C. The government had to do something, just like they're going to have to do very soon. You know, people aren't going to sit back and let them kill 'em with hunger and starvation.

Anyhow, with the NYA job I got twenty-seven dollars a month. That is what my mother, father, and I lived on. We rented this little house for ten dollars a month. On that twenty-seven dollars a month we never paid [were able to pay] one dime of rent, but the house was not vandalized while we lived there, so the owners let us stay. At the time, radishes, onions, beets, carrots, turnips—all those root vegetables were a penny a bunch. Frequently we did not have the penny. Sometimes we got food boxes through relief, and that's how we survived.

I got married in nineteen thirty-seven and we headed up to Oregon. On the way we stopped off and topped onions for twenty cents an hour. In Oregon, Lew and his dad cut wood to make a living. Our oldest daughter was born there. We raised hay, grain, and cattle and had a big garden. We sold butter and cream for cash to live on. The cream checks were two to four dollars a week. Six of us lived on that.

Finally we sold some cows for beef and went back to California. I was gonna try and get a job teaching, and Lew was gonna go to school to become a boilermaker. It didn't work out. The schools wouldn't hire married teachers, and then on top of that I got pregnant again. I miscarried, but got pregnant again not too long afterwards, so I never did get to do the teaching.

Just before World War Two, Lew got a carpentry job on defense work. We still lived pretty much a hand-to-mouth existence because we had such a backlog of poverty. I used to go into dime stores, where you could buy just about everything. Sheets were fifty cents. Well I would *have* fifty cents, but there would be so many things I needed to spend that fifty cents for, I couldn't make a decision. Sometimes I would just go out and not buy anything.

Lew worked in a number of the defense plants—Paso Robles, Bradley, and then Los Angeles, where I had my third daughter, and from there to Sacramento. We just followed the defense plants. While in Sacramento we left our oldest two daughters with relatives, because I had quite a difficult birth with Marjorie and needed a lot of rest. When we left Sacramento for Medford, we took all three kids with us. From there we went to Idaho and finally down into Vancouver, Washington, where I went back to work as a nursery-school teacher.

I think I made about eighty or ninety cents an hour, so my husband and father-in-law said, "This is terrible. You should get a job at the shipyards, because there you can make a dollar twenty an hour." So then I got my job at the shipyards as a carpenter and joiner on a permit. Being on a permit meant I was not allowed to join the union. I was born thirty years too soon. The permit workers were all women.

It was a fun job. You'd go in there with your tape measure and your cutting knife and cut the insulation to size. I was always proud of the fact that I did a very good job. I measured to the sixteenth of an inch and seldom had problems. I put insulation on the bulkheads and deckheads and, because I was small, usually got sent up into places that were difficult to get into. I worked on the outfitting dock. You see, after the ship was built and went down the ways and had the bottle smashed on it, then it came over to the outfitting dock. That's where they put all the equipment in. And before they put the equipment in, wherever possible, we would put the insulation in. Sometimes we had to tuck the insulation around the equipment, and once we had to work in a hot boiler room while the boiler was on. We could only stay in there for a minute, minute and a half, and had to come out. We took turns going in there and getting this job done. We'd go in and take a measurement and rush out and cut. I don't remember all the details, but I know it was insufferably hot.

In the winter we stood on corrugated cardboard or the insulation itself to keep our feet from getting chilblains. And in the summers those metal decks were blistering hot. There were many times when we just worked steady, steady, steady, and times when we had to wait while another guy does his job. If they weren't ready for you, you'd just sit on a box somewheres and hide out. That's the way the job was organized.

The insulation crews were almost all women because the carpenters wouldn't do that stinkin' work. It was scratchy, itchy stuff and it made you itch all over. My husband used to complain that I took it to bed with me.

Of course, we always had men foremen. One time a directive came down from on high: "You're spending too much time in the restrooms." The restroom was a couple blocks away so it took a few minutes to go there. But the poor foremen had to give us the word, and then take our flak. "Oh," we'd say, "Jimmy, I've got my pants unbuttoned. Can I go now?" "Jimmy, can we use your hat?" Well, that directive didn't last too long.

We made lots of good friendships. One woman I've been friends with to this day. Another I was friends with until she died.

I had begun to get political by this time. My father-in-law educated me, really. He corrected a lot of the *mis*education that I got in college. From him I learned that women *did* have rights and about the fallacies of religion. A lot of the political struggles in the shipyards were won before I came in in nineteen forty-two. One of them was the Fair Employment Practices Act, which said they had to hire blacks. The whites said they wouldn't work with the blacks, so the company told them, "All right. Do you want your check now or later?" So the whites worked and they never quit.

Irene Hull, shipwright/bindery worker

What I did get involved in was the Democratic Party elections. We were struggling to get people out to vote. We weren't telling them *how* to vote, but the Democratic Party put out flags and we put 'em on our hats. Then the order came down, "Take those flags off." I think that's very significant, considering the fact that the Moral Majority uses the flag so consistently now, but at that time it was unpatriotic to urge people to vote. But we won that one. We kept on wearing flags on our hard hats.

Oh, my goodness, I almost forgot to tell you about the nursery schools. Lew worked graveyard and I worked swing, so I'd take the kids to nursery school in the morning and he'd get them at night. The nursery schools were open twenty-four hours a day. Once in awhile if we wanted to go out, we'd take them back and they'd stay all night. In nineteen forty-two, as part of the war effort, the Lanham Act was passed by Congress. The federal government paid most of the total cost to keep a child in the school. The parents paid only fifty cents a day per child to keep them there. And those were good nursery schools. They taught the kids.

Anyhow, in nineteen forty-four things began to wind down. They weren't building so many ships. I got laid off. There were a lot of layoffs and no organized struggle about seniority for permit workers. The permit workers, who were all women, went first, of course, and so did the blacks. Last hired, first fired—always. We were terribly un-class-conscious and unaware, disgracefully so in some ways. I wish now I had put up a struggle. I never thought of it. I never dreamed of seniority being a right that I should have had. I don't know if I would have wanted to stay being a carpenter or not.

One of our daughters was hard of hearing, so when I got laid off we moved up here to Seattle so she could go to a school for the deaf that was here. Lew got another shipyard job and I went back to nursery-school teaching. I think I made a dollar an hour then. This is probably a good time to tell the story of how they closed those Lanham Act nursery schools. It's kind of a sad story. In nineteen forty-five, Fleming, the superintendent of public instruction, came down with an edict, "We're going to close the nursery schools October thirty-first." Well, I'd never heard about having a meeting to protest anything. Even though I had gotten involved in some struggles, I hadn't gotten that far yet. Well, a friend of mine and some of her friends knew about having meetings and called a meeting of the parents to protest the closure. The men hadn't come back from the war yet, and a lot of the wives still had full responsibility for children.

I got elected secretary of the organization that we called the Citizens' Child Care Committee. We arranged to have someone go and meet with the school board at their next meeting. Well it turns out the school board was real clever. They changed the time and date of the meeting, but somebody found out and went. So then we made arrangements to go to the second meeting and had a hundred fifty people there. So the school board went out of town and said they didn't have anything to meet about. So there was a third meeting and we had as many, maybe more people there. And the school board said they had to have a private meeting first. Well most of those nursery schools closed at five-thirty, and when the meeting dragged on, Fleming came out and said, "This private meeting is going to take so long that the Board sent me out to give you the message that they won't have time to talk to you." So all these people started gathering up their books to leave. I happened to have my kids in one that closed at six P.M., so I could stay longer.

"Could I just ask one question, Mr. Fleming," I asked. "Would the school board refuse to meet with us who could stay?"

He swelled up seven feet tall and said, "Certainly the school board would never refuse to meet with anybody." And he stomped into the little room, and they all stomped out and threw their books on the table and rustled their papers and passed the resolution that we asked for, which was a simple

Irene Hull, shipwright/bindery worker

little request for Congress to continue the Lanham Act funds. As a result they kept those child-care centers open for three more years. They kept closing one here and one there by a divide-and-conquer strategy. Of course, when the nurseries were closed, I was out of a job.

I think it was in forty-six or forty-seven when I got on in the printing department of Lynden Chickens. Well, I thought I was an apprentice printer, but actually I was an apprentice bindery worker. At the time I didn't know enough about the printing industry to know about the divisions in the industry. The ones in bindery do everything to the paper *after* it's printed. And that's the part I was learning first. I ran the cutter. It wasn't electric. It was just one of those hand-pulled cutters and very sharp. I also did collating and embossing. Then I was learning to run some of the machinery before I had to quit because of family problems. I always regretted that.

Finally I got a job in a laundry and that is a terrible place to work. They put me in the shakers, which is where people shake the sheets after they came out of the dryer and folded them. It was terribly hot. People were passing out from the heat. I'd put cold water on my wrists, back of my neck, on my forehead, and I was all right as far as survival was concerned. Shakers made something like eighty cents an hour.

I decided shaking was going to make me old before my time, so a friend told me all about what she had to do to be a pantry worker. So armed with that knowledge, I talked myself into a job at one of the grandest hotels. When I got onto the job, the workers kept saying to me, "Where did you say you had worked?" You can fool the boss, but you can never fool the workers. They know when you're ignorant, dumb. But I held that job for five months and worked in other restaurants for several years.

I was working in one when I was named by the Velde Committee in nineteen fifty-four. The Velde Committee was part of the House Internal Security Committee. It was the anti-Communist witch-hunt committee. The head of it in Seattle was named Velde. Barbara Hartl was a Communist Party member who had gone to jail during the Smith Act trials, and then they brought her back here as a stool pigeon. I don't know how many people she named. Anyhow she said I was expelled from the party as a Trotskyite. Well, the reason I've always thought I was expelled was I disagreed with some of the leadership. I was called anti-leadership and a few things like that, which I never was. But when Barbara Hartl named me as a Trotskyite, all I could think was, "Why can't they say some of the good things I did?" I didn't want to be labeled a Trotskyite.

After I was named, one of the business agents from my union said to me, "Well, what about your husband, Irene? Is he one of them thar Commies, too?"

And I said to him, "You know better than to ask anybody a question like that in this day and age." See, this was in fifty-three or fifty-four and the McCarran Act was already on the books. The McCarran Act silenced the unions. If you questioned, you were a Communist. If you didn't agree, you had to be a Communist. And Hubert Humphrey, the great liberal, who wanted to prove that he was no longer the tail of labor, helped pass it. It destroyed a lot of good union people. Folks clammed up. Young people refused to support their parents morally and to be known as their parents' children, sometimes. Many were deported. I joined a committee here in Seattle called the Washington Committee for the Protection of the Foreign-Born in the nineteen-fifties, and we managed to prevent any deportations here, although several attempts were made.

That union business agent made it his business to go over to the restaurant I was working in and told the guy that hired me that I was named by the Velde Committee. The guy called me in and said, "You're a nice girl, Irene, but we don't want you here

Irene Hull, shipwright/bindery worker

any more." That's all the explanation he would give me, but I knew what had happened. I was just devastated. Six weeks later I went back to get some uniforms of mine which had been in the laundry. The boss was gone and the chef hired me back part time. The chef was a good guy. Before I knew it, I was working seven days a week. It was too much. I still had three kids at home.

A friend that worked in a printing shop sent me to the business agent of the Bindery Workers Union, who gave me the names of some shops to go to. It was in fifty-five that I started looking, but it wasn't until fifty-six that I got a job. The day I got the job, I started out at one end of town and walked the whole length of the town before happening into a place that had a big job. That's one thing about bindery work, it's feast or famine. There are long periods of just go, go, go, go, go and you get a lot of overtime, and periods of nothing to do. Well this place was really busy and the man said, "I been trying to talk them into hiring an apprentice. Are you sure you want it?" I said I was, but every so often for months he'd keep saying, "Are you sure you want to do bindery work?" I completed a three-year apprenticeship, and when I quit bindery work in nineteen-seventy-nine the wages were seven dollars and twenty-two cents an hour. I served on the executive board of the Graphic Arts Union and ran for business agent, and came within seventeen votes of beating the guy. After that I never got another job. See, we have a union hiring hall. But I feel that I made some contributions to my local. One of the contributions that I got, because Lew was an alcoholic, was alcoholism as part of our treatment in health and welfare. I feel really good about that.

I've tried to be class conscious all of my life. I have tried to avoid a feminist attitude because, as I always say, "We have to work together—men and women." When they started the struggle for the ERA, I opposed it, because I said, "We have got to have equal rights for *all* workers and not lose the protections that women have got." I felt the professional women were short-sighted. They wanted to work ten and twelve and eighteen hours [a day] so they could advance and get status. They weren't thinking about health. I know. I've worked in the shipyards.

Occupational Safety and Health

Every year 14,000 Americans die from on-the-job accidents; another 2.2 million suffer disabling injuries. In addition, there are annually 390,000 new cases of occupational illnesses brought on by workplace exposure to chemicals and other irritants. Because of the difficulty in diagnosing these diseases as being definitively caused by job-related exposure, their actual incidence is probably far greater than these figures indicate.

Although much of the literature on occupational health and safety blames worker carelessness for the problem, virtually every women I interviewed stressed the importance of working in a safe manner. Laura Pfandler, whose job requirements include welding on live gas lines, has a healthy fear of inadvertently setting off a gas fire. Diana Clarke takes every possible measure to protect her fire-fighting crew, but nevertheless worries about abrupt changes in the wind that might cause a fire to turn upon them. For Michelle Sanborn, the main danger comes from breathing toxic chemicals while working in an unventilated room. In fact, none of the seven women injured on the job had been behaving in a reckless manner at the time of the accidents. Instead, injuries just seem to be a natural part of working in a trade.

This does not, however, address the often asked question of do women get injured more than men? Thus far there has been minimal comparative research done on this subject. Critics assert that women's bodies are simply not strong enough to withstand the physical abuse associated with blue-collar jobs. But I do believe that the women in this collection can add some insights that traditional academic studies might miss. First off, safely performing blue-collar work can involve brains and common sense as much as brawn. After studying how men lifted heavy weights, Amy Kelley evolved a system that relied upon her hips more than her back. Beth Gedney found that men on her ship appreciated her refusal to perform unsafe acts because it gave the men themselves a way out of their macho peer group's pressures to lift too much. And finally, across-the-board comparisons of male and female accident rates will miss the impact sex discrimination has on inflating the women's rate. When Beverly Brown first sought employment in the mills, she was told horror stories of how the only woman to ever work in the plant had gotten injured. Instead of being daunted, Brown asked for more details and discovered the men had refused to show the woman the proper procedures for working with the machinery. This theme of discrimination leading to injuries also appears in Lydia Vasquez' and Teresa Selfe's stories.

For some of the women, the physical pain caused by their accidents is only a small part of their suffering. Whether due to callousness or oversight, encounters with the medical establishment have turned into bureaucratic nightmares. Kathryn Brooke was sent home from an emergency room with two aspirin for a broken tailbone. Lydia Vasquez, who has been unable to work for three years, is still being bounced around by different agencies and has collected nothing in disability. One cannot help but wonder if middle-class male patients receive the same treatment.

Even though on-the-job injuries are of concern to both male and female workers, sex discrimination intensifies the impact it has upon women. It is more difficult for women to receive adequate training, fair job assignments, and decent medical care. And finally, as long as a woman's chance of getting another well-paying job is minimal, women like Nora Quealey will continue to work in life-endangering conditions because they have children to support.

Plumber

ANGELA SUMMER

An advocate of solar energy, alternative lifestyles, and the term "journeywoman," she has more than sex separating her from construction industry co-workers.

My father was a tankerman. To be more explicit, he unloaded and loaded barges on, like, oil and gas. And he was like a dead man a lot. It was really just labor. There wasn't much skill to the job at all. He didn't make much money. My mother was a housewife, a frustrated housewife. Ours was a big Catholic family and my parents put expectations on some of their kids, but they didn't seem to have any designs on me. But everything I've done—and I've tried a lot of different jobs—they've supported me in doing it.

I guess the only traditional work I've done is a month and a half of waitressing. I've done apple picking and some taxi driving when I was eighteen. Let's see, other things, I guess it's all been pretty non-traditional, like housepainting. No, let's see, when I was nineteen—I think I was nineteen—I worked in a can factory in Baltimore and that was very traditional work. I mean it was all women who worked at the machines. They paid a dollar ninety an hour. I remember that very clearly. It was piecework, so you could make more money if you worked faster. One time in an eight-hour day I did thirteen hours' worth of work. It was the hardest work I have ever done in my life. I can still say I haven't done anything harder. It was all women working on the machines, and there were some men doing maintenance, but women did all the assembly line work.

What I really disliked about the job was it was real shit pay, and I stood on my feet all day long in one spot. You know, now I stand on my feet all day too, but I get to move around. But on that job I'd stand in one spot all day long, or I'd move a few feet, but that was it. And my feet would kill me. I thought it was terrible how much money we were making, especially like the other women; a lot of them were raising their families. They had like six or seven kids. Some of them were married, but their husbands didn't work. They hung out in the pubs. It was a very sad scene. I disliked that a lot, but I really liked the women I worked with. They were really neat. They were all over forty and all the young girls that'd come and try to work there, they'd all just quit, because you couldn't keep up with them. And they wanted me to stay, so they would just say, "Don't worry about it," when my table would pile up to the point where if there was just one more box of cans the whole thing would fall over. Then everybody would stop and go to my table, and in about two seconds it would just be done. They would just do it. And it was a really hard thing to accept, you know, because I always thought I was a good, hard, fast worker. Like I had done picking, and my dad worked us pretty hard, and I thought I was pretty fast, but I couldn't keep up with those women. It blew me away and it was real hard to, like, not quit. And to feel like even though it was just a few pennies, maybe, I was slowing them down when they were making such shit wages anyway. When, after about a month, I could keep up with them, it was just wonderfully satisfying.

They were typical housewives—no causes like feminism and stuff. I would talk about things with them, and they thought I was just a little out of it, but they liked me. I had hitchhiked all around the United States and they had never been off their block in Baltimore hardly. I learned a lot from them.

After I came back to Seattle, at one point I decided I was gonna get a good skill and make some money. That meant something

Angela Summer, plumber

which had usually been thought of as a man's job. At first I thought about carpentry. I think that's what most women think of. It's more of a romantic feeling to work with wood and make beautiful things. The only reason I didn't do it was I was scared by the math. So I took up plumbing, which has more math and more complicated math than carpentry. But I thought there would be no math when I took it up.

I knew a woman who had gone to welding school at SOIC [Seattle Opportunities Industrialization Center]. It sounded great to me. I was gonna get paid to go to school, and it was pretty good money, too. She made a hundred eighty-six dollars a week while training and that was six years ago. When I heard that, my eyes got big and I ran down there. And that's pretty much how I got into plumbing. The attraction was being able to use my body and be physical, which I love to do, plus being able to use my mind. And feeling like it would be a way to use my mind that was more practical than schools, where they want you to write essays; that felt like a lot of busywork. That and the money were the attractions.

I didn't have much fear except about the math. If I had known at the time what lay ahead, I would have had more fear. But I didn't realize how creepy it might be out there, so I went into it pretty blindly, thinking that it would work out like everything always does. Going with the flow used to be more my way of doing things. I probably had some fears about being qualified, about being able to do things as well as a guy, since you've been told all your life that guys are better at fixing things. I work on that a lot, and it's definitely not as bad as it used to be, but it's there a little still.

At first I was the only woman in the class. There were other women in the school, because there were also very traditional jobs for women taught there, like secretarial and such. The last couple months there was another woman in the plumbing class with me. Two-thirds of the class were black men. Some of them had gone to high school with me at Garfield, so I was pretty comfortable. We had pretty different lifestyles. I lived in collective housing and was into the alternative scene. I don't know exactly what they were doing. They'd have their cars and girl friends and stuff, but we got along pretty well. Some of them I've seen on jobs and they've made it, and some of them I knew wouldn't make it. That was kind of sad and depressing. They were doped up too much and couldn't get the discipline to come to school all the time.

I was at SOIC for about six, seven months. I learned the vocabulary, the names of tools and how to use them. I learned basic stuff like how to do diagrams, but not much hands-on stuff. It helped me when I got into the union. I already had a foothold. There were a lot of guys starting out in the union that didn't know anything. And I knew a lot more than them. So the school was good in that way.

It was bad in that it's only a few months, and then you have to go out and sell yourself. You know some stuff and if you're lucky maybe you have worked on a little job, but you don't have a lot of knowledge.

I felt comfortable with some of the tools like crescent wrenches, screwdrivers, pipe wrenches, and basin wrenches. I used a threading machine and a cutting machine, which were really nice to learn before I went into the union. I also learned how to solder pipes together, which was the only practical hands-on thing I learned. I didn't learn how to fix a toilet or anything like that.

The school really pushed us to get jobs. When Washington Natural Gas was on strike and they were hiring scabs, I got a lot of pressure from the school to go down and apply. I decided to apply to get the experience and see what was going on, but I knew I would never take the job. So I went down and applied and they liked me, which I knew they would. I was supposed to call them back, which, of course, I didn't do. I was called into the school office and given a lot of shit by my instructor and counselor and told I should take the job. I told them there was no way I was gonna work for a scab shop or cross a picket line. They said everyone needs to make money and I shouldn't feel that way. It was ridiculous. I needed a job and should go down and get a job. I thought that was real bad. I didn't expect them to be that way.

After leaving SOIC it took three years for me to get into the union. I filed suit, applied twice, and I was finally accepted. My first job was as a helper. When I first applied, I was told the books were closed and they weren't accepting anyone except blacks. I filed a discrimination suit. Maybe I should explain how it happened that they were just taking blacks. Six years before, UCWA [United Construction Workers Association], a group of black construction workers, had taken them to court to get into the union. At that time there were no women or people of another color who had applied and been rejected, at least that they knew about. So the judge said, "Okay, you'll have to take blacks," but that was all. They weren't told they had to take anybody else, so I got a thing in the mail saying, well, we're taking blacks, so if you qualify, come on down. That's when I filed suit. I didn't hear anything about it and finally got something from the EEOC when I'd been in the union for about a year. Then they opened their books, I applied, and was told I was number fifty-something on the list and they only took twenty. So I just went on with my business doing other things, applied again, and finally got in.

I was hired as a helper during the summer, and right before school started I became a first-year apprentice. From being a helper I pretty much knew what to expect. I was very fortunate on my first job. We were converting an elementary school into a school for retarded or handicapped kids. My journeyman and foreman was the first black man to get into the union. He was a wonderful, nice guy. Since I already knew how to do a lot of things, I was on my own quite a bit. We worked together basically like a team.

We were changing around toilets and things so we were using sledgehammers and malls. Busting up stuff is a heavy kind of work. I also used drills and saber saws and heated up lead until it was cherry red and poured it for showers and different joints. And rotohammering—that's a drill made for going through concrete. It acts like a jackhammer going back and forth, pushing its way into the concrete. Rotohammering isn't that hard, but it's a drag when you're drilling into the ceiling all day long. It's hard on your arms, and a couple times I wasn't given eye protection, so you get little pieces of concrete in your eyes. Now I'm real good about making sure I have eye goggles.

There's no such thing as a typical job. I've been on jobs where I work with just one other guy and a lot of times with a small crew of four or five. Then I've worked on big jobs with fifteen or twenty guys, so it just depends. I've never worked on a crew with another woman. I have been on jobs where there have been other women in different trades and only twice did we have the same lunchtime even. Some of the men I've worked with have been really decent, and some haven't been decent at all. Usually if I'm working with one guy, even if he doesn't like me, we both do our best to get along and do the job well. But if there's another guy for the man to talk with, I might as well be dead. They're real friendly if I'm the only person they have to talk to, but with another man around, first they talk sports and then they start talking about women and stuff. They're real two-faced a lot of times. I haven't developed any friendships where I see anybody off the job.

I haven't been discriminated against in the work too much— just in a social way. I don't know how to explain it, but you're very aware the whole time you're hanging out with these guys that you are different from them. I feel excluded a lot of the

Angela Summer, plumber

time. If I'm in a situation where I can go off and do something else, I don't mind it. A lot of times I like that. During break or lunch is the only time I can be by myself. Sometimes if I am stuck in a place where I can't go away for lunch it can be creepy—but I'm almost used to it. I bring a book and I read. I don't know. . . .

My supervisors—some have been real jerks and some have been real nice. My last foreman was very surprised to see me, but open and thoughtful, a very nice man. Another time I worked for a year with a man who was wonderful. He was in his late fifties and a pleasure to work for. He was very honest, got upset with me a couple times and let me know it, but wasn't a jerk about it. I think it's easy, for a white man especially, to put a white woman like in the role of their kid. Even if they don't think it's good for you to be doing the work, they have a family feeling for you. A lot of their kids are doing things they didn't plan or want 'em doing. They kind of take you under their wing. They're always shocked and find it hard to believe that I'm over twenty years old. It kind of destroys this little girl image.

But they're not all that way. There was this one Mormon man I worked for that was a real jerk. We were a small crew of only four or five guys and all got along pretty well before he came on the job. As the only apprentice, I did a lot of "gofer" work but also got to do things on my own, too. That relationship was destroyed when this new supervisor arrived. Every joke he told was either racist or sexist. I don't remember a lot of them, but one that stuck in my mind was, "My wife didn't mind that I was bringing home scalps, but not ones with holes in them." Something on that order—pretty gross. It really infuriated me 'cause I could feel, I understood how he could get off on that—the idea of scalping a woman—a woman's cunt, as he called it.

Another time on that job we were working sixteen hours a day and under a lot of pressure to get things done quickly. One night when we were working on the fifteenth floor, I was under a sink undoing a nut with a basin wrench. It was an awkward position, a drag, and I was just starting to get it done when he came over and said to me, "Run down to the basement and get me a couple copper fittings."

I said, "Okay, in a minute. I'm almost done." It was gonna take me a half a second to finish that job.

He said, "Get off your cunt and go get that." I was shocked. It just didn't make sense. Like it made a lot of sense for me to finish what I was doing before I got out from under the sink and ran down to the basement and took twenty minutes. I would have to crawl back under there and get into this position again. I wanted to cry and scream.

Finally, I started screaming, "You fucking asshole!" But I didn't feel any better. He just smirked like he'd gotten what he wanted. It's so fun to get women fired up. What really hurt me was there was this guy standing around that I had been working with and felt really good about, and he didn't say a damn thing. It made me feel rotten. I felt like we were friends and had good rapport. None of the other men would have said something like that to me, but with him they felt like they had to stick up for another guy. Behind his back they would tell me he was a creep, but there was this peer pressure with him around.

The union hasn't been much better. They didn't want me in and the big-wigs haven't given me support since I got in. One time I ripped some porno off a wall, a poster-size crotch shot of a woman, and the apprenticeship coordinator said I should have called him in, but that I had to understand I was in a man's trade, and that the men shouldn't have to live by my rules. So I showed him the crotch shot and asked him if he found it objectionable. He said, well, he guessed so. Some other pornographic things have disappeared, and I've been told I could be in trouble and sued by the union for taking personal property, although nobody has seen me take personal property.

The last thing that happened was that there's a Rigid Tool

Angela Summer, plumber

calendar—you might be familiar with them. They don't show naked women. They show women in sleazy bathing suits looking like they're almost fucking tools, and these calendars appeared in our apprentice classrooms last year. So for three nights a week, three hours a night, you're supposed to look at the front of the class at the blackboard with that calendar on it. That's all there is to look at. I talked to the teacher and he took it down, and then it was back up, and he took it down again while I was there, and turned it around for my class. Another woman apprentice, who's not in my class, asked the apprenticeship coordinator to remove it. He wouldn't, said it was a tradition and Rigid Tool calendars have been around for twenty-five years. And she replied that so has woman beating and child abuse been around for twenty-five years, and you could consider them to be a tradition, but that doesn't make 'em right. Then he started screaming at her and said it stayed. At that point, I went to him and said I wanted it removed also. He said no, it stayed.

I found out through this calendar thing that if I went to EEOC the only thing they could do is file a suit. They can't call up and say, "You should stop doing this thing." I called the Washington State Human Rights Commission and I got a guy that actually called the coordinator up three different times. Then he said that he'd done more than he should have, and all he could do is file a suit, and if I wanted to file a suit he'd love to take my case. But if I file a suit, I'll be completely ostracized, so for now, all I can do is scream and rant and rave and kick things. And I talk with my friends.

You know, your friends change when you change. Most of my friends are women in non-traditional work. I hang out a lot with women that are in my union. I need the support of women who do what I do. Like I lived for a while with a woman medical student, and it just didn't work out because what we were doing with our lives was so different. We couldn't support each other or understand what we were going through.

My body's changed a lot from the work, too. I feel really strong. When I'm not working, I feel out of shape and look forward to going back to work. I don't push myself too hard physically. You can build yourself up, and if you go slower, it'll just take a little longer to get there. In the last year the union has taught us about taking care of our bodies and there's more consciousness about not doing more than you should. I did once put my back out picking up four-inch cast-iron pipe, but usually I'll ask for help. With older guys it's pretty easy to get help, but younger guys are still into the macho thing.

I've also done some obvious things to my body, like smashing my fingers so they'll never be the same. I had done some core drilling and was carrying the core drill, that probably weighs eighty pounds or more, back to a shaft. It was a messy job site with a lot of stuff laying around, and I tripped over some rebar that was sticking out. Rebar's a half-inch-round metal bar used to reinforce concrete. So I tripped over it, and I think I could have regained my feet, but I forgot about the weight of the core drill on my shoulder. When I realized I couldn't stand up, I threw the drill away from my body, but there was no way I could pull my hand back out. It bounced off my fingers and smashed them. I mean they were split open. The foreman came running out and ran around in circles until I got in the van, honked the horn, and said, "Get over here and drive me to the hospital." It took us about three minutes to get to Harborview, and I spent five days in the hospital having pins put in my fingers.

I was out of work for ten months. The bones didn't grow together right on my ring finger, so they decided to do a bone graft. I went into the hospital again for four days, and they opened up my elbow and took bone out of it and added the bone to the finger. I did physical therapy for my little pinkie, too, and everything was supposed to be fine, but it's pretty stiff. It won't curve beyond a forty-five-degree angle. Actually, not to minimize it, but if you're gonna hurt some fingers, those are the best two to hurt. It hasn't really been a problem—just a drag when it's wet and cold. They get stiff.

I'm a fourth-year apprentice, almost a journeyman now, and I'm kind of scared by that. I've gotten into this mold of the subordinate. I mean, I'm so used to having someone tell me what to do that I worry about having to just go out there and do it on my own. Lately though, I've been getting more feedback as far as people telling me that I'd done a good job. It's not something that men do. It's hard. People don't always give you strokes or good feedback. But I usually get the feeling, even if they don't tell me, that they're pretty happy with my work, because sometimes you get into a rhythm, really producing, and you're partners. I hope that feeling carries over to when I'm a journeywoman.

I think plumbing is a good field for women. Oftentimes carpentry is harder physically. Plumbing sounds like dirty work. You think you're going to be working with shit or toilets all the time, so women don't think about doing it much, but it's a good job with lots of security.

Soldier / Long-Haul Trucker / Bus Driver

KATHRYN BROOKE

*Kathryn Brooke describes herself as a "blue-collar baby,"
meaning that she has floated from one blue-collar job to
another. A profession was never an option in her life.*

I grew up in Chicago. My parents were Catholic and thought I
should be a nun. You see, I was adopted. They got me from the
Catholic Home Bureau, the Catholic supermarket for unwanted
babies during the war. So, of course, I went to parochial schools
all the way through. The teachers were convinced that I was
there just to harass them. I wasn't a rebel, but when things
didn't add up, I'd ask questions and be pinged for it. Like one
time in catechism class we were supposed to go through this
book and memorize long explanations for simple questions.
One of the questions was, "What is the difference between a
mortal sin and a venal sin," and they were talking about steal-
ing. If you stole a penny from someone who made X number of
dollars a year that's just a venial sin, but if you take like five
dollars from the same individual, that's a mortal sin. Well I
popped up and said, "What about inflation?" I was told to leave
the room.

In high school at St. Thomas it was the same old stuff. I didn't
fit in with the program. My mold kept cracking and they would
have to wet down the clay and start over again. I was *really* a
rebellious piece of pottery there, and so they finally just gave up
on me and asked me to leave after my junior year. I said, "That's
cool," and started waitressing in restaurants.

Kathryn Brooke, soldier/long-haul trucker/bus driver

When I was seventeen I made one of my many mistakes. At that time the only way a good Catholic girl left the house before she was eighteen was to get married or join the convent. By then I knew I would never be in a convent, so I got married to someone I'd known for three weeks to escape from the house. I got pregnant and didn't even know how it happened. Right after the baby was born I left my husband and had to work two jobs to make ends meet. Well, he sweet-talked me into going back with him, but by this time I knew how to get pregnant. I'd been told if you drank orange juice that it would help. I was trying to figure out how the citrus fruit prevented pregnancy—did you drink it before or after?—when I got pregnant with my second son, Danny. Later I learned you drank the orange juice *instead of*—so after Danny was born, I left him again. I couldn't take the beatings any more. This must have been nineteen sixty-three through sixty-four.

I got a nineteen fifty-five Dodge with no reverse and went to Los Angeles. I knew if I got far enough away from home I wouldn't be tempted to go back with him. But then I made another mistake. I like mistakes. I thought, "Well, I gotta go to church," so I talked to a priest about what my condition was. Great! Six days later my husband was knocking on my door. The priest said he told him where I was for the benefit of the children. So I thanked him very much for his assistance. One night after a bad argument, my husband raped me and that's how my third son came along. I said, "That's it," and left for good.

By this time I was up in Washington and had heard of welfare. So I went down to my friendly welfare office at eight in the morning, got a number, waited in line, and they saw me at about a quarter 'til four that afternoon. They said to come back the next day. When I came back, they told me I hadn't been in the state long enough to get welfare money, but I could have low-income housing. They put me in a place out in White Center that rented for thirty-three dollars a month. That little thirty-three dollars a month back then was a fortune to me. I could hardly make it.

I went back to restaurant work. I'd work the breakfast shift, stay through lunch, and then come back to work the dinner. By working the evening shift I wouldn't get out of there until eleven-thirty at night. The kitchen would be closed by then. It was an Italian restaurant and they'd put the meatballs, spaghetti, and ravioli in a big can over night. This was before the days of plastic bags, but not before the time of Tupperware. Everyone wanted to know why I carried such a big purse. Well, it was a grocery bag. I'd reach in as I walked through the kitchen and grab a handful of meatballs, cheese, or sausage and put it in a Tupperware bowl in my purse. After awhile my purse smelled like oregano, and I had all the dogs in the neighborhood following me as I walked down the street.

Just when I was thinking there had to be a better way, along came Jim, who was overwhelmed by my strength and stamina. I'm five foot six and weighed ninety-eight pounds at the time. The energy had to come from God, because otherwise I never could have made it. I was twenty-one years old and the mother of three kids. Jim was twenty-seven years older than me. I really fell in love for the first time. He came when I needed a father for myself so I could be a mother to my kids, and he needed a daughter. Our needs were met in each other so we got married. Nine months and one day later our daughter was born. By the time Michelle was a year old, I didn't need a father any more. I needed a husband and the children needed a daddy.

Jim wasn't a very good manager of money. He tried selling real estate and cars, but we were in the midst of a big Boeing recession. So we moved to Elma and started a restaurant. I worked my butt off—went a year and a half without a day off—but we lost the place. Jim never paid the taxes, so it was shut down. That was real hard on me. I knew then I would never be able to have the yellow house with the white picket fence and my little girl dressed in pinafores. "Leave it to Beaver" or "Father Knows Best" weren't going to be for me.

After we lost the restaurant, I became a born-again Christian. A neighbor lady had a Bible time every Wednesday afternoon for the little kids. I said, "Wow, a free babysitter," and sent my kids. Every time I saw that lady she was so up, exuberant, happy. I couldn't understand it, because her husband beat her, drank, and smoked. And all the time she talked about this Jesus. It got to the point where I told her, "It sounds like this Jesus is your best friend."

She said, "Oh, but he is." And I thought, "This lady needs help. I better get away from her." Then she asked, "Are you saved?"

"Saved? Saved from what? Of course, I'm saved." I knew I didn't come from a monkey. Good Catholic girls know that.

But one afternoon I laid down. I fell asleep. Now I'm not saying I had an out-of-body experience or a vision. Call it a dream. I had died. Jim and my kids and my mother were there, and I saw a little cloud leave my body. It was going to a place called Hell, where there was going to be torment. Right then I woke up and said, "I give up. I give up." That's how I got saved. I was born again and felt it immediately. It wasn't religion, but a definite relationship with Jesus Christ. I was charged and the charge is still with me. Not too much later, I was praying one night for my son, Matthew, when I hear a voice—not with this ear, but the one behind it, inside of my head. It said, "I will show you how." And then I started speaking in tongues. I mean, I took Spanish and I can't roll an R if I tried, but all of a sudden there were these words coming from me. It was beautiful. This was before the charismatic movement, so I got thrown out of the Baptist church I had been attending. I heard about a church called the Full Gospel Pentecostal Church on KBLE radio, and that's how a good Catholic girl became a Pentecostal.

During this same time I finished up my high school degree

and started taking community college classes in commercial foods. An Army recruiter at the college was pushing a new Army program called Stripes for Skills. He said you go in as an E-3 and two months after basic pick up E-5. Well, I didn't know what an E-3 or E-5 was but I soon learned. Normally it takes six or seven years in the service to make E-5. The recruiter said the only problem was that I was married and had kids. He said I could petition the court for a legal separation, giving all the care, custody, and maintenance of the kids to my husband, then go through basic and get my E-3. As an E-3 I could reverse the court order and have my family as dependents. This was March of nineteen seventy-four. We were awful broke, so about a week later I did it.

I had seen the recruiting films about all the fun you had in basic training. You know, everybody is out there doing PT [physical training] and saluting the flag and looking patriotic. It didn't look too bad. And, well I guess my husband and I thought it would be a new beginning for us. So I kissed Jim and the kids goodbye and went to Fort Jackson, South Carolina, for basic. That was one of the most sad times of my life. It was the first time I was separated from my kids. On paper I was single, so I had to think and act single. There was a real conflict of interest between on paper and in heart. But I knew I had a job to perform. It was like when I went through labor with my kids. I learned on my second child that with every pain you are closer to birth. And so I just conditioned myself to thinking that every minute that passes I'm closer to being home with them.

What was basic like? Well, the PT was not like in the training films. It was a pain in the the tusch. And it wasn't like "Private Benjamin" either. It was what you made of it. I thought it was kind of neat to learn how to iron fatigues on the floor and be able to make a bed so a quarter bounces off it and how to stand in line at three-thirty in the morning so you can be the first one down to the mess hall to eat by seven. It's just a bunch of razzle-dazzle that they use to try to break you, and in trying to break you, they make you. I'd been through a lot of crap in my life and this was the first time I felt like I had accomplished something.

When I got my permanent party station at Fort Ord, we reversed the court order and my family came down. I'm not going to say it was because of my situation, but it wasn't more than a month later that the military changed the rules so you had to have an actual divorce decree to get in—no more legal separations. I guess it got expensive for the military to move my family and all my personal effects down. Since I had dependents, I immediately qualified for housing. That was something! Okay, they write the rules and you play the game, so if you go by the rules in getting over, then you shouldn't get pinged for it.

When I started doing my job, I didn't know what in the world I was doing. But the thing I've got going for me is I don't mind doing paperwork. You can have grease three inches high and cockroaches crawling across the counter, but by God if that paperwork is squared away, "You've got it together, Sarge!" So the mess sergeant, Sergeant Lawrence, put me in charge of paperwork. He was an alcoholic with about four months until retirement, so he didn't care about anything. But the one thing he cared about was me. He said, "They aren't going to screw you out of that E-5. I'm gonna see to it that you get it." So he schooled me in all the essentials, like what a lieutenant was and how to talk back to a warrant officer without losing my military bearing. Thanks to him I made my E-5 on October fourth, nineteen seventy-four.

The trouble started when I made E-5. I had to put in a lot of extra hours to justify having those stripes. They were hard to hang onto. Everybody in the world wanted those stripes. You know, they wanted to know how come I'd gotten E-5 when they'd been in for ten years and didn't have 'em. Then my husband started getting upset about the long hours I worked.

When he couldn't take it any longer he left me. I felt totally rejected. I had done this for him. It was my name on the dotted line, but he packed up and left. I could have gone to the NCO club every night and gotten bombed, but I turned to the Bible where it says, "All things work together for the good." I was where God wanted me to be, so I served out my three years.

The military doctors screwed up some surgery and messed up the sphincter muscle for my bladder. As a result I have to drain my bladder a couple of times a day. No one knows about that except for the Veterans Administration. So I get three hundred eighty dollars a month, fifty percent disability, because they screwed up, but I did my duty.

After getting off active duty, I kicked back and collected unemployment for eighteen months before getting into trucking. I knew a guy who worked for a trucking firm, and one weekend he said, "I have to take a load down to L.A. Do you want to go?" That's when I learned what a Kenworth was. I needed a challenge. My kids were older, and I was ready to do something different, so I hit the road.

I worked partners with an independent trucker. There was no sex involved. He was a married man and his wife was one of my best friends. It was just a business relationship. He respected me for who I was, and he needed someone who would work cheap, and I worked cheap. It was a split after expenses. You couldn't get most partners to work for a split after expenses. They'd want a per diem and meals and stuff, but I was going through a period where I needed to get loose, get away. I could not have afforded to pay for a vacation to all the places I went to. I was bringing in two thousand dollars a month and getting piles of job satisfaction. My kids were real proud to have a mother on the road, a trucker. A young couple took care of my daughter when I was gone, and my mother lived only three blocks away, so it was very convenient.

A woman trucker had to constantly prove herself. When you come out of a truck to get some coffee at a truck stop, you're not

Kathryn Brooke, soldier/long-haul trucker/bus driver

seen as a trucker. You're not a driver. You're a beaver. A beaver is a term given to female truck drivers. They have gross bumper stickers about beavers. I'm sure you've seen them. One says, "Save our forest. Eat a beaver." I don't know if it's because of the tail—piece of tail. I sure don't know. I don't have buck teeth. But what's important is to do your job and not lose your integrity. Fools are gonna talk so you just have to carry on.

There was a lot to learn about trucking. There's two basic truck models. The conventional is the one with the long snout. The COE, or cab over engine, is the square one like BJ in "BJ and the Bear" had. Also trucks take diesel, not gasoline. You don't ever say gasoline. The first time into a fill-up station, I asked the man to fill it up with gas. He just refused, and I didn't realize my mistake. It's fuel, not gas.

Our truck was real comfortable. It had a sleeper, a little color tv set, a microwave oven, and was all padded. When you lay down in the bed, you strap yourself in. One drives and one sleeps. That way you keep it rolling all the time. Course, how long you really drive it, and how long you put down on paper for the State Patrol are two different things. According to the Patrol, you're only supposed to drive eight hours in a twenty-four-hour period, but you don't. You drive until the coffee buzz wears off and your partner takes the wheel. When you put more miles on in a day than the Patrol allows, that's an overload. Then you take the back roads and wait for the scales to close. Where did you think all these trucks came from on Saturday and Sunday nights? They're all overloaded.

I never thought of it in terms of hours a week, but as trips or loads. Like, say we had a trip down to Phoenix. Well, rather than drive back up to Washington empty, we'd go through a broker to find out who needed a load brought up here. Then you get paid for both ways. It's real uncertain, though, how long you'd be gone. My longest time away from home was twenty-three days. We'd had a breakdown and I flew home.

Most truck drivers, if they see you back up a truck, jack that trailer around, let your fifth wheel down, and hook up, know you can handle the job. I think a lot of women bring heartache onto themselves. If you put on Levis that are three sizes too tight and walk around with a blouse open down, then you're gonna get sexually harassed. I don't care if you're a monk. But if you maintain your integrity and do your job, it'll be recognized.

I really loved that job, but it got to the point where I said, "Kate, you've gotta grow up." I had to change my short-range goal of just getting that quick buck to a long-range goal. I wasn't always gonna be thirty. Pretty soon I was gonna be forty, then fifty, and then sixty. I was gonna want to retire someday and knew I had to get into a job where there were some benefits.

That's when I started thinking about driving a bus. I loved driving and the transit company had the most benefits. Well I got hired for part time and went full time two-and-a-half months later. I thought it would be pretty much like driving truck, but I was mistaken. God, it's like the difference between sweeping the rug and using a vacuum cleaner. Driving a bus is a lot more secure. You know where you're going and spend every night home in your own bed.

When you start there, they train you on every kind of bus imaginable from a 200 American Motors General, which is a nineteen fifty-two vintage monstrosity, to the Articulateds, which are sixty-foot-long bending buses from Germany. All of them are diesel except for the trolleys, which are electric. Before you even get behind the wheel, you're taught defensive driving techniques. The cardinal rule is summed up in what they call the Three S's—Safety, Service, Schedule. That's the order of priority you must keep.

An example of a safety rule is keeping your distance behind another vehicle on the freeway. You pick a point the car is going past, and then count the seconds 'til you reach it in the bus. One, two, three, four on a regular bus. On an Artic you count to six. Another safety point is checking your mirrors every six seconds.

Kathryn Brooke, soldier/long-haul trucker/bus driver

The supervision uses fear as a tactic on new drivers. It is just like coming out of basic training and not knowing what you're getting into, and before you know it you're caught like a fly on flypaper. Supervisors are people who used to be drivers the same as you are, but now they stand on corners waiting, anticipating, praying that you'll make a mistake. If you ask me, it's a bunch of bullshit. When a ten-year driver does something wrong, they look the other way, but let a new driver do something— Like in downtown Seattle, have you ever been sitting in your little Volkswagen and got stuck behind a bus and said, "Those damn buses"? Well, that's cool; you can afford to swear, but when you're driving that bus it's a whole different story. There you are in that bus and see three buses in front of you that the traffic won't let pull off the curb. Well, if you can do it, you stick your ass end in the curb lane and pull your front end out to where the traffic can't get by you, so those three buses in front of you can pull out of the zone. You gotta protect each other out there. It's like a war out there on the streets. So if you're an old-line driver and you do that, it's fine. But let a new driver do that and a supervisor see you, you're standing before "the man." It's called an RDA, report of disciplinary action. Each infraction is worth so many points. The maximum you can get during your probationary period is fifteen. The points stay on your record for a year. One morning I got stopped by a policeman on the way to work and was two minutes late; I got pinged with four points for that.

Another thing you get hit with right off the bat is the union. You pay, I think, a three-hundred-fifty-dollar initiation fee and then seventeen fifty a month. It don't matter if you work sixty hours a week as a full-timer or only an hour and a half a day as a part-timer, you still pay the three-hundred-fifty-dollar initiation.

Have you ever had a fancy on a Saturday night to steal a bus? I'll tell you how to do it. It's not just a simple matter of going out and turning on the key. What key? They don't use keys. First thing you do is find a transit base and get on a bus. Now if the doors are locked, you squeeze them open. They open very easily. Once on the bus, you push a switch marked, "Day or Night." Then you hit the tiny button that says, "Start." Give it some fuel, just a little bit, and it should start right up if it's in neutral.

We're also supposed to check the oil and water, but the union says no, that we're not mechanics. But we do have to go around the coach and make sure there's no scratches and all the lights are working. If there's a scratch when that bus comes in at night and you haven't reported it, then you get pinged for it. You gotta cover your tail all the time.

I'm not working right now. I haven't worked since October twentieth, nineteen eighty. I had finished my morning run and stopped to help this new driver back up her coach. It was her first day. Anyhow, to make a long story short, when I stepped off her bus, I slipped in some wet cement and landed on my behind. I told the chain of command about it and was taken to the hospital, where they rubbed cotton all over my arms and legs, and I was told to blink, and they put a pin in each thigh and said I was fine. I said, "I've got spots in front of my eyes. In fact, there's a great, big green blob on the end of your nose." The doctor didn't understand what I was trying to tell him. He sent me home, said to take two aspirin, and report to work the next morning.

That night I had a splitting headache and real bad pain in my back and down my legs. I went to another doctor the next day. He said to take Valium and stay in bed for three weeks. The pain got worse and worse until one night I passed out during dinner. They took me to the hospital in an ambulance. The next day an orthopedic surgeon said the nerves in my back were screwed up because I had broken my tailbone.

Up until then no one had even taken an X-ray. This was a good three to three-and-a half weeks after the accident. They gave me

Kathryn Brooke, soldier/long-haul trucker/bus driver

pain killers and muscle relaxers and said to go home and rest. That's what I did until New Year's Eve, when I started vomiting up this stuff that looked like coffee grounds. It was blood. Happy New Year! I ended up in the hospital with a bag of blood hanging over me and a needle stuck in my arm. The medicine this one doctor had given me for pain had eaten holes in the lining of my esophagus and going down into my stomach. So now, not only have I got a broken tailbone, but I've got a restricted diet and ulcers and they're talking about sending me to the pain clinic.

Sailor

TERESA SELFE

*Very slender, almost fragile in appearance, and soft-spoken,
she defies all the stereotypes of tough lesbians.*

I remember having friends of mine changing tires and being
extremely impressed at their abilities and thinking I wanted to
be able to do that and why not? But I'm very slight physically
and had always assumed I was not strong enough to attempt any
type of labor that involved physical stress. It didn't really scare
me. It's just that I basically didn't like to work and avoided it as
much as possible, only making enough money to take trips and
things. The financial aspect was a hell of a lot of the reason I got
into non-traditional work. I was tired of not having made
enough money and having traveled enough and lived long
enough that I was coming more realistically to terms with the
amount of money needed to survive. I mean, I have picked
cherries in the Okanogan and later cucumbers, worked in restaurants a whole lot, sold shoes, and worked in a bookstore.
Yeah, that's about it. And with the way wage scales and everything go, what was a livable amount of money back then would
not be now. I wasn't really poverty stricken but it was always
very difficult for me to make enough money to save any or to
even think about buying a car. I probably lived on anywhere
from say three hundred fifty to five hundred dollars a month.

One of the things I particularly disliked, aside from the
money involved, was that a good percentage of what I had to do
was inside, and there were only minimal rights for my fellow

Teresa Selfe, sailor

employees and myself. It was very limiting to have to be focused into using only certain parts of myself. I was also very rarely given anything to do that made me feel I was really accomplishing something. It was always the kind of never-ending tasks that just go on forever.

Over the years I have known men who were involved in various aspects of construction and always seemed to have enormous amounts of money. Never wanted to spend it on you, but always had amazing amounts of money. Always had suntans and muscles and cars and seemed to have a more general control over what was happening to them. They could change jobs, and that always made an impact on me. I was also involved for a while with a woman who worked in the water department and made extremely good money. She was the first woman who I knew intimately who was involved in a non-traditional trade. That influenced me, made it a possibility. But it wasn't until I moved to Seattle when I was surrounded by organizations and groups that seemed encouraging of this—just seeing flyers about workshops on women in non-traditional trades, having Mechanica available where you could learn the details about steps in joining a union. That's when it became a real possibility.

In the summer of nineteen seventy-nine I needed a job very badly and was thinking very seriously of getting one outside, when I saw this huge apartment building being renovated really close to where I lived. There were a few women working there, and at that point in time it seemed exactly what I should try. I was persistent in going back and asking for a job, so I was eventually hired. I did a lot of painting, basic sanding, put in baseboards, countertops, linoleum, deadbolts, rehung doors, did a substantial amount of finish carpentry, built a railing, and did a lot of sheetrock. The work involved all kinds of tools—everything from very sharp saws to certain kinds of power tools, that I had no familiarity with before, to certain kinds of chemicals, to odd balancing situations where I had to do a lot of heavy stuff, dropping things on my feet, hammers and nails, sharp, sharp, heavy things that I could not anticipate how they would respond.

Quite frequently I had to ask someone for help in figuring out how to do something new. Rather than have the men acknowledge my question, I would sometimes have to ask them two or three times because they were ignoring me. Then instead of simply answering my questions, I would have tools actually physically removed from my hands and the job practically done for me, and I'm talking about things that were very simple to do, that would involve only a small how-much-of-this-should-I-cut-off type of thing. At first I just allowed that to happen. After a certain amount of time, when I got to know the tools of the trade a little bit more, and I knew the question I was asking was something that could be easily answered, I would very often express irritation at them taking the tool out of my hands— almost to the point of sometimes taking the tool back and saying, "That's all you had to say," or "I can do that myself. I've done that before. I know how to do that. You don't have to show me. Let me do it myself." Some of them got angry to the point where they would not speak to me for two or three days afterward. I didn't pay much attention to their reactions.

I met a man working at the company who told me about a seamanship school he had attended in Ballard. He was just working construction while waiting for NOAA [National Oceanographic Association] to call him. We had many discussions about the frustrations of trying to get your Z card. To work in the marine industry you had to have a Z card. But if you don't know anybody, or haven't had a substantial amount of experience on the private level, or aren't willing to put out two or three hundred dollars to bribe someone, you can't get a Z card and can't work. But this man mentioned there was this school

Teresa Selfe, sailor

where I could get my Z card if I graduated. Now I had always liked the sea and wanted to travel, so I decided it was time for me to see what I could do about getting my Z card once and for all.

I went to the school with only the expectation of getting my Z card—seaman's papers. I did not know enough about the marine industry at the time to know it would be extremely difficult for me to get into the unions and work even if I had my Z card. I was not aware of the way the marine industry had changed and how difficult it was going to be for me.

There were a few other women in the school, but they were mostly in the engineering program, while I was in the deck program. The engineering program is more concerned with the mechanics of the ship, whereas the deck is more concerned with navigation, meteorology, road-map type of stuff, laws, rules of the road concerning behavior towards other ships, legalities involved, signaling, and nautical terminology. The school really did try to cover just about every aspect of working on ships that one could encounter and that could be presented in a classroom form. I also thought that in actuality they were fairly encouraging to women in the school. You didn't find yourself completely blacklisted or getting automatic bad grades or having people slashing your tires so you couldn't make your class.

But when dealing with men there are a few guaranteed things that come up to one degree or another, particularly if they feel you are entering into an area they have designated as their own. I can remember numerous incidents where I felt that as a human being I was being singled out to have fun poked at me in one way or another. You know, just for the fact I was there, or my response was being looked for, searched for, either by somebody provoking me or attention being called to my reaction. They would insinuate that something I asked was a dumb question or continually turned the fact that a woman was in the classroom into a joke situation. When someone said, "seaman," another would say "seaperson" and kind of joke about it or they say, "With ladies in the room this or that is goin' on," and act as if they were doing me a big favor by pointing out that I was there. They never seemed comfortable with me being there. I was either an entertainment or ignored. That is except for the navigation teacher and the meteorologist. These two men were very objective in their treatment of women.

There were a couple teachers in the engineering department who fancied themselves to be ladies' men to some degree, and I thought their choice of humor was extremely tactless. I've blocked out a lot of the crap they said, but all I will say is there were continual references in class to women's bodies, other women's bodies, *my* woman's body. You were always being called "cutie" or "good-looking." A number of the women in the school were continually being asked out socially by these men. It was just a very general lack of respect. It was like being in a Green Bay Packers locker room and either being ignored or on stage.

There were two other lesbians in the program at various times. One was in engineering class and just quit coming to class one day. I don't know why. The other one was in the deck program. She was in her early twenties and very much a soft-spoken pleaser, not one to confront anyone with this issue. I'm sure no one else there knew she was a lesbian. We didn't have much in common, so I stopped extending myself to her just strictly because we were lesbians.

The straight women were mostly supportive of my being there. Of course, they didn't know I was gay. Like most straight women, they were much more concerned with what the men thought of them and their interaction with the men than their interaction with me. They did not treat me unkindly. It's just that interaction with me was not a top priority for them. They basically seemed to enjoy being in a majority-male-type situation, incredible as that seems. There were a couple women in the program that I became close friends with. As far as support went, I relied mostly on them. My roommate and ex-lover was pretty supportive, too. But in general, the area itself was so foreign to people outside the school that talking with them was pretty useless.

I did learn in the school how self-destructive it is to continually keep your mouth shut just to keep harmony. Maybe expressing your opinion is better. I remember one incident, a pretty low-key one, where a teacher in the middle of a marine law class began going on at great length about this woman who had been a secretary of his and didn't shave her legs. He kept going on and on about how disgusting that was and equating his disgust at her not shaving her legs to her complete person being distasteful. I didn't say anything, but it hurt so much. I had come from a very isolated lesbian community and had not had much daily contact with men for a long time and generally found their presence disruptive to my peace of mind and self-worth. I learned how to ignore certain actions and comments that were not worth being unsettled about as long as the school was important to me. The actual school situation was a lot more like daily life a woman would experience in the city than the extremes my jobs were. As such, I wasn't really prepared.

In the spring the oil company comes to the school to recruit new employees. Their method was to hire people as summer workers and try to lure them into becoming permanent employees. They specifically came with the intention of hiring women and other minorities. I was interviewed and hired as a summer employee in the spring of nineteen eighty.

I went out to sea on an oil tanker in June. I had not anticipated the cumulative effect of being away from all support systems other than those that could be found on the ship. Other than that everything I encountered was pretty much what I had expected. I had expected to enjoy the sights and sounds of the sea and the various animals; to find a fairly monotonous routine, a regularity about life, every day being the same; a separation from events on shore; emotionally, intellectually, as well as physically, an increasing introversion with myself. I expected to learn a lot about myself through contact with people from many different walks of life and areas of the country. I did. I also expected a substantial amount of harassment from the men in being female and as a being which can be approached sexually. I expected to have my capabilities invalidated, which frequently happened. It was fairly much what I expected in a lot of ways. It was only *my* actions that I had not expected.

I had just come from an extremely upsetting personal situation with my ex-lover. I was physically and emotionally drained, so when I got on the ship my self-image was not particularly high. I was frightened about being around so many men and nothing but men. I also worried about the effect my being a lesbian would have on the people around me and, therefore, their treatment of me. I had very mixed feelings about whether I should come out to anybody there. That first trip I only came out to a couple individuals and not for quite some time.

Being on a ship is very confining. The hallways are narrow. The rooms are narrow, so you are constantly hitting things because it has an unbalanced state to it. You are constantly being walked past or walked around or having to walk around. You are dealing with materials that are always metal or plastic or wood—usually metals that are very cold or very hot and are usually heavy. There's a lot of dirt, especially on a tanker. There's grease on the floor. There's always grease somewhere. It's very difficult to stay clean. There's a strange physical sensation of a large body trying to suck you into it, becoming one of the masses, because it is very hard to get away from anybody. It's difficult because you are never really physically alone. You're either completely alone in your little room or you always have somebody next to you, in front of you, or behind you.

Teresa Selfe, sailor

When I was working in the galley my specific duty was to serve food to the officers and clean up afterwards. Most of the non-white people on ship ended up working in the galley. Most of the people in positions of authority in the galley were, in my opinion, completely crazy in a really negative way. One steward with a hair-trigger temper used to sit and glare at nothing for hours, constantly repeating nonsense to himself. Another one that comes to mind was a man who was extraordinarily obscene, and to the point where a good percentage of the other men on the ship actually thought the guy was gross, which really says something. He insisted on doing things like discussing his first sexual experience when he was eleven years old in the alleyway with a number of other guys and some young girl who was giving them all blow jobs. He discussed this in great detail with the man who was washing dishes in the sink beside me, and when I asked him if he could please continue the conversation at some other time, he asked me why, and I said because I found it extremely offensive. He then said, "Good," and that I should go somewhere else. I did.

When I worked on the deck my specific duties were to stand the eight-to-twelve watch both in the morning and the evening, to help with the tying up and un-docking, to stand various bow watches, to take in and put out fire hoses and other fire equipment, to degrease decks, and to keep the upper deck, the interior upper deck, and the crew's lounge clean. The big, heavy ropes and lines you are pulling in are extremely heavy, particularly when they've got ice frozen on them. I damaged my wrist that way. You're constantly under physical strain—in part because the number of days off are very limited, so it had a cumulative effect on you. But also you have to carry big boxes of Chlorox around and pick up seventy-pound cargoes and haul them up and down ladders. It's hard on your body.

While on the deck crew I had an extremely nice, older man, who was Swedish or something, as boatswain. He was very quiet in his dealings with us. That was in marked contrast with all the other men in positions of authority. I appreciated that man very much.

The other part of the ship I worked in was the engine room. There I had to clean the lower deck, laundry room, and exercise room. Then I did anything else that was requested of me. Mostly it involved painting walls and machinery in the fiddly, which is part of the engine room. It's very high up and extremely hot. I also degreased decks, cleaned up oil spills throughout the engine room, cleaned up any messes involving insulation, changed the filters on the big oil fuel transfer pumps, let people know if there were any leaks, swept up behind the boilers, cleaned out the big inert-gas-system fans that had this very abrasive, poisonous soot on them that used to get on your skin and burn it, and anything else I was told to do.

In the engine room I worked under the first assistant engineer. He was a bright, energetic man who had a thing about women— liked them socially, but basically, I think to be very honest, did not like them at all as people. He was extraordinarily offensive to me and used to make comments about my breasts being small. At one point he said to me that he didn't know I had a hysterectomy. Somebody, I guess, had told him about that, and he then proceeded to go into great detail about how he had noticed most women walk a little funny a few days out of the month, and he had noticed that I didn't walk funny. Then he started talking about how amazing it was that some women could fit two Tampaxes, one right on top of the other, in there and wasn't that an extraordinary thing. I replied that I was not in the least interested in discussing female genitalia with him in any way, shape, or form. He later approached me to come up to his room and play my fiddle for him and asked me to give him a kiss. I ignored him. There were comments like that going on all of the time on the ship.

A couple of the other men in the engine room refused to look at me or talk to me the whole time I was there. Actually the ignoring didn't bother me that much. I would rather have them ignoring me than trying to interact with me personally. I mean they're a lot less trouble to deal with if they're not trying to get into your pants. I just have certain reactions to male heterosexuality obsessions. Specifically, there were men in the engine room that were very sociable to me until they found out I was gay and after that refused to have anything to do with me. I just basically figured that when people are acting like twelve-year-old children who are angry, then you've got enough negative reactions in there. I wasn't going to lower myself to that level.

I was on a ship for a while where there were four other women. Also at one point I was the only woman on the ship. Basically the women got along fairly well. A good percentage of the time we would be spread out. There would be a female radio operator; there would be a woman working the galley; and maybe one on deck or whatever. In situations like that, the women had a tendency to get along quite well. Most of the women that I saw on ships were much more interested in their relationships with the men than they were with the other women, so they were just as glad the other women were working in other departments so they could be the center of attention in the particular department they worked in. It changed a bit when you got a number of women working in the same department. Nine times out of ten there was a lot of competition among the women for the men's attention. If a man appeared to get along with or like another woman, the first woman would flirt with him, try to be more attractive, and make sexual inferences. You know the way straight women have a tendency to be.

This whole situation was very difficult for me for many reasons. Until I came out I had a terrifically hard time dealing with my own conscience because I was not being honest about my sexuality, and that was difficult because I had been an active, functioning homosexual for a while. It was hard for me to be in a situation where I had to shut up about it. There was nobody to reinforce my visions of what was going on. I felt very alone. These people were functioning in a very different reality than I was. There was nobody there to tell me that I was okay, that I wasn't sick, and that I wasn't strange. You know, I didn't see any happy homosexuals around me, and therefore it was very difficult for me to maintain any kind of positive self-image because I certainly couldn't relate to the role models around me, the straight people. My discomfort came out in various physical ailments. The first summer I was out there my stress was such that my hair started to fall out. I was getting tremendous rashes and not sleeping well. I was having nightmares and felt like some kind of semi-freak. I declined any offers of friendship because I didn't want to get close enough to anyone so I'd confide. I thought at that time being out of the closet probably would be, in the long run, much harder. After the first time out I decided to come out. It was easier to live with myself. Then I was ignored—hostilely ignored, but ignored. That wasn't such a difficult situation because I am moderately accustomed to negative reactions from people.

As far as my treatment by the other women, there's a few things I have to add here. The first time out there was a woman that I knew slightly from the school. I did not know at this time if she was gay or not. She knew I was and happened to be of the temperament that she needed a lot of attention from everybody and had enough homosexual tendencies to be jealous of any other friendships I had on the ship. The first couple months were extremely difficult for me because she would flirt with me and even ask me to sleep with her, and yet she was doing so only to get some kind of attention, and when it came down to being supportive of me in any respect, she was not there.

The other straight women also were flirtatious with me if they knew I was gay. They somehow thought of me as some kind of sexual ego gratification on their part. They got a kick out of me thinking they were attractive. They just basically treated me in many ways the same as they gamed around with the men. You know, flirting and even coming into your room at night. They enjoyed watching me open up to them emotionally, be drawn to them, and then immediately would retreat back into their safe heterosexual role. That took a lot out of me even though these things are more easily dealt with when you're out. If women are the only people you're inclined to open up to or feel any emotional attachments to, the double message really takes its toll. It was very difficult being on ship with other women and having their attention directed to the males that were around them.

There is another thing about a lot of straight women on ships. Many of them didn't try to do their jobs competently. They liked taking long breaks and to do whatever because they knew that as minorities, if they got fired, they could throw sex discrimination at the company, so the company wasn't likely to fire them. See, most of the minorities there could get away with a lot of stuff that a lot of the basic white males could not, and that's another reason why the basic white males resented women and minorities.

It was always very important to me to do a good job. Yet it seemed like I got criticized more. In the engine room I got an unfair evaluation from the first assistant I mentioned earlier who was making the comments about Tampaxes. On the evaluation was a question which asked, "Is there anything about this employee's health which could make it possible for them not to do their job well?" There were "Yes, No," and "Unsure" boxes. He checked "Unsure" and wrote, "Complains of chronic tiredness." I had turned down overtime a few times because I was tired and that was all. There were men on the ship who did not work much overtime, and there were men who were extremely materialistic and wanted to do nothing but make lots and lots of money at the expense of everything else in their lives—their marriages on shore, their physical health, everything. This evaluation was even more unfair because the last few weeks I was on the ship I was the only wiper on board. The wiper is your basic engine-room "gofer" and does everything. During that last period I worked nonstop doing the work of three people because I knew we were coming into port, and the engine room had to be especially clean to make the first assistant look good. So how could he complain about my work? Then he gave me this big spiel that I might think the evaluation was because I was a homosexual, but the people on the ship were cosmopolitan enough to accept homosexuals, and my evaluation had nothing to do with my unwillingness to kiss him and play my fiddle for him in his room.

Everything that was going on during that time made me incredibly angry. But for the most part I could not express that anger without being fired or hit. I would never have survived then. I did occasionally make good friends. The first time out I became close to someone and the last time out also. In between, there were occasional people I found pleasant to me for varying periods of time depending on how long we had been out there. They became less supportive the longer we'd been out because they'd become more horny and interested in me sexually. You know, their human nature would start leaning over into the sexual aspect. How can I explain it? You're in a situation where you're constantly being disappointed, and it gets to the point where, because you're being treated like shit, you start feeling like it and aren't that surprised when people are unkind to you. You confide in people less and less so you're being let down, at least in that respect, less and less.

I damaged my knees very badly when I was on the ship. While working under that particular first assistant I was going up and down extremely steep ladders, carrying heavy things, and developed severe tendonitis and chondromalacia [preternatural softness of the cartilages] in my knees. They're still affecting me after six months, and I've been going to a therapist, doing exercises, and trying to stay away from knee-stressing activities, but I've been told that probably all my life my knees will be sensitive, and I can expect this pain to be a recurring thing. I know it has a lot to do with how hard I was working, because when I had a different first assistant and kept up the same pace, everyone around me kept saying, "Why are you working so hard?" and "You don't have to go so fast."

It's different now, in that I am much more in touch with Number One, just how miserable I can make myself if I'm not careful about what situations I involve myself in. I have shown myself through doing this what can happen when you start thinking in terms of money being the answer. Even though I have bought myself a truck and have a little bit of money in the bank and am grateful for these things, nothing could be worth to me what it cost me. My priorities are not in the area of material gain, and I have no reason to go back.

Now I'm much more conscious of my own efforts to treat myself well, and I am also kind of relearning to accept myself and like myself and trust myself and my feelings towards other people. I've also had to retrain myself to remember that if I don't like a situation I am capable of turning around and walking out the door, that I am capable of walking away from that person. I'm not going to have to work with that person for the next three months and therefore must swallow my anger.

Basically my own self-image is the big point I'm working on. It went way down, and I'm working on getting in touch with it again, because I can't remember what I was like before going to sea. It's almost like watching a movie. Occasionally I will talk with an old friend who will bring up an incident from my past, and it will show a particular amount of self-confidence, and I will find it difficult to relate to. It didn't happen that long ago, but it is hard to recognize myself as being that person who could do confident things. It is like talking about somebody else completely.

I have a very deep sense of sadness at the human condition, the way humans treat each other, the way men are, and how possibly unchangeable that situation is out there. I have a fatalism about the marine industry, at least tankers. The young men that go out there become like the old men are. These old men have been out for twenty, thirty, forty years and they are the way they are, and they're not going to change, and that's definite, but the young men replacing them are becoming just like them. All this jive about young men being more open-minded is a bunch of shit because it's an extremely male-dominated environment. The men bring out and reinforce in each other these same male values, male attitudes, male emotional reponses, male treatment of each other. They're just reinforcing it, and they've only got women there because they're getting tax breaks and have to do it.

I think the way to handle it would be to just stay away from it as far as possible. How do you handle Ku Klux Klan meetings? There's always people who are into it, and you can either choose to be there or choose not to be there. I do not choose to have it affect my life anymore. I used to feel a certain kind of semi-spunky, well, I'm doing this for the cause of furthering women's desires, choices to do new things, to go out here and have the opportunity to try this. I felt a certain sense of reponsibility as a female and as a lesbian in that respect when I first went out there, but as far as I'm concerned, and this might sound a little strong, it's like being around some kind of rotting corpse. You know, you don't go in there and clean it up. You get away from it. There is no place out there for intelligent, sensitive people, much less women who give a damn about themselves.

Truck Assembly Line Worker

NORA QUEALEY

*She still dreams of meeting someone who can take her
away from the assembly line and back
to being a housewife.*

I was a housewife until five years ago. The best part was being
home when my three kids came in from school. Their papers
and their junk that they made from kindergarten on up—they
were my total, whole life. And then one day I realized when they
were grown up and gone, graduated and married, I was going to
be left with nothing. I think there's a lot of women that way,
housewives, that never knew there were other things and people outside of the neighborhood. I mean the block got together
once a week for coffee and maybe went bowling, but that was it.
My whole life was being there when the kids came home from
school.

I never disliked anything. It was just like everything else in a
marriage, there never was enough money to do things that you
wanted—never to take a week's vacation away from the kids. If
we did anything, it was just to take the car on Saturday or
Sunday for a little, short drive. But there was never enough
money. The extra money was the reason I decided to go out and
get a job. The kids were getting older, needed more, wanted
more, and there was just not enough.

See, I don't have a high school diploma, so when I went to
Boeing and put an application in, they told me not to come back
until I had a diploma or a G.E.D. On the truck line they didn't

mind that I hadn't finished school. I put an application in and got hired on the spot.

My dad works over at Bangor in the ammunition depot, so I asked him what it would be like working with all men. The only thing he told me was if I was gonna work with a lot of men, that I would have to *listen* to swear words and some of the obscene things, but still *act* like a lady, or I'd never fit in. You can still be treated like a lady and act like a lady and work like a man. So I just tried to fit in. It's worked, too. The guys come up and they'll tell me jokes and tease me and a lot of them told me that I'm just like one of the guys. Yet they like to have me around because I wear make-up and I do curl my hair, and I try to wear not really frilly blouses, see-through stuff, but nice blouses.

We had one episode where a gal wore a tank top and when she bent over the guys could see her boobs or whatever you call it, all the way down. Myself and a couple other women went and tried to complain about it. We wanted personnel to ask her to please wear a bra, or at least no tank tops. We were getting a lot of comebacks from the guys like, "When are you gonna dress like so-and-so," or "When are *you* gonna go without a bra," and "We wanna see what *you've* got." And I don't feel any need to show off; you know, I know what I've got. There were only a few women there, so that one gal made a very bad impression. But personnel said there was nothing they could do about it.

But in general the guys were really good. I started out in cab building hanging radio brackets and putting heaters in. It was all hand work, and at first I really struggled with the power screwdrivers and big reamers, but the guy training me was super neato. I would think, "Oh, dear, can I ever do this, can I really prove myself or come up to their expectations?" But the guys never gave me the feeling that I was taking the job from a man or food from his family's mouth. If I needed help, I didn't even have to ask, if they saw me struggling, they'd come right over to help.

I've worked in a lot of different places since I went to work

Nora Quealey, truck assembly line worker

there. I was in cab build for I don't know how long, maybe six months, eight months. Then they took me over to sleeper boxes, where I stayed for about two-and-one-half years. I put in upholstery, lined the head liners and the floor mats. After that I went on the line and did air conditioning. When the truck came to me, it had hoses already on it, and I'd have to hook up a little air-condition-pump-type thing and a suction that draws all the dust and dirt from the lines. Then you close that off, put freon in, and tie down the line. Then I'd tie together a bunch of color-coded electrical wires with tie straps and electrical tape to hook the firewall to the engine. Sometimes I also worked on the sleeper boxes by crawling underneath and tightening down big bolts and washers. Next they sent me over to the radiator shop. I was the first woman ever to do radiators. That I liked. A driver would bring in the radiators and you'd put it on a hoist, pick it up and put it on a sling, and work on one side putting your fittings on and wiring and putting in plugs. Then they bounced me back to sleeper boxes for a while and finally ended up putting me in the motor department, where I am now. The motors are brought in on a dolly. The guy behind me hangs the transmission and I hang the pipe with the shift levers and a few other little things and that's about it. Except that we have to work terribly fast.

I was moved into the motor department after the big layoff. At that time we were doing ten motors a day. Now we're up to fourteen without any additional help. When we were down, the supervisor came to me and said we had to help fill in and give extra help to the other guys, which is fine. But the minute production went up, I still had to do my own job plus putting on parts for three different guys. These last two weeks have been really tough. I've been way behind. They've got two guys that are supposed to fill in when you get behind, but I'm stubborn enough that I won't go over and ask for help. The supervisor should be able to see that I'm working super-duper hard while some other guys are taking forty-five minutes in the can and having a sandwich and two cups of coffee. Sometimes I push myself so hard that I'm actually in a trance. And I have to stop every once in a while and ask, "What did I do?" I don't even remember putting parts on, I just go from one to the other, just block everything out—just go, go, go, go. And that is bad, for myself, my own sanity, my own health. I don't take breaks. I don't go to the bathroom. There's so much pressure on me, physical and mental stress. It's hard to handle because then I go home and do a lot of crying and that's bad for my kids because I do a lot of snapping and growling at them. When I'm down, depressed, aching, and sore, to come home and do that to the kids is not fair at all. The last couple of days the attitude I've had is, I don't care whether I get the job done or not. If they can't see I'm going under, then I don't care. And I'll take five or ten minutes to just go to the bathroom, sit on the floor, and take a couple of deep breaths, just anything to get away.

The company doesn't care about us at all. Let me give you an example. When we were having all this hot weather, I asked them please if we couldn't get some fans in here. Extension cords even, because some guys had their own fans. I wasn't just asking for myself, but those guys over working by the oven. They've got a thermometer there and it gets to a hundred and fifteen degrees by that oven! They've got their mouths open, can hardly breathe, and they're barely moving. So I said to the supervisor, "Why can't we have a fan to at least circulate the air?" "Oh, yeah, we'll look at it," was as far as it went. We're human. We have no right to be treated like animals. I mean you go out to a dairy farm and you've got air conditioning and music for those cows. I'm a person, and I don't like feeling weak and sick to my stomach and not feel like eating. Then to have the supervisor expect me to put out production as if I was mechanical—a thing, just a robot. I'm human.

You know, I don't even know what my job title is. I'm not sure if it's trainee or not. But I do know I'll never make journeyman. I'll never make anything. I tried for inspection—took all the classes they offered at the plant, went to South Seattle Community College on my own time, studied blueprinting, and worked in all the different areas like they said I had to. I broke ground for the other girls, but they won't let me move up. And it all comes down to one thing, because I associated with a black man. I've had people in personnel tell me to stop riding to work with the man, even if it meant taking the bus to and from work. I said no one will make my decisions as to who I ride with and who my friends are. Because you walk into a building with a person, have lunch with him, let him buy you a cup of coffee, people condemn you. They're crazy, because when I have a friend, I don't turn my back on them just because of what people think. What I do outside the plant after quitting time is my own business. If they don't like it, that's their problem. But in that plant I've conducted myself as a lady and have nothing to be ashamed of. I plant my feet firmly and I stand by it.

Early on, I hurt my neck, back, and shoulder while working on sleeper boxes. When I went into the motor department I damaged them more by working with power tools above my head and reaching all day long. I was out for two weeks and then had a ten-week restriction. Personnel said I had to go back to my old job, and if I couldn't handle it I would have to go home. They wouldn't put me anywhere else, which is ridiculous, with all the small parts areas that people can sit down and work in while they are restricted. My doctor said if I went back to doing what I was doing when I got hurt, I had a fifty-fifty chance of completely paralyzing myself from the waist down. But like a fool I went back. Some of the guys helped me with the bending and stooping over. Then the supervisor borrowed a ladder with three steps and on rollers from the paint department. He wanted me to stand on the top step while working on motors which are on dollies on a moving chain. I'd be using two presswrenches to tighten fittings down while my right knee was on the transmission and the left leg standing up straight. All this from the top step of a ladder on rollers. One slip and it would be all over. I backed off and said it wouldn't work. By this time I'd gotten the shop steward there, but he didn't do anything. In fact, the next day he left on three weeks' vacation without doing anything to help me. I called the union hall and was told they'd send a business rep down the next day. I never saw or heard from the man.

Anyhow, I'm still doing the same job as when I got hurt. I can feel the tension in my back and shoulder coming up. I can feel the spasms start and muscles tightening up. Things just keep gettin' worse and they don't care. People could be rotated and moved rather than being cramped in the same position, like in the sleeper boxes, where you never stand up straight and stretch your neck out. It's eight, ten, twelve hours a day all hunched over. In the next two years I've got to quit. I don't know what I'll do. If I end up paralyzed from the neck down, the company doesn't give a damn, the union doesn't give a damn, who's gonna take care of me? Who's gonna take care of my girls? I'm gonna be put in some moldy, old, stinkin' nursing home. I'm thirty-seven years old. I could live another thirty, forty years. And who's gonna really care about me?

I mean my husband left me. He was very jealous of my working with a lot of men and used to follow me to work. When I joined the bowling team, I tried to get him to come and meet the guys I worked with. He came but felt left out because there was always an inside joke or something that he couldn't understand. He resented that and the fact that I made more money than he did. And my not being home bothered him. But he never said, "I want you to quit," or "We'll make it on what I get." If he had said that I probably would have quit. Instead we just muddled on. With me working, the whole family had to pitch in and help. When I come home at night my daughter has dinner

Nora Quealey, truck assembly line worker

waiting, and I do a couple loads of wash and everybody folds their own clothes. My husband pitched in for a while. Then he just stopped coming home. He found another lady that didn't work, had four kids, and was on welfare.

It really hurt and I get very confused still. I don't have the confidence and self-assurance I used to have. I think, "Why did I do that," or "Maybe I shouldn't have done it," and I have to force myself to say, "Hey, I felt and said what I wanted to and there's no turning back." It came out of me and I can't be apologizing for everything that I do. And, oh, I don't know, I guess I'm in a spell right now where I'm tired of being dirty. I want my fingernails long and clean. I want to not go up to the bathroom and find a big smudge of grease across my forehead. I want to sit down and be pampered and pretty all day. Maybe that wouldn't satisfy me, but I just can't imagine myself at fifty or sixty or seventy years old trying to climb on these trucks. I've been there for five years. I'm thirty-seven and I want to be out of there before I'm forty. And maybe I will. I've met this nice guy and he's talking of getting married. At the most, I would have to work for one more year and then I could stay at home, go back to being a housewife.

Race

Racial minorities have been in this country for as long as whites. In fact, when Christopher Columbus "discovered" America, there were already about one million people living on this continent. Today, minorities in general occupy the bottom rungs of the economic ladder; their unemployment rates double that of whites. Levels of pay and years of education are also lower. Few minority women have the option of becoming housewives; work is a clear economic necessity for them and their families. It must be noted, though, that each of the minority groups has its own distinct experience.

Both blacks and Chicanos have historically been rural farmers. In the early twentieth century, 75 percent of all blacks were rural, Southern tenant farmers. This changed dramatically during World War II when blacks migrated north to work in the war industries. Now only 2 percent of blacks are rural farmers. Chicanos, or Mexican-Americans, had traditionally been farmers in those Southwestern states ceded to the United States by the Treaty of Guadalupe Hidalgo in 1844. Now, however, many are urban industrial workers while only 2 percent remain as farmers. The stories of Katie Murray and Lydia Vasquez capture the transition from rural farm labor to urban industrial work.

Sylvia Lange talks about the disruption of traditional native American fishing. As these people are driven out of salmon fishing, will they too be forced into urban industries?

Asian-Americans have not traditionally been quite as depen-

...shing or farming for their livelihood. Their education
...come levels have been somewhat higher than other
...norities', although the degree of difference varies among specific ethnic groups.

While cultural differences among minority groups are important to note, it must be recalled that all non-whites are viewed by the majority as something different from the norm. This sense of being different is a common point among minority groups. Amy Kelley, who views herself as quite assimilated, says the racial discrimination she experiences is the same as that experienced by all racial minorities. And yet neither Amy Kelley nor Geraldine Walker experiences racial discrimination as the dominant factor in her work life. This is in sharp contrast to Katie Murray and Lydia Vasquez, who feel the racism they encounter overshadows everything else about their jobs. For non-white women, it is clearly a case of double discrimination. Even the sexual comments, as Amy Kelley and Katie Murray point out, have racial overtones.

Machine Operator

LYDIA VASQUEZ

*Although she does not consider herself to be a very
strong person, Lydia Vasquez has struggled
for many years to support her family despite race
and sex discrimination and physical injuries.
She attributes her perseverance to faith in God.*

When I started school I didn't know a word of English—only
Spanish. But the teachers objected if we Mexicans spoke Spanish because then they didn't know what was going on. What was
I to do? The teacher would tell me to do something and I had no
idea what she was saying. It made for a very difficult situation.

It didn't last long though, because my parents felt girls didn't
need to go to school. Your life was cut out to be at home and
raise a family. That's the way it was among Mexicans. I quit
school in the fifth grade when my mother was hospitalized for a
long time. At that point I became fully responsible for cooking
meals, watching six younger children, and keeping up the
house. When my mother came home from the hospital I helped
her until she was able to be up and around.

Then I started working for the white people in Los Fresnos,
Texas. That was the town we lived in. I did their housework,
ironing, and babysitting. That went on for a couple years until I
got on washing dishes at Refugio Hospital. For fifteen days of
work I got paid forty-five dollars. In those days that was a lot of
money. I turned most of it over to my parents to help out. The
little bit I kept went to buying clothes. I've always been clothes

crazy, but short on money, so I've forever been a person to dress off layaways.

I stayed at the hospital for two years until I got married. My husband made enough money as a carpenter that I didn't have to work outside of the home. We had three boys so I had plenty to keep me busy in the house.

When we separated after six years of marriage, I went to work in the fields. By that time I was already here in Washington—Sunnyside, Washington. I did all kinds of field work—thinning beets and mint, cutting asparagus, picking potatoes, and picking peaches, pears, plums, and apples in the orchards. It was very poor pay, always under minimum wage. The way you make better money is for families to work together, contracting out to work several acres a day. Even so, it doesn't pay. The hours are long and the heat is horrible. There is always poverty in people doing that kind of work, because they don't make enough money and it's seasonal. After doing work in the fields for a season I found work in town as a cook and waitress in a restaurant. After it closed down, I got a job packing Mexican sweet rolls and making tortillas. For the next three or four years I went back and forth between field work and temporary jobs like that.

In nineteen sixty-five I married my second husband, a serviceman. I don't know everything he's done, but he served several years with the Green Berets and has been up at the front line many times in battles. At first I didn't work when we were married, but when he went overseas to Vietnam I started working in a day-care center in Othello. I really enjoyed those years in the day-care center. Even little babies can learn by how you treat them. I could see the difference in children when they'd be gone over the weekends with the parents. On Monday mornings it would be a disaster to see some children come back dirty from not being bathed over the weekend, and with a rash on their bottom because they were not changed frequently and cleaned properly. I felt my heart go out to the little ones. Ninety-nine percent of the children were Spanish-speaking, so my being bilingual helped the white supervisor understand the problems of the children. When my daughter was born, I kept her in the nursery there while I worked.

When Rudy returned from Vietnam in nineteen sixty-seven, I left the day-care center because we moved back to Fort Lewis. In nineteen seventy-three I started working outside of the home again, because I knew things were so bad at home that I was sure we were going to end up in another divorce. I hated the idea, but I had tried the best I could for almost ten years. My husband felt he was always right and refused to get counseling from anyone. I started working so that when he went his way, at least I would be working, and the kids would be adjusted to that.

This time I got on in a Mexican restaurant. For three dollars and twenty-five cents an hour I did cooking, the inventory, ordering the day's groceries, and helped out the girls waiting tables. I felt I was working too many hours and had too much responsibility for the money I was getting, but there was no sense in even talking to the owner about a raise. No one was getting a raise. So when a friend mentioned that there was an opening for a janitoress in a machine shop, I went down and filled out an application. I was hired even though I had no idea what a machine shop even looked like. The pay was three twenty-five an hour.

Most other machine shops have men for this kind of job, but it was not a very big shop and the work was not tremendously heavy, so I fit in rather well. One day, after two weeks of janitorial work, I mentioned to the supervisor that the machines looked intriguing and if there was ever an opportunity I would like to run one. That two weeks were all of the janitorial work that I did, because after that I was put to work running machines. Of course, I was under a supervisor, because I had no idea how to run a machine or what to do with it. While there I ran a milling machine, a lathe, drills, a piece-marking machine, sanders, and a sand-blasting machine. When I moved onto the machines, I got my first raise up to three fifty. By the end of three months I was getting three seventy-five, so I could see the raises were coming in quickly. At that point I realized there was more money in doing jobs that have been mainly men's work.

The men did not seem to have anything against seeing a woman running a machine there. They were so willing to help me do things, make a set-up, bring parts, or whatever, that I had no fears at all. If somebody was willing to teach me, I was willing to learn.

Like many small outfits in Seattle, the company did ninety percent of its work for Boeing. At this particular time, Boeing was going downhill and laying off, so all the smaller shops doing their work were affected by it. Naturally, being one of the last hired, I was laid off.

I knew I would not be able to live on unemployment alone, so I started to look for another job. I applied at different places, but mostly with machine shop in mind. SER, a job placement service for Spanish-speaking and other low-income people, referred me to a truck manufacturer. My first day of employment was February second, nineteen seventy-six. I don't know what I expected, but it was a much larger outfit than I anticipated. I guess I had just thought a machine shop was a machine shop, and when I went in there with all the different shops, it was just like a sea of machine shops all over. Actually they were all different departments, not everything was a machine shop. At that point, I became a bit fearful and kept getting the feeling it was not going to be easy.

I could see machines that I recognized, bench drills, lathes, and mills, so they didn't really shock me. But there were other larger machines doing different jobs and I started to hold back. I couldn't very easily say that I would like to know what's going on. I think there were about a thousand people employed there. The majority were white. I started on swing shift, where there

Lydia Vasquez, machine operator

were maybe thirty to thirty-five working in my area. None were women.

The swing-shift supervisor was careful about what he would ask me to do. He called me the little girl and felt I was too small for some of the jobs. As a result he tried to find smaller jobs for me to do. At first I used a hand drill. Later I was put to work drilling long aluminum pieces for sleepers on some of the trucks. The pay, five dollars and seventy-one cents an hour, was the most I had ever earned.

I was told that I would have to join the Machinists Union within thirty days. I didn't want anything to do with the union, because in one of my earlier jobs I had been in a union. When people had been injured the union had never done anything about it. So I had hostile feelings toward unions. If a union's not going to be for the people, why join it? But I had no choice, so I started paying my dues. I wasn't acquainted with anybody that had anything good to say about the union, so there was no reason to change my feelings.

In the first part of September, when my children started school, I was switched to day shift. Lord behold, day shift totally turned me around. Everything was so different. The supervisor, and even some of the workers, had a hostile attitude towards me coming on day shift in the machine shop. This supervisor didn't want women in the machine shop and tried to keep us away on nights.

That's when I started to learn what discrimination was. One time the supervisor suggested I slip him a five or give him a bottle to get a better job. That disturbed me because I was not used to buying my jobs by bringing gifts or giving money to anybody.

Everything that came from that supervisor was crude in some way or another. Once he said the reason I was brown was that I drank too much coffee. Since I only drank one cup of coffee before starting to work, I guess the coffee must have been an awfully strong dye to make me turn brown before his eyes. He was always telling me that I should be married and at home. After hearing that particular line several times, I asked him if he wanted me married so bad why didn't he marry me and support my family. I don't think he ever mentioned my being single again. Another time that man told me, if I was going to do a man's job, then I had better look like a man.

The lead man was no better. He always teased me about being short, brown, dumb, and about what an ugly man I made. "Here comes the ugly man" was his favorite line. He also put me down because some of the truck parts were made in a factory that they have in Mexico. He said the Mexicans were dumb and didn't know what they were doing. Sometimes I think the harassment was more because of my race than because I'm a woman. I did get some support from other workers, mostly minorities and other women.

I guess the supervisor decided he was not getting rid of the women fast enough, so he asked us to do more and more. The lead man tried to intimidate us by saying that we had to do more, we had to hurry up, we had to speed up even though I was working as fast as I could. To him it was never good enough. Then they started giving me much heavier jobs. After awhile I began to have physical problems, especially when I was lifting heavier objects. Many of the parts I could barely move, let alone be lifting all day. Because of that I ended up having surgery on my right hand.

Then, after I had been with the company not quite a year and a half, I was terminated. It's a rather involved story, but I had been in an auto accident the night before and called in the morning to let them know I would be late because I had to get three insurance estimates and make out some accident reports. When I got to work, my hair was down, and I realized I had been in such a hurry to leave home that I forgot my pins that I normally use to put my hair up. I did have a hair clip and a scarf, so I pinned the

Lydia Vasquez, machine operator

hair to the nape of my neck and put on the scarf. At about two-thirty the supervisor told me that I shouldn't be wearing my hair down and put his hands on my hair, trying to stick it down under the band of my safety glasses. That really upset me, because he had no business putting his hands on my hair or head or anywhere else. I explained the reason my hair was down and thought everything was taken care of. It wasn't, because at three-ten the plant superintendent came out to talk to me, and I went through the story again. Neither he nor the supervisor mentioned that having my hair down was going to hurt me in any way. Both of them seemed to accept my explanation.

The next day I came in with my hair up and was immediately sent in to see the superintendent. He sounded angry and right off the bat said, "You're fired." Then he shouted at me saying he had asked me to pin my hair up.

I said, "You didn't ask me to pin it up. You asked the reason and you seemed to have accepted it." He insisted that having my hair down was the reason he was firing me. It wasn't fair because men in the shop had hair down to their shoulders, beards that would come down to their chests, and none of their hair constrained in any way. A lot of times they didn't even wear a hat on their heads.

After packing up my tools, I immediately went to the union hall. The business rep could do no more than sit there and laugh when I told him my story. He couldn't believe what I was telling him and assured me that he would look into it. At home I started thinking. What could I do? I couldn't sit still; I had a home; I had a family and responsibilities, so something had to be done. Meanwhile, people at work passed a petition around saying I should get my job back and raised money to help my family out. Some of the people who helped me were close friends. Others I did not even know. I can never express what these people did for me.

Three days later I went back to the business rep at the union and found out that he had not done anything at all. All of my anti-union feelings flared up and I said, "This is exactly what I meant when I said that the union doesn't do anything." Further, I told the business rep if he didn't contact the company he would also be hearing from my attorney.

At the union meeting that night there were men from day shift and swing shift. When the business rep saw the number of people there, he knew he had a real problem. The members passed a resolution saying they supported me in this action that the company had taken against me. It was the first time a resolution was passed in Local 79 to support a woman, and a Mexican woman at that. I felt really good knowing the people were behind me. For the first time I knew for myself that union members were the ones that'll either make it or break it. If they're gonna stick by you, then you can make something of it, but if the people aren't gonna stand by you, the name of the union doesn't mean anything. I really appreciate the support of the union members.

After several meetings with the union and personnel, we agreed that I was to go back to work and the union would continue fighting for my retro pay. Finally the union won me pay for eleven of the fourteen days I was out. I continued to fight my case with the Human Rights Commission and after two years ended up collecting my other three days. In fact I got a total of fifteen hundred dollars for damages, which is not to say that I got paid for the amount of time and harassment that I had to go through. I don't think you can measure in dollars what people go through in that place. Nobody could ever be paid enough for all the harassment.

I didn't expect it to be smooth going back, but I must say I was very proud to walk in there and to know I was right and that I wasn't going to keep quiet about it. The supervisors were very bitter that I'd gotten my job back and found ways to retaliate. They'd tell me to work on a machine that practically didn't

Lydia Vasquez, machine operator

work and expected me to do a perfect job when there was nothing around to do the job with. Some of the comments from supervisors and lead men were pretty nasty. A lead man in the tool room even called me a "fucking cunt." Others said things that were derogatory towards me as a Mexican. I think my race played a big role. If you were not white, you were not good enough. Just because you had a different shade meant you were dumb or an idiot or ignorant. To them only white was the supreme, the only ones that could do anything, even though many times I knew I did a better job than some of the white guys. But just because they were white it was all right for them to make mistakes. If we non-whites made any mistakes or scrapped anything, it was always pointed out. Race played a big part in this little game of theirs.

I think they wanted me to get hurt physically. For a long time I worked on radial drills, which are quite large. They're a high machine, so I had trouble reaching all the levers. So between working with the heavy objects, lifting constantly from the table onto the machine and running levers, my head had to be in a looking-upward position for long periods of time. Over a number of months I had constant pain in the back of my neck. It never went away and continually got worse. Finally, I couldn't take it any longer and went to a doctor, who took X-rays and had me go through a myelogram. The doctor said I had a ruptured vertabra. Now I'm not a sickly type person and never had injuries of this nature before I went to work there, so I'm pretty sure it was work related. The company fought me all the way, and I never got any type of compensation. In fact, somewhere down the line the doctor changed his diagnosis from ruptured to deteriorating vertabra. I feel there's a lot of difference between ruptured and deteriorated. Anyhow I had surgery to fuse two vertabrae and I was not supposed to do much bending. It left my neck stiff and hard to move. I could turn slightly to the left and it was almost impossible to turn to the right.

When I came back I was given the job of running the Heald, a borematic-type machine. The parts we ran on that machine weighed no less than sixty pounds. There were no hoists to help lift these heavy, awkward parts into and out of the machine. I had to handle each part three or four times before the process of running a piece was complete. By the time I was done with a part, I had lifted it four, five, maybe six times. I did that all day long. Due to this constant heavy lifting of parts I hurt my lower back. But to this day I have gotten nothing out of it. They keep saying it is the same thing I had with my neck and now my lower back vertabrae are deteriorating. I still find it hard to believe, because I never had any problems with my health before. Do they think I hurt my back pushing a broom at home?

I have not worked since December twenty-seventh of nineteen seventy-nine. I had a sinus infection, and the doctor said I should not use heavy vibrating tools for a short period of time. The supervisor said there was nothing, then, that I could do and terminated me. I haven't been able to find other work. It seems like the other places that I have gone to are fearful of taking someone who's been injured.

My body is all messed up now—my lower back, neck, and hands. But I have gained through my experience something which no one can take from me. Now I understand prejudice. Now I know what racism is. When someone is being discriminated against, believe me, I feel for them, because I know, and if I can do anything to help the individual I will. This knowledge is something which I have gained. Plus I gained a lot of good friends. I know there's still a lot of good people out there in the world. Had I not gone through all this, maybe I would not be the person I am now.

Shipscaler

GERALDINE WALKER

*Geraldine Walker is nothing short of amazing—a single
parent raising five children, one of the first black
supervisors at the shipyards, and vice-president of the
Shipscalers Union. Instead of being frazzled by her load,
she radiates a calm serenity.*

I had this girl friend and we were both out of work and she heard
about jobs down in the shipyards. That was back in nineteen
seventy-four and it paid five dollars and seventy cents an hour. I
probably thought about it for a month. I wasn't really sure I
could do it, because you had to start working at seven o'clock in
the morning and I was used to sleeping late. And I wasn't sure
whether I could hold down a full-time job. I have five children. I
knew nothing about shipyards and maybe I was just afraid of the
men.

I decided to just kind of bluff it. The day I went down to the
union hall, I didn't really have time to think about being afraid
because I was watching a little girl for a friend of mine. When I
got dispatched out, I only had an hour and a half to find somebody to watch her, find some clothes to wear, and then go out
there. So I really didn't have time to think about it.

The first thing that struck me was I didn't get any instruc-
tions from the union hall on how to get there and what I was
supposed to do once I got there. I don't know how I found it, but I
did. I had a hard time parking. They've got big lots out there and
I expected rules, but everybody just parked where they wanted

as long as it wasn't on the street. Once inside the yard, I still didn't know where to go. I just stumbled on this little office that was personnel. It wasn't like somebody met you at the gate and took you around. Down there you just happen to find what's happening. The office sent me to a man on drydock. First I went with a quarterman and then a lead man. I remember walking down the passageway of a ship and him walking very fast and kind of losing me. One time he *did* lose me and had to come back. I remember telling him, "Did you do that on purpose?"

He said, "Oh, no, I wouldn't do that." But I kind of thought they were giving me the run-through. I expected it because I was a woman.

I felt very uneasy. Everything was in a jumble. A ship being built looks like confusion. You smell smoke, paint. Often it's noisy—machinery, saws going, just a lot of noise. And a ship is gray or an ugly drab or black. Ugly! Everything seems awfully drab to me. Even the people look drab. My first impression was of dirtiness and everybody wearing the same clothes and everything torn up. But the people wear different-colored hats. There's a lot of different-colored hats depending on the craft. Scalers wear orange hard hats and supervisors wear white— white cowboys.

Of all the crafts in the yard, the scalers had most of the women. At that time there might have been twenty or thirty women. There were one or two woman shipfitters and a few female welders. I think scaling was easier to get into because in the other work you had to know something before you started.

Another thing is there weren't many blacks in the other crafts. In the total yard, besides scalers, there were one or two black fitters, one black electrician, and two black machinists. I think at one time black people would work at any job they could get and nobody wanted the scaling jobs, so for years and years blacks had control of the Scalers Union. Now more whites are coming into scaling. With the economy the way it is, more whites are looking for any job.

I'd never worked with so many men. Well, I did when I sorted letters at the post office, but there were also a lot of other women. And the men there didn't make you feel like you were out of place, but they did at the shipyard. They were rude and stared and talked dirty about me. I've forgotten a lot of the feelings from when I first started, but I can remember after a big layoff there were times when there were maybe three women in the whole yard. You would go into a room where there were five or six men talking, and as soon as I walked in, they were all quiet, staring.

Back then my lead man was acting funny, very friendly. I decided to overlook it. I didn't get angry or mad. In some ways I still overlook a lot. I figure it's better than making a big deal out of it. You learn to be grateful to the men that are glad to have you there. For whatever reason, they were more pleasant than the others to be around.

When I was a firewatcher I especially heard a lot of really gross jokes about women. I didn't like it, but tried to ignore "the man." After a couple days maybe I would talk to him. When a man found out I did my share and sometimes helped him on his job, he would begin to accept me and find another woman to be rude to.

On firewatch you follow a burner around. You clean out the site and make sure there is nothing flammable. Then you make sure the asbestos covering was wet and cover all cables. If they would be hunting through bulkheads, you'd have to go check the inside of the bulkhead. Basically it was dragging a steel water can around the yard.

Some men resented my standing around with a water can while they worked and others didn't. Some knew I was just doing my job and liked having me around for company, somebody to talk to and stuff. And then there were the others. I did get an awful lot about "You make good money for doing that."

Scalers also do the cleaning around the yards. You start at the top of a tank and wipe it down and clean it out. We also use sandblasters to clean. You use a high-pressure hose and a fan to blast. You wear a special suit and boots and a respirator to protect yourself. It's an awful job, but those that do it, like it. I think they like it because they can see what they're accomplishing. A good one can sandblast very fast. Scalers also scrape the ships. One job that I never had, but some of the women did, was when a ship was out of the water, scraping the hull of the ship. Basically we just try to clean the ship up. For that we make around twelve dollars and fifty cents.

The greatest discrimination women face is not being taken seriously. For a long time there were just certain jobs that women weren't allowed to do. I've worked on ships where women could just clean. They couldn't lift or carry. The supervisors wouldn't allow them to do more. Say a ship came in that needed the bottom power-washed. They wouldn't pick a woman to do it. There were a lot of things we were not asked to do. They automatically picked men. Even if we were willing, they didn't want to think that we could really do the job like a man could.

Particularly in the early days I did more than I should in order to prove myself. You know, ships have big, huge anchor chains that go all the way down and all this muck and mud collects in the bottom. Once I shoveled out a whole bottom by myself. A man was timing me, so I did it fast. I never should have done that. I wouldn't say it was unsafe, but it was scary being way down there. The other people were on top, pulling my bags out. There were two sides and a wall with cutouts. There was a man on the other side who was crazy! Just loco! I think he was a little psycho. He tried to get another woman to throw a hose down over the side. It would have made the water come in over me! He

Geraldine Walker, shipscaler

yelled and cussed at her when she wouldn't, and she cussed him back. That guy's not allowed to work at the docks any more.

. . . For the first few years it wouldn't have made any sense for me to get angry at the discrimination. It wouldn't have done any good. But things have changed since then, basically because of legislation and lawsuits. They have to watch it more now. We women got tired of being pushed too far, tired of going along with whatever and not making trouble. Now we talk back a lot more.

In September nineteen seventy-eight I became a supervisor, so now I get to assign the work. With people it's important that they work as a crew. There are some jobs that some people are better at than others, but there are some things, like knowing how to wind hoses and string them up, that everyone needs to know. Sometimes I try to give the women different things that they might not have an opportunity to do working with a man. Sometimes things happen because a woman just doesn't know how to do a job. Like I had one woman pump out a bilge. Well, she turned on the pump, which was fine. The discharge from the hose went off the ship over the pier to a huge tank. When she started pumping, she didn't even think where this oily water was going. It went over into this tank, which was full, and it overflowed. It's not our job; it's a pipefitter's job to make sure those tanks are pumped, and a lot of times they don't do it. The next time I had a woman work on the job, I told her to think about where the water was going. On little things like that I try to show the women how to do the job. I won't just get a man to find hoses and check tanks. I'll *show* a woman. If she knows how to do it, she might not avoid it [checking the tanks] later. On the whole, I've found women to be excellent workers. They're grateful to be making that money, so they get out there and they work. Not like a man, who expects it. The women don't mind getting dirty.

Being a supervisor is a lot of responsibility, and some days I feel like I would rather go back to just being a scaler. Sometimes I would like to not be responsible for anybody but me. I wasn't sure I could do it at first, but mostly I like it. We're nearing the completion of a ship that we've been working on for almost two years. Most of the hard work is done now and it's more relaxed. A year ago my answer would have been different. Then it was dirt and water everywhere.

I'm trying to think. I might be the only black woman supervisor. I'm not sure. There was another black woman who might have been a foreman. I'm not sure.

I get so mad at the racial stuff. I've heard a lot about race from blacks, from whites, from Koreans. In the seven years I've been working in the yards, there has been more slurring of other minorities, more so than the blacks. Maybe they don't feel so threatened by blacks any more. But I hear more about other groups. Not from females, though. I think women are less likely to pigeonhole someone because of color. But there's always somebody who gets it. It's really hard. You can't make someone like you. If somebody is getting bothered about race and it's not too much of a problem, I'll advise him to ignore it. Sometimes I go to another supervisor about it.

It's been hard working and keeping up a home. During my first year of work my husband was off work, so that was very difficult. I'd work and then I'd come home and work some more. I don't think my husband liked me working there, so I couldn't tell him about all the things that went on. He would have gotten too mad if I'd told him about the sex stuff. It would have been nice if I could have talked about things that were bothering me, but he probably would have started throwing things if I had.

Since I started working I don't do nearly as much around the house as I used to. I would say one of the most important things is that my children have become more independent. I used to have kids who didn't know where their socks were. I never

Geraldine Walker, shipscaler

thought I would leave my children to pretty much fend for themselves, but I had to do it. They've gotten used to it, so much now that I wonder how other kids learn anything when they don't have to do it on their own. For the past two-and-a-half years, since their father and I split up, they've really been doing for themselves. The girls do their own hair. They sew. They iron. They wash clothes—everything. They don't always get the good meals that they should, but they don't starve. And I think they're more self-sufficient this way.

I think working in the shipyards contributed to the divorce, but it was a lot of other things too. It was hard for him to adapt to my making good money and becoming very independent. Also I got involved in the union. I think if my marriage had been better, I probably wouldn't have gotten so involved. I was basically bored. What sort of happened is that I went to a nominating meeting and got nominated for vice-president. As I started serving my term I got more and more involved. Our business agent wasn't doing his job. He was a do-nothing and didn't process grievances. At one point the Shipscalers was a good union, but under his leadership, or lack of leadership, it didn't do well. So one thing lead to another and a bunch of the members got really frustrated and decided to make a change. In July of nineteen seventy-nine an opposition slate won all but one position. With all of this I was spending most of my time talking with people about the union and doing union work.

That's pretty much where I am now in my life. I'm a lot stronger now than when I started in the yards. I don't doubt now that I can take care of myself. Financially, emotionally, I'm more confident. Before I started in the shipyards I don't think I would have imagined that I could be my children's sole support. Now I know more what I *can* do and that's good. But in some ways I am still adjusting to the divorce. Since the divorce I have put on weight. I thought it would be much easier. The first few months were okay, but as time goes by a lot of different problems come up. I feel insecure. My two older children are getting to the age now where I can see them leaving and it worries me.

Machinist

AMY KELLEY

Amy Kelley's traditional Japanese relatives believe she has strayed too far from her proper role, but her husband happily leaves the house repairs in her capable hands.

My parents were divorced when I was nine. My father was a cook at a twenty-four-hour cafe. My mother used to work two jobs—a pressman at a drycleaner's and also as a janitress. After the divorce, my mother moved in with my aunt, who is a widow. My aunt was a journeyman printer—negative stripper— and she was very independent, so I learned a lot of that from her. She's also one of the first women in her field, which subconsciously I wonder if that's what got me into this, but somehow I really don't think so. My aunt was more influential in my life than my mom. Although my mom was around, she was always working.

When we moved to Ballard I was in the fourth grade, and I made some friends out there, but found them to be more closed-minded than neighborly. I didn't really care for the types of kids that were out there, which is why I continued to commute to the Central District to go to school. I felt more comfortable there than I did out in Ballard. Being a minority made it kind of awkward. The school I went to was more or less for low-income students, so we didn't have a lot of classes, and it wasn't coed, so we didn't have classes like shop. There was home ec and sewing, basic women-type classes. From the time I was a freshman in high school I worked to put myself through. Right after school I had to go straight to work, so I was never able to take extracurricular activities like volleyball.

I started out when I was fourteen years old working for a knitting company based in Ballard. They made ski sweaters. I started out as just a packer. I'd pack the sweaters in plastic bags and get them ready to ship. Then after awhile I got really interested in learning to run the knitting machines. There were no women running the knitting machines. I wasn't supposed to run the knitting machines because I was under age. Because of the child labor laws I had to be sixteen. But I would be able to sneak over and learn when I didn't have much else to do. The boss didn't care as long as I wasn't actually running them. I was just learning how. The knitting was minimum wage. I don't know what minimum wage was in nineteen sixty-nine. It was like a dollar twenty-five. It got slack and I got laid off, so I got a job working in a drive-in restaurant. I started that in nineteen seventy-one—waitress, whatever you want to call it. When I turned eighteen I was making a dollar sixty-five an hour. That was minimum wage, so it had to be a lot less when I was working at the sweater company. It was not so great, that's for sure. The conditions at the knitting mill were not that great. I didn't like the fact that the people who owned the place took advantage of immigrants. They'd pay them the minimum wage and work them like they had no feelings. Just produce the work and no money. I didn't like that. But the drive-in job, I enjoyed that. I really liked working with the public. It was fun, and I had a neat boss who was an older guy. He was really good; there are not many places like that. But the pay was lousy.

I started thinking about non-traditional work seriously when I was a senior in high school, because I realized there'd be something I'd have to do when I got out. I had just met my husband. When he came back from Vietnam he eventually found employment as a machine operator at a big machine shop in Seattle. At first, during all this time I had known him, we

Amy Kelley, machinist

discussed what he was doing at work. I found it fascinating. It was not necessarily machine-type work that I was thinking about. It was more like something automotive.

When I finally thought about machine shop work, I liked the money, and I always wanted to do something different. And then, of course, I like working with my hands. But I thought that maybe I might not be smart enough—whether my education was enough or did I know enough to do it. That was probably my biggest fear, because I think the education I was given in high school was inferior. If I had it to do all over again, I probably would pick a superior high school, but when you're in high school you're not thinking about your education, per se, you're thinking more about getting the heck out of there.

My husband (at that time he was my boy friend) suggested I take some training courses, so he looked around. He had been going to a private fellow who had a private course he was giving in his house, teaching people how to read precision instruments and blueprints. Well, I'd only taken the precision part of it, learning how to use the instruments and stuff. My husband was working in the aircraft industry, and by then they were looking for women and minorities with non-traditional skills. The federal contracts wanted to see more minorities and women in the non-traditional jobs, so they were essentially out looking. They were asking people in the shop if they knew women that would qualify for that kind of thing, so I kind of fell right into place. It helps to know somebody on the inside out there.

When I was hired, I was hired as a milling-machine trainee, which is a twenty-two-month program. I didn't know what to expect, because I had never set foot in a machine shop before in my entire life. I didn't know what it would be like to work with a bunch of men. I felt like I was very naive when I went in there. I had just come out of an all-girl high school and I didn't know a four-letter word from a five-letter word.

It was a big, huge place. They don't have anything small.

Everything's a zillion times bigger than you are. When I walked in there I thought, "Here I am, I'm walking in, I'm eighteen years old." As it turned out I was probably the youngest person in the whole shop. And *all* these guys that I saw! I thought, "Gee, these guys don't look very friendly at all." And I'm trying to get enough courage to say, "I'll do all right." The first room was awesome. It was closely packed with machines and noisy. It was the largest machine shop in the company—the machine fabrication shop. The head count at that time was over twelve hundred people on all three shifts. It averages three hundred to four hundred people per shift in the entire building and everybody has plenty of space to breathe. They're not real crowded or cramped. They could easily get two or three airplanes in a building that size. It's like a giant warehouse. And the amount of men compared with the amount of women was—really—I didn't think there were so many men in one place. At the time I was the youngest female in there. Now it's changed, but when I walked in there in nineteen seventy-two all the women were either dispatch clerks or tool room clerks, and all in their upper forties and had been there a long time. There wasn't any woman in the non-traditional jobs, so when I went on the machine it was like I was there all by myself.

When I went in I was wondering what it would be like to work with guys. I was wondering whether the guys would like me, whether I could work with them. I knew at least one person there and that was my husband, so I didn't feel like I'd be totally lost, but the others—they were all white, all male, and probably starting at age thirty-five and up.

After the first or second day there was a supervisor that kind of took me under his wing. He was Japanese and he always reminded me of the way I'd like to have my father be. He made me do and think on my own, but it was like he was looking out for me, which I really appreciated.

After eight months of learning the milling machine, I was

approached by the apprenticeship supervisor and asked if I'd be interested in the apprenticeship program. It sounded fascinating, because I was getting bored with what I was doing, so I filled in the application and had to go before the review board, which was made up of three representatives of management, generally from upper management, and three members from the union. They jointly vote on who's going to be an apprentice; they evaluate apprenticeship applications; they make sure apprentices who are on the program are doing their job, not getting bad grades, not having any problems with supervision, and getting proper training. They have to run the apprenticeship program essentially to the state guideline—what types of courses, what kind of machines you're supposed to run. When you apply for an apprenticeship, you send in an application along with your high school transcript and anything that's favorable, and they evaluate it and then ask for an interview.

My entire interview was tape recorded, and I understand I was the only one tape recorded. The main concern was whether I was going to get married and get pregnant, and I got so tired of hearing it. And then also why I really wanted to become an apprentice, did I really feel I was going to stick it out. Was I going to be there the whole four years or was I going to get pregnant? I would have liked to answer it one way, but I just said, no, I wasn't going to, but I wish I'd told them that nobody has to get married to get pregnant any more. I must have been asked that question four times in my interivew. I passed—five people voted for me and one person did not.

I got spoiled in my apprenticeship. Everybody was so willing to teach me everything. Like I was saying earlier, women at that time were such a novelty all the guys were hands on, they wanted to train a woman. I think it was a macho thing for them—"Hey, we got a woman here." The only thing I found was some areas in which I worked I think they were afraid to let me go on the machine, because they were afraid of the fact that they didn't really know whether I could handle it or not, so I feel like sometimes I suffered in that respect.

I started out making three dollars and fifteen cents an hour, something like that, and I don't even know what it is now—twelve forty-three? Right now I'm working on a sixty-two-inch lathe. A lathe is a machine that turns metal, makes it look round on the corners. It doesn't square 'em up. It doesn't make it look square or boxy. It makes it look round like the spindles on a bed, if you can imagine them being metal. The machine I've got can take over a five-foot-in-diameter piece of work. It works on a single cutting tool.

We do anything from the front end to the back end of the plane. The skin of the airplane and the outside shell and the wings are done by a subcontractor, but basically all the smaller parts, the intricate pieces, are generally done by us. I've learned everything from the leading edge of the airplane, which is the part under the flaps that filters up and down. . . . We have aluminum, which is a lightweight metal, and steel, which is what the engines are made of, or the older engines, I should say. We have exotic metals like magnesium, which is flammable and dangerous, and titanium, which is similar to stainless steel, like your pots and pans.

Right now, because of the lathe I'm on, I do only large work. I run all the large jobs on the machine. It's not really hard. It's kind of funny to see a woman on this machine. You think, "Oh, she's gotta work hard." But it's not really that bad. I do work hard just to get it set up so I can actually get the job going. But you have cranes to work with. You do have to use brute strength, and I'm not afraid to ask somebody else for help if there's something I feel is beyond my capability.

I'm quite union active. I'm a shop steward now. I was elected two months ago as a shop steward in the machine shop. I am the first and only woman to be a steward in a machine shop, and I had to work hard at getting that. It's been real political, as far as

Amy Kelley, machinist

just getting to *have* the election so I could become shop steward. The union's political for two important reasons. One is whether you support the incumbent that's in office right now, and two, the political incentive. Most men just aren't ready to take on a woman on a committee that's going to speak for them all. They feel uncomfortable with the fact that a woman has any self-confidence at all. They feel like it's a threat. Basically, they start near the bottom and head towards the top—down the road, like a business rep or staff assistant. They've got some really weird jobs in the union. I don't even understand why they even have those positions. I may not agree with what the elected officials are doing, but I believe in the causes and principles of the union. I believe that every person has a right to fair pay and decent working conditions and somebody to represent them in case of problems. I think the approaches of the union have got to change from what they used to be, like way back in the old days, in how you succeed in getting the things you want. But basically the union is only as strong as its membership, and I'm a firm believer that the union should involve its members more, so it can become strong, not alienate themselves from it.

In relationship to women in non-traditional trades, I don't think the union's done all that much. They just look at it as something they don't talk too much about. If you're a woman and you've got any vocal tendencies to speak your mind, you might as well forget anything for yourself, unless you support their ticket. It's not really a fair game at all, so to speak, within the union. The union, as far as representing women or minorities, is just starting to come out and seeing that justice is done. Basically they don't like to work on problems with women or minorities because it upsets the rest of the membership—the white Caucasian males. They [the rank and file] think that women and minorities are getting preferential treatment, so they [the union officials] keep it all low-key and quiet.

I treat people with respect if they give me respect. And I don't appreciate supervisors, just because they have a little badge that says "supervisor," to treat me just like another employee, another number that doesn't have any feelings. I feel like there's no reason why he can't say, "Please," or "Thank you," or "I appreciate your work." I'm not hesitant to say that. I've had supervisors say, "I need this job done," and I'll say, "What about please?" Or some boss will ask me, "Where the hell were ya?" And I'll ask, "Who the hell wants to know?" I've been wanting to advance in the hourly positions, but I can't seem to, mainly because I'm too outspoken. They want people who are gonna say yes, not why or no, or how come. And I think being a woman doesn't help either. Also, Japanese women are supposed to be diminutive and quiet and do what they're told. I shock a lot of my co-workers.

When I first came into the shop I was a naive girl and I was afraid. I went in one day and opened a cabinet door and there was a nude centerfold. It set me back, but then I realized at the same time that women shouldn't expect to change attitudes of the men. I think, with time, we are showing men we know how to do the work. Then they'll change just naturally. They can't help but respect you if they find out that you can do the work. I think it's very important for women to become more involved with their union and use it to make men realize that they have feelings; they have special problems that men don't understand, like sexual harassment, sexual discrimination. And most of these guys, unless they see it happen to their wives, are oblivious to the whole thing, so they have to be educated, and it has to start with the union, because the management's sure not going to do it.

I have had cases of sexual harassment. I have complained to the EEO commission. The company has an EEO office. I had one supervisor that used to come up behind me and pat me on the butt, and I didn't even know he was back there. And I had another supervisor that would come around, when I didn't

Amy Kelley, machinist

know it, and snap my bra strap! It was just something that they thought was cute. I told the supervisor who used to come up and pat me, "Hey, maybe you'd better cut that out, because if *your* supervisor saw you do that, you'd be in a heck of a lot of trouble and I'm not real keen on that." Sexual harassment is one touchy subject. This other supervisor—it wouldn't have done any good to talk to him. I filed a report and it hasn't happened since. They had a meeting and told us that they were getting some complaints, not from who, and it's gotten a lot better. I haven't had to worry about it from the fellow employees. It's the managers. I get a lot of teasing, a lot of jokes from the fellow employees; that doesn't bother me, and I think they have a little more respect for you because they're working *with* you. The supervisors, they're so away and detached from you. They feel like, "Gee, I'm a supervisor, so she should be flattered."

My husband understands my position. If you say too much then you can end up—you know, as much as they say they're not supposed to retaliate, there's other ways they can retaliate. They can make your work a little difficult for you, or they can give you jobs that they know you can't handle, or assign you to a different machine that's a little tricky.

I feel like I've been sexually discriminated against. I guess that's all I can say. Nobody's gonna come out and say, "You're being discriminated against because of your sex." I think that there have been jobs in which I have been sexually discriminated against—mainly the jobs that pay in the higher grades. About two years ago I was able to work a lot of the different jobs that pay higher than I get now. No problems. I was always asked to come back. They would always come and get me for a higher-paying job if they needed someone, if someone was sick or absent. And I'd keep going, keep going, keep going in, and the only time there was a permanent opening I didn't get it. There's no selection process. It's a popularity deal. If the boss likes you, he gets you in the job. They'd put guys in the positions that had less time than I did, who had less experience and less qualifications. And if that's not sexual discrimination, I don't know what to call it. Because they've put me in the positions temporarily before, they're telling me that I'm qualified. All of a sudden the jobs open up permanent, and I'm *not* qualified. That doesn't make sense to me.

In the area I'm working in I'm the most senior employee on second shift. I feel I am respected because I do know quite a bit more, as far as the procedures and where everybody in the area works, which jobs should be lathed on what machines. It makes me real mad when the lead man is not there they will not give me the lead position. I think it's because I'm vocal. I'm not a yes person. If you're not a yes person, you don't get the position. Although it doesn't help that I'm a woman, because there isn't a single woman in our shop that makes higher than a grade 8, which is what I am.

I went to the company's EEO office on a sexual discrimination claim when I thought I was being discriminated against in not getting the higher-paying jobs. The guy that got the job had less time than I had, and he didn't even have to go through the connecting jobs like me. I was not really satisfied with the results. They told me I didn't have enough running-time experience, which I disagree with, but I felt like there wasn't a whole lot I could do internally and I wasn't quite ready yet to go on the outside. I think I could have been successful going to the outside, but at the same time I didn't want to cut my own throat. If I had gone to the outside and started a sex-discrimination case and won, then the supervisors may retaliate by giving me hard jobs or putting me in an area that was wrong. I'm not the kind of person who likes to make a whole heck of a lot of trouble. These supervisors know that I want to get ahead. I think they also know that I could go to the outside if I wanted to. That's why I'm sort of biding my time. They're gonna realize that I'm gonna run out of patience.

Amy Kelley, machinist

I filed a sex-discrimination case with the EEO several years ago. I had been trying and trying to get on the apprenticeship board. EEO said there had never been a case like that before. They said there wasn't anything they could do because it wasn't a paying job. So I was up a creek. But I wanted it real bad, and a group of apprentices wrote up a petition. The men sent it down to the union hall and the next thing I became an alternate to the committee. Of course, they say it's not because of the petition, but funny it didn't happen until the petition had been sent in.

Race hasn't been too much of a factor. I think most people realize I'm more American than I am Japanese. Race has only been a problem on the men's bathroom walls. There's stuff about me on the bathroom walls, but, you know, it's kind of touching. Somebody will make a comment about me. Amy is a so-and-so, and somebody will put underneath the graffiti, "What difference does it make, she's nice." And it makes you feel good to think that somebody thinks that the clown who put this up there was crazy. But it's no different than blacks or Chicanos or anybody. There's racism in that shop just like everywhere else. I just live with it. When I first heard about it on the bathroom walls, what am I gonna do, tell 'em to erase it? It can still go back up there again, you know. I believe there are ignorant people out there, and I'll just ignore those ignorant people; I can't waste my time with them.

I like doing things around the house. I like to build things—small carpentry things. I built a sixteen-foot work bench in the garage. I've put light fixtures in our house. I've found that my job has made it a little easier to understand all these other things I do at home. My husband doesn't like doing things like that at home. So it's kind of like, if I don't do it, it won't get done. Our marriage is very different. My husband has always been in favor of me becoming better, becoming more independently capable, taking care of myself.

My family doesn't quite understand what I do. It's just a

language barrier. I feel it's almost like they have learned to respect me making almost thirteen bucks an hour. And they also realize I'm a lot more American than they probably want. Most of the women in our family have been taught to be traditional Japanese. They're from Japan, where the wife obeys the husband. When he says to get something to eat, you hop to it and do it right away. Where I'm more likely to tell him, "There's the kitchen; if you want something to eat, you can get it yourself." I'm more independent than they'd like to see a Japanese woman be.

But sometimes I miss being able to look like a woman. There's a purpose behind the way I dress. I don't dress to work at a fashion show, but I mean it isn't glamorous and there are times I'd like to dress up. That would be the one thing about work that I don't like. It's hard to relate to other women about what I do. I get tired of getting stared at in department stores when I go in with my grubby jeans and my flannel shirt and my steel-toed shoes. They kind of look at you like, "What in the world?" It's a whole different attitude.

As soon as I walk in the door at work it's like I'm not any sex at all. It's no sex at all. It doesn't matter if I'm a man or a woman. I'm a machinist. I can do the work. The guys look at me, not because I'm a woman, but because I'm a machinist. And that feels real good.

I think this is a good job for a woman, but only if she's strong, and I don't mean just physically. I mean mentally. They need to be strong, secure, emotionally stable, and able to take some stress. There's more pressure than on other jobs I've done. You have to make a good part. Because if you don't make a good part, that's gonna make an unsafe plane. She has to be able to cope with the stress of wanting to do good. Somebody that's physically capable—who knows how to compensate for their weakness. The women I've noticed, and myself too, they find little ways of doing things a little different, because you can't do it the

Amy Kelley, machinist

same way the guys do. They didn't build a woman's hip the way they did unless it was on purpose. I use my hip to a lot of advantage. I don't have the strength all on my own, so I'll put my weight into it also.

Some women just don't have the brute strength to do it, but I think the biggest *dis*advantage is from the moment they're born. Somebody's gonna raise them to be a "woman"—not to get their hands dirty, not to go out with Daddy and his hammer and nails. She's not gonna develop the mental skill or the agility. I know I have that problem with hand-eye coordination. On my job it hasn't been a problem, but it has been playing baseball. I think if I had been taught when I was a little girl that it was okay for little girls to play baseball, I would have developed that hand-eye coordination. There are other things that men take for granted. Boys, when they're growing up, learn how to fix their cars, learn what a feeler gauge is or how to set spark plugs, how to understand mechanical levers. Women don't have that advantage, no matter how much training they get. They aren't brought up with it, so I think it's important that they realize that and try to compensate. Also I think it's important they realize not to raise their little girl to do the same thing.

Sheet Metal Worker

KATIE MURRAY

Deeply religious since her son's near-death from drowning, Katie Murray finds it hard to comprehend the hatred whites feel for her black people. She wonders why God allows the racial discrimination to continue.

I always wanted to be a beautician. I never thought of anything but a beautician 'cause, you know, I used to do my sister's hair and my mother's hair, and I'd do it pretty good. But when I was home in North Carolina, working on the farm, we didn't have money for school. We didn't have time for nothing. We would get up at four o'clock in the morning and work until seven or eight at night and stop for supper. I didn't get a chance to go to school much, really. In the spring of the year the only time we got to go to school was when it rained 'cause we was always out farmin'—tobacco, corn, wheat. And in the fall of the year we'd go to school maybe two weeks out of the month, two weeks straight maybe. In my high school years they brought in French and typing, but of course they were special courses. You had to pay for them. My parents couldn't afford it, so I never took them. Anyhow, I just barely made it through high school.

Then after I went to New Jersey I was thinking of making a decent salary and sending money back home, and then I got pregnant and I had to raise the child. You know, most black people at that time were really poor, so I thought I wouldn't make any money being a beautician.

In New Jersey the first job I had was workin' for a mattress factory where I made bed mattresses. It must have been around nineteen sixty-two. It was piecework, and we got twenty-two cents for a double mattress and eighteen cents for a single. It had to be divided between two people because two people had to work on the mattress together. You had to make at least thirty mattresses a day to have a decent salary. I liked the job. I got a chance to go to different places. I don't like to sound conceited, but I was a good worker, so whenever they came up with a new bed mattress my supervisor would always ask me to go up to their other plant in Boston to show the girls how the mattress was done. They paid the hotel fee and plane fare and took you to lunch at the Whitman. Boston was a very prejudiced place and they didn't have no black people working at the plant there. When I went up there and showed them how the job was done, they told me that they had never taken an order from a Negro and weren't about to then. So I had to report back to my supervisor, and a woman who had been there for forty years got fired for making that comment, though I understand that she was rehired after I left. That time I stayed two weeks. Then I went back to New Jersey and they come up with another new mattress, so I had to go back, and that time they wanted me to stay a month. But those women gave me such a hard time. I went to work with a headache, and I came home with a headache. I wish I had stayed. I probably would have been the first black woman to make supervisor.

But I left there and went to work at a sewing-machine plant. That was commercial work and we was on a labor grade. I was labor grade ten. That was the lowest. Even if you could make over a certain amount a day, they wouldn't pay you for it. We was only making a hundred and thirty dollars a week. I liked that job real well. There wasn't anything about it I didn't like. It was a sit-down job, plenty of people. The people in New Jersey are much friendlier than the people here in Seattle. They didn't stand on black or white. You all workin' together. There are a lot of Italians in New Jersey. Italians and blacks get along pretty good there. I stayed there until nineteen sixty-eight. That's when I got married and didn't work for two years.

Next I did motel work—chambermaid. It was minimum wage, about a dollar forty an hour. Then I had domestic problems, left my husband, and came to Seattle. My brother was out here working where they make trucks. When I told him I was thinking about coming out here to live, he said, "Good, I hear they're hiring women out here now."

I said, "I've never driven a truck before."

He said, "Then you should try it," and sent for me.

I checked the place out when I first got here. I said, "If anybody else can do it, I can do it too. If you got men doing it, I can do it, just give me a chance." They told me they didn't have an opening, but according to my brother they *did* have an opening. Finally they let me take this physical exam and told me I had back problems. Course I never had back problems in my life. So when they told me that they couldn't hire me, I said, "That's okay, but I'm goin' to my own private doctor tomorrow, and if he says there's nothing wrong with my back, then I get the job." The personnel man said it was okay. I left, went on home, and about five o'clock the phone rang, and it was the personnel manager.

He said, "Katie, we're gonna overlook your problem. You come in tomorrow and go to work." So that's why I knew I didn't have no back problem. They just wouldn't hire a black woman. I got the job on May twenty-ninth, nineteen seventy-four.

When I first started working there, they gave me a hard time and wrote dirty words on the ladies-room walls about what they would like me to do for them—sex and all that. After awhile I just got tired of looking at it and I spoke to my supervisor, who finally got the walls cleaned off. And when I would walk up the aisles they would make wise cracks about what they would like

Katie Murray, sheet metal worker

to do. I just kept on walkin' and pretended I didn't hear 'em. It made me feel trampy. That's because I was a black girl. I'm sure you've never experienced this before, but the white men think that they can take advantage of a black woman. They think that she'd be proud to be with a white man. That's true. But I don't want no white man. I love my own black people. That's what I feel.

I guess I should have felt that there was gonna be some racial prejudice, but I didn't. I thought they'd treat me the same, 'cause I was a woman tryin' to feed a family, and I needed the job just like a man. I got a son to feed and I'm out here with no money. I was uncomfortable, I think mainly because I was the only black woman there at the time. They had one other woman there, but she was white.

I can't really describe how I felt when I first walked in there. I was scared. At that time I never said much, but the more I live the more I learned I had to speak up to defend myself.

In the plant the smell is terrible. And the sounds—you have to wear ear protection. The sounds are awfully loud because there's a lot of riveting and screwdrivers, especially in the cab shop. I don't know how anybody could just walk through there without ear plugs. When I first started I was in sheet metal sub-assembly, where it's very quiet. It was pleasant except for my lead man. He was a Southerner from North Carolina and he was very, very prejudiced. He made me have a lot of depression headaches. I never relaxed around him. He talked so much and you couldn't trust him. He was always telling the supervisors something or other, whether it was true or not true. He always put you down. It was very uncomfortable. That's why I transferred out.

Now I'm building doors for the superbox. When I get the work it's just an inside panel and an outside panel. I put in insulation first and then I rivet the two panels together, put a hinge on, and put on the lock and air vents. We have a jig sit on the table for the hinges to fit down in. Then I use a rivet gun on them. Every day I do more than I should because they have people laid off and they won't call 'em back. My supervisor has me go help them catch up in sleeper boxes so run over here, do this job, run back and do my own job. It's too much. I can't do it. Everybody told me to stop doing it, because the longer they see you can do it, they'll never call them people back in. I was so tired at the end of the day. Yeah, I do more than I should, I really do. I don't mind helping when they get behind, but sometimes, you know. . . .

The lead man, he's supposed to be there to help. The lead man we have now is very helpful. The lead man we had to have before wasn't like that. He was always telling me he was tired of babysitting. If I went to him for help, he said, "Niggers are more trouble in this place."

My supervisor, he has been into it so many times with me 'cause I feel that he can be very discriminating. He has a paper-work job getting in the orders for the day or week. When he got ready for this job to be done, he went and asked one woman to do it for him. And I questioned him as to why one of the black girls couldn't have done it as well as her. He said, "Well, I felt she could give me a good day's work."

And I said, "Do you feel like a black person couldn't give you a good day's work?"

He said, "Katie, I don't want you to feel that way."

I said, "Well, this is the way I feel. Why not let her do it for a week. Let this one do it for a week, let another one do it for a week, and then let me do it. This way we all can learn how to do paperwork. Besides, I understand to make journeyman you got to know how to do the paperwork, too."

He said, "Yes, that's true."

Then I said, "Let us all do it." And from that day to this day he still hasn't let us do the paperwork even though he'd always tell me what a good job I do. Can't nobody keep up with me on the doors. Still I don't never get a chance to do nothin' but make doors. I asked him once to let all of us learn to do different jobs, because one job can get boring at times. He won't let us do that because he's afraid that if we learn to do more than one job, we can make journeyman. That's all it is. I'm a production worker right now. When I first started I was a helper. I was a helper for eighteen months before they made me a production worker. And the union got behind me in the end. That's the only reason I made production worker. Most everybody else was a production worker in six months, three months, but not me. If I don't get journeyman in the next three years, I won't get it at all. I been ten years on it.

Most of the people I work with are white males and a black person never gets a chance that way. Take, for example, an incident that's going on right now. There's a man giving a three-day seminar out at the Holiday Inn. You don't have to come in to work, you just leave home and go to the seminar for three days with pay. Every week twenty-seven people go to the seminar. Out of all those people they haven't asked a black person to go. And it's sad; we're all out there workin' together, payin' our union dues just like the whites are except they haven't asked a black to go. And whenever I bring up something like this, they say I'm trying to cause trouble. But it is not that I wanna cause trouble. It's just that I wanna be treated equally. I want a fair chance just like the white folks do, male or female. I never caused a bit of trouble since I been there, but with this I'm gonna start a grievance tomorrow.

The racism is a continuous thing, maybe not with me but with some black person. Just when you think you got something settled, then something else pops up. It runs all the time. It never ceases. I think they have more of it there than anybody else. I really do. Let me tell you how that place has affected me. Because of the way it is, I had begun to drink quite a bit. When I drank I wouldn't go to work because I knew I couldn't do my job if I was drinking. There was a white man who missed the same amount of work as I did and for the same reason, but they called me into personnel and told me if I didn't go to Cabrini for alcohol treatment I would lose my job. The white male, he didn't have to go, but to save my job I had to go. Now that's on my record.

And another thing I felt I was discriminated on was when I had domestic problems and filed for a divorce. When my husband got the divorce papers, he threw me out of the house and I didn't have no place to stay. And I went to AYD, a division of United Way, for emergency help. I had been a member of AYD for four years, but when I went to them for help they told me it wasn't an emergency. I had a broken jaw, a broken hand, and no place to stay, but it wasn't an emergency. But when our lead man had a heart attack, they gave him assistance and he had a pile of money. If my situation wasn't an emergency, I don't know what one is. So I had this friend working there, and I was telling her about it; when I told her my problem she said, "Katie, you can stay with me tonight," and I stayed with her for three nights, and then I went to the YWCA. But AYD never gave me a cent and I got out of it the next day.

You know sex, it does play a part, but not as big a part as racial, because a white woman can get much farther than a black woman. And here I'm a black *and* a woman and it's hard. So I think sex is on one side and color's on the other.

I wouldn't say this job's changed my home life as far as being tired. Yeah, I be tired, but I'd be tired anyway. It has made me cranky. And made me be short with my husband when I come home. When I get cranky, we don't have no sex life and I think that's what made the domestic problems that we had. 'Cause I would come home after a bad day, like today, and I didn't know what I was gonna do. You know it really hurts, the way they discriminate against us.

Tell you the truth, my life is different because I pray every day

Katie Murray, sheet metal worker

that the Lord will take this feeling I have away from me. I have this hatred for the white male. Every night, every morning, I ask the Lord to take this hatred from me. This job has changed me so much. When I came here I didn't feel this way towards white people, but I think it was because I wasn't treated this way. It *has* changed me. If they would treat everybody equally, it might be a nice place to work, but I think they've got more suits against them than anybody I know. If they wasn't so prejudiced I'd love working. As it is I wouldn't tell nobody to work there.

Unions

American trade unionism was born shortly after the Revolutionary War, when, in 1786, Philadelphia printers struck for the one dollar a day wage. But American women were not welcomed with open arms by unions, which saw them as economic competition. Although women who worked in 1833 were estimated to earn only a quarter of what male workers made, they still were excluded from all national unions. In its 1866 convention, the National Labor Union, a short-lived federation of national unions, started the effort to break down these barriers by resolving, "We pledge our individual and undivided support to the sewing women and daughters of toil in this land. . . ." The following year, the Cigarmakers Union made history by becoming the first national union to allow women to become members on an equal basis with men. Still unable to get into most male-led unions, women workers formed their own, such as the Collarmakers and Laundry Workers Union, and the Daughters of St. Crispin, a union among shoemakers.

In the 1880s, women, who comprised 17 percent of the workforce, gained some acceptance in the Knights of Labor. when the Knights of Labor disintegrated, women tried to become part of the American Federation of Labor, but were not encouraged. Many of the early organized AFL craft unions still are reluctant to let women in, as is illustrated by Angela Summer's lawsuit to join the Plumbers Union. Even though not totally welcome, women workers persevered. The radical Industrial Workers of the World, or Wobblies, which was founded in 1905, aggressively organized women as well as male workers. In 1909, women led "The Revolt of the Twenty Thousand," the famous New York garment workers strike.

Today women are still not equally represented in unions. While three out of every ten American men are union members, the rate for women is one out of every seven. Women continue to be a rarity in the higher levels of union leadership even in unions with a majority female membership. The Coalition of Labor Union Women, a national organization of women unionists from all different major unions, is seeking to change this situation. One significant step forward was the AFL-CIO's decision to endorse the equal rights amendment. But as many women union members will tell you, endorsing the ERA is only the first step. Equally important is getting states passing the ERA to extend protective legislation to male workers. In Washington state this never happened and, instead, all protective legislation was removed. As a result, lunch breaks, weight limits, ventilation requirements, and cots in bathrooms were eliminated; in other words, the actual working conditions of women factory workers declined.

The stories in this section illustrate that unions can either be a force for justice on the job or a stumbling block. Barbara Shaman has had to fight her union as much as her employer. Jo Ann Johnson's union work fills her need for a greater challenge than her boring job provides. Laura Sarvis' and Linda Lanham's stories provide a remarkable contrast between a woman trying to survive and organize a shop, and a more polished union professional battling both the company and male hostility within her union.

Painter

JO ANN JOHNSON

She gave up a job with social status for an entry-level position as a painter trainee. Why?

I don't remember ever being given any direct guidance by my parents or teachers about what I should do with my life. I decided to become a nurse because my parents would pay for two years at a junior college if I lived at home. I think they were somewhat proud—most parents like the idea of their daughter becoming a nurse. It has social status. Besides, nursing was one of the few things at that time that you could put in two years and have something for it.

After I got my associate in arts degree in nursing I went to work on the surgical floor as a staff nurse in a small Seattle hospital. I was twenty years old and extremely green. I wasn't on top of things. I remember one patient, an old lady, who had surgery, went home, and then came back in with complications. I knew she was going to die, and there was nothing being done. It was my first experience with death, and I kind of knew her, because she had been in before. She actually did die on my shift. It was very gradual, and it would have been beautiful if her daughter had been able to sit there with her. But she died with no one there, except for me popping in and out whenever I could. Her daughter couldn't stand the emotional trauma of being with her. So I remember going in and out and holding her hand, which gradually got colder and colder. I really thought it was a sacred moment and somebody should be with her. Anyhow, while I was doing all this, I neglected my other duties and received complaints that I wasn't responding in a timely enough fashion to the other patients. The gist of it was that I got fired from that very first job.

After that, I got married and went to work at a hospital in Tacoma. I worked in their psychiatric unit from nineteen sixty-seven to nineteen seventy-five. When I first went to work there I really liked the job. You shared charge duty with someone else. Each of you had equal standing and responsibility. Our job was first of all to make sure the patient was all right and ascertain their level of mental health for the day. We did a lot of one-to-one counseling. That all changed as it became more and more medical as opposed to psychologically oriented. What can I say? Nurses don't make these decisions. I think the most exhausting thing about psych nursing was some of the doctors. I didn't agree with their medical treatments and felt some weren't very beneficial to their patients. They'd send people back into the same home situation, and then they'd come back in a year or two, not really changed. I quit there in nineteen seventy-five, tried selling real estate, and finally went to work in the other Tacoma hospital, which had a mental health unit. But I really couldn't do it. I didn't feel medically qualified, and there was a lot of lab work that I was supposed to be knowledgeable about that I really wasn't. I don't know. I really liked the unit, and the way they ran things, but I just felt increasingly stressed. At work I covered the stress as best I could. Yet I didn't feel I was doing the job as well as I wanted to.

I promised myself that I wouldn't leave there without a job and flounder around, so on my day off, I went down to see if they were hiring at the aircraft plant. I was determined to get a non-responsible job. In nursing you are responsible all of the time. I wanted to not have to take care of anybody, but I was also afraid. I wondered if I could function in that type of environ-

Jo Ann Johnson, painter

ment. I've always been good at theoretical things, but not good at just logical, ordinary, everyday situations, so I questioned if I had enough horse sense to handle it.

I filled out an application card that I would take an hourly job. At that time, after filling out the application, you were called to a window to talk with someone. Now, no one ever gets to talk with anybody. All of these people were going to the window and coming away without papers. And I told myself that I was not leaving until the person at the window gave me some papers. So I happened to get this man who had warm, brown eyes, and I think that's the only reason I got the job. He had apparently heard something from headquarters about hiring women painters. I believe I got the job because I'm a woman. They had to meet their quota. I told him I would do anything, even clean the toilet, but he told me I couldn't do that because you had to have two years' experience. Still I wouldn't leave, so finally he went to check with his supervisor about giving me a painting job. The supervisor said, "Well, maybe she got tired of emptying bedpans." After that he gave me the papers for an interview, but that was just a formality.

I started work in July of nineteen seventy-seven, making eight dollars an hour. I was really nervous the first couple months, but then I liked it. At first I worked in tooling, painting large fixtures that held big parts in an airplane. I painted these with a brush. My arms got tired, and more often than not my hands would get cramped. Tooling is very cut and dried and boring. After about two months they decided to put a woman on the construction crew. Construction painters get to mud and paint and do all kinds of things. It was kind of like an honor when I got chosen for that crew. But I wasn't allowed to do as much as I could have, because the supervisor didn't supply me with the taping and mudding tools—a mudpan for doing drywall and knives. Without the tools on a mud job, there's not a whole lot you can do.

We were supposed to be given those tools, but the supervisor didn't want me to learn. The attitude was that women can't really do this.

Along about this time I got a transfer that I wanted from swing shift to days. At one point I got a below-average evaluation, and I was quite upset and asked to have a copy of it. They didn't want me making waves, so the next day I was taken off the construction crew. There appears to be a lot of favoritism as far as the people who get the good jobs and bad jobs. I've been getting bad jobs for several years now.

They hire painters as learner-progressors. They hire people off the street without any background and train them on the job. It's a way of not paying much. You also don't get the training unless you happen to be favored. If you're favored then you get the training that you should get. At the end of two years, you're at the target level, which means you should be able to perform a certain job description. And they have not been allowing people to learn the different areas that are included in the job description. I talked to the supervisors about the problem and very little was done so I went to the union. One of the business reps told me that the company could sit me in a chair for the whole time. As long as they paid me, they didn't have to let me do anything.

It isn't fair because men don't stay in tooling. Usually men who take the time to talk to the supervisor and get into the in group move right into construction. And even if they start in tooling, they don't stay there long. Most women stay in tooling.

It is hard constantly being in the inferior position and having to ask all the time to be able to do things. Sometimes I get the feeling that maybe I can't do the trade. If you want to learn a trade well, you have to put yourself out all the time. Whenever I'm in a situation that requires more than what I know how to do, I have to go and ask, plead with them, you know, I wanna do this. You have to continually do that, but if you allow yourself

Jo Ann Johnson, painter

to *believe* that you can't do it, then it's hard to go and do anything. It's very frustrating. Sometimes when I'm wearing steel-toed shoes, I go and kick something; garbage cans are great.

The union, in theory, treats women equally with men. At most positions, even shop steward, you'll find women, but when you get to the thirteen business reps, they're all men. Women in the union recently formed a women's committee to help women with work problems. We are having a workshop next week to get women's input on priorities to be working on. We think that day care and job training will probably emerge as priorities. Most women are in the lower-paid grades and don't know about any upper-level jobs or what training they might take.

I've been a shop steward for two or three years. My job is very boring and gives me little except the money. The union allows me to be involved in another level. It gives me an opportunity to be active and hopefully work towards justice.

It is hard, though, because a supervisor can come in and make all kinds of mistakes, do wrong things to people, even go against the contract, but it seems like that's all forgiven. When the shop steward makes one small, little error, everyone's talking about getting rid of him, all behind his back.

I've had some difficulties the past few months because I didn't handle a situation right in my capacity as shop steward. I was technically correct, but didn't handle it in my best interest. In the morning you take down paint buckets, cut rings out of them, and put handles in them. One woman decided that some of the rest of us were taking her buckets and made a few scenes about it. The next day before the shift started, I was trying to read the paper and heard all this clattering and banging of jamming buckets down. I was disturbed and told the woman doing the stuff with the bucket that she shouldn't do that until the shift started because she'd have to be paid for it. Any time a person works before or after a shift, he is to be paid for it. The woman didn't seem to know what I was talking about, which kind of made me mad. Anyway, as it came down, I talked to the supervisor about paying the person overtime, which I shouldn't have done, but I did just because I got upset and angry. A couple days later the woman came to me and demanded to see the business rep. I can't materialize a business rep on demand, but did finally reach him on the phone. He said to have the woman stop by the office because he would be in. Well, that was totally unsatisfactory according to the person, because it was too late in the day. And there was another person who more or less said that, if I couldn't get a business rep within an hour, then I wasn't any good. Anyhow there has been a lot of flak flying around about what a lousy shop steward I am.

I definitely wouldn't want my daughter to be a painter. Painting is a lot harder than it seems. In thinking about it, people say, well, I painted this bathroom or this living room, which is very easy compared to most painting that I experience. In regular painting you don't have to do much prep work, for one thing. And really, the painting is the easy part. On most all our jobs, painting is not the problem. Like right now I'm doing a lot of scraping. I scraped all morning with a putty knife and hammer in an area where they sprayed part of the airplane. What I'm scraping off is essentially an overspray that got stuck and hardened. It's hot, uncomfortable, and damn tedious work. The scraping makes a dust that is hazardous to your health.

Believe me, painting is not the safest job to have. I don't know if I have done anything out of the ordinary that other painters don't do, but working on ladders all the time, up and down. I've been in some really high areas. Sometimes, if there's not a ladder that's tall enough, you have to use one that's a little short, and that's hard to handle. If you're aware of it, you're usually okay. If you're not, or sloppy, or don't think about it, then you could get in trouble.

Jo Ann Johnson, painter

I think spraying is hazardous, particularly lately, because we've been spraying ceilings on these jigs. We spray with an airless sprayer, and it's really hard to use any eye protection, so we have paint all over our eyes. Now I stop and put on eye protection. It takes me longer to get set up, but I won't do it without goggles any more.

Often I work in areas under construction and have to wear a hard hat. You have to be very aware of things at all times. Once I was injured on the job because I stepped back into a hole that I didn't know was there and broke a bone in my foot. They're supposed to put up barricades around holes but don't always do it.

When I worked part time as a nurse, I had more time for my family. This job is hard because, when I'm tired, I'd like somebody to take care of me and there is no one. I get behind on my housework and have been working on different methods to get my daughter to help more. This last weekend I got really upset. I go to school every other weekend, so I got home at six o'clock Sunday night and the house was a mess. The dishes were still stacked up from Friday night. I cleaned up the kitchen and then put up a sign saying, "This kitchen will no longer be serviced." The sign was a little harsh, but I had to do something. It's helping, too. My husband was kind of mad, but sometimes he'll make dinner, sometimes the laundry. Sometimes he cleans out the shower, but it's not structured. His response is, "Are you going to change the oil in the cars?" He maintains the two cars, truck, Jeep, camper, and boat. We both have too much to do. But when I finish school in June, I hope to leave there for a better job.

Concrete-Truck Driver *

MARGE KIRK

With a waitress' smart mouth and a soft spot for little kids, she uneasily wends her way through the burly world of construction.

I went to a Catholic high school in Seattle. It's hard to remember what the nuns wanted me to do, just that I should do something respectable. I went to college and ended up doing one of those interdisciplinary study things. It was in the nineteen sixties and I couldn't quite figure out what to do. I would have loved to have figured out a way to work with kids, but the opportunities weren't there, and if you did go into something like that, you were just buying into this whole other garbage about professionalism, or so I thought at the time.

I'd always worked. My folks encouraged us to earn our own money and, as we lived in a farming valley, jobs were fairly available. I started in the strawberry fields when I was in the third or fourth grade. My first paycheck was a large amount— seven dollars. On the way home I lost it and my mother blew her stack and said, "You go find it." I went back and forth along the road until I found it. The money had fallen out of my pocket into the ditch by the side of the road.

In the summers we all worked in the fields—strawberries first, and when you get a little older in the spinach and flower bulbs. Later if you get to be a good worker, you go to work in the

---

* Cement is the dry stuff and concrete the wet mixture with sand and gravel—fascinating, right? [Marge's correction to manuscript]

Marge Kirk, concrete-truck driver

barn, which is hourly pay. The field work is all piecework. After that I worked in the canneries for two summers. Then I turned to waitressing, which was my main job until I started driving truck. I mixed waitressing with janitorial work all the time I was going to school.

In nineteen seventy-two, after I got out of school, an employment agency sent me down for a waitressing job at the Heritage House. It was a black club for the most part, but they wanted to draw the big money people. So they figured they needed some white people to work there and draw the white people in to eat there. It was this black guy's dream to have a real hot club that was sophisticated down in the Central area, and he did a pretty good job, but there were other people who wanted to siphon money off on the side and kinda got in trouble for that. It was pretty interesting working there. The guys I was working with were mostly these young Black Muslims and were really dedicated to seeing an all-black area. Like they really wanted it to be like Chicago, where they wouldn't see any white people for blocks, you know. Anyway they were really neat guys, good people to work with.

I quit there when the management changed and got on with the phone company. They were terrible to work for. I was a long-distance operator. They were always pushing you, timing you to see how fast you were. I used to come home at night and just cry. It was so depressing. I don't know what it was about the job, whether it was sitting inside, or being so controlled, or being hooked up to this electronic thing or what, but I would just come home and cry. It was awful. I couldn't stand it any more and went up to Juneau, Alaska, with a girl friend of mine. I waitressed up there in this neat old cafe that was kinda the working people's place to go. Everybody went there. The Indians and the state people, even the governor. The guy that was running it was this Japanese guy that'd toss a cup of coffee down the counter to the guy that wanted it and throw the spoon down after it. Everybody liked him. He had a heart of gold. Stayed there for a year and then ended up going up to Fairbanks hoping to get on the pipeline. Couldn't get on because you had to have so many hours out of the Fairbanks union local, so I did cocktailing at this hotel that had the hookers upstairs and the pimps downstairs. It was quite a place, but I did get my hours. Money was real tight. It was like you got your paycheck and then ate it in about two days and that was all there was.

Just when I was about to give up and leave town, my name came up at the union hall for a job in the kitchen of one of the camps connected to the pipeline. That was the best pay I'd ever seen—ten dollars and seventy-one cents an hour for kitchen work. But I watched all the other people on the line, and they had quite a few women in all the trades. They were all making more money and working about half as hard as I was, and I says to myself, "Hmm, there's got to be another way." Before that I'd always thought I couldn't do those jobs, that I'd just be a waitress. I knew I could always figure some way to take care of myself, but the frustration of not having a specific job skill that paid decent money was getting to me. I've always liked waitressing, but you rely on tips for money. It's a little like being a prostitute. It's how nice you are to these people, even if they're jerks, that determines whether you get tips or not. Working with the public can wear anyone out eventually.

So when I came down off the pipeline in the spring of nineteen seventy-seven, I started a two-quarter truck-driving class at South Seattle Community College. You know, I don't think I ever dreamed of being a truck driver, and I didn't really have those romantic ideals of driving across the country in some big truck. But I wanted to learn something so that as the years went by I could get a job and make some money if I had to. Even if you're married and had a kid, so many people end up getting divorced, it's really nice to be able to make a decent wage.

It was a pretty good program. They did a lot of defensive

Marge Kirk, concrete-truck driver

driving things. The teacher was somewhat attuned to women. You know, he did like it if you were cute a bit more, but he did encourage all types of people to get their confidence. I think back on a lot of the things he told us, and I'm glad I took the class because they are the little things that in an emergency you would just want to have thought about once before—perhaps only to get some idea of what the options were, or heard somebody with more experience say, "This is what I did." Like lower gears plus light braking going down hills, using a little throttle going around curves and such. Mostly it does take experience.

Oh, I had terrible fears that I'd never learn how to back up a semi. I still wonder how well I can do it. In a semi you turn the front wheels the opposite direction of how you want the back end of the trailer to go. But the trick is to have a very light touch. There's a tendency to over-turn the wheel. It drives you nuts. It really was a matter of practice—to just keep doing it until you got it and *believe* that you could get it, because anybody can learn it. Pretty soon you'll be able to back up a semi and shift the damn gears. The other girl in the class and I were perfectionists. The guys seem to have a natural confidence that if you jam it in gear, it will go. But we tried to get it in their "right." We had a little higher expectations of what we needed to be doing than the guys did, I think.

The illusion about going to school is that you'll be able to get a job. Getting a job is really hard. My girl friend didn't get one. I went everyplace looking for a job. I talked to dispatchers. I went through the phone book. I walked. I looked. I mean if you try finding some of these places, they have the weirdest addresses. So you spend most of the day finding these places and they all give you this kind of blase "Well, why don't you make out an application?" In reality, they aren't even going to look at it. The freight offices—there is nothing that's going to make them hire a woman unless you're related or sleeping with somebody. But I had no idea then.

One outfit had women in the personnel office, which really can help, and I got sent over to the dispatcher's office. In reality, the dispatch office did as they pleased and were not into hiring some "woman" and I really didn't have the experience. It ended up a big mess, but I did get some practice in backing their trucks and worked a few days for them—enough hours to join the union.

Finally, I started trying construction and concrete companies. This one company had a real friendly woman working in personnel. She sent me down to the superintendent, who said, "Come on down and ride with us and we'll see how you do." Actually, they needed another woman on their list for minority quota and I came at the right time. Those drivers were all big, heavy-set guys, like construction guys. It was this real gray place with concrete all over it down by the river, and the offices were ugly. And it was all full of people—men—and they were all standing around, very much in charge of *their* world there. I just had a scary feeling about it. That was the beginning of nineteen seventy-eight.

There were some disastrous moments while I was being trained, more than I care to remember. One day we were in this really tight place trying to get out of this job, and I was finally getting around this corner, and there were trucks behind me waiting to get into the job, so they were all watching what was going on. This concrete truck has this big front end and I'm going forward, backing up, and going forward and backing up. And this guy who's training me is directing me forward, and I kept stopping and saying I should back up 'cause I'm getting too close to this car that was parked there. And he kept saying, "Come on, come on, come on." He was looking real mad and "Come on, you dumb girl, get up here." Anyway, he got me right next to the car and then had me back up. Of course, not being real together on the truck, I didn't put the hand brake down. Well anyway, I rolled into the car, made a little scratch, and had

Marge Kirk, concrete-truck driver

to call in. I think I had only been there a week and I thought, "Oh wonderful, here goes my job!" I was so shaken up. One of the younger drivers saw the whole thing and told the dispatcher what led into the thing, so they decided to give me a break. Thank my lucky stars! I don't think the older driver meant to get me. I think he was just challenging my driving ability or maybe thought I knew better. I don't know. We're friends now. As I think back, he wasn't sure how to relate to me. If I related to him like a woman, he would help out in a patronizing way. But when I was trying to be just a truck driver, it was a little bit harder. He didn't know what to do with that.

But what else happened when I was just starting? Once I had this old truck and I don't know why the dispatcher sent me, a new driver, out on this one job. You had to back up this narrow dirt road, and it was like straight up, and then you had to get around this corner. Every time I got the truck up there, the front wheel would be ready to run into the forms on the corner. I tried again and again and then finally I tried to swing out wide, but I got the duals, the back wheels, too close to the side of the road and sank in a soft spot. So there I was, stuck, petrified, shaking, going, "Oh, no, there goes my job!" Here I was with this top-heavy truck leaning into this ravine. The big fear with concrete trucks is rolling them over, and this was one of those moments. This load of concrete had calcium in it to make it set faster, so it was getting harder and harder. I called in a mechanic and another truck driver came down, too. And pretty soon all the guys that were working there, probably fifteen in all, came down. We started adding water to the concrete because it was getting harder and stickier. So finally what they did is they brought the pump down and I got my load into the pump, which pumped it into another truck. Then they took the other truck up the hill and dumped from the other truck into the pump and finally onto the site. They had a lot of trouble getting it through the chute, but after all that hassle and all that help it worked out okay and I was able to drive out of the hole. When I got back to the plant I was really shaken, and the dispatcher actually showed some empathy, took me to lunch and calmed me down. I will give him credit for that. It was definitely my mistake, and he really gave me a break.

The dispatcher is your immediate supervisor. He has a lot of power over a driver. There's a real difference in the jobs you're sent out on, and he can really play havoc with that. If you kiss up to the dispatcher, you *may* get better jobs, you may get on the wash-up rack earlier. When you're new and inexperienced, being sent to a difficult or nasty job is a real fear. It takes a lot of experience to know where to back in, what's the best angle, what to do when the customer doesn't know what they're doing, et cetera. So when you're not playing the game the way the dispatcher thinks you should, you may get the less desirable jobs. With a few years' experience the fear is gone, but it's still a tiresome game.

As dispatcher, the guy wants "loyal soldiers"—drivers who will do whatever. There's a lot of effort to manipulate new drivers into this position. As a woman it's even harder. The dispatcher is the big cheese and you're the new girl. You're coming into a mostly male workplace where there is always the male competition to see who and if anyone's gonna "score." So the pressure from the dispatcher really used to get me when I first started. The worst part was that he had been successful with one of the women that came before me. At the time, I didn't have a particular boyfriend that I could use as my "protector" (bad practice anyway). So it kind of makes you fair game according to male thinking. You put up with a lot of sexual innuendo, like this dispatcher's standard, "Should I call you in the morning or should I just nudge you?" And you can't take it serious. It takes a lot of energy just to stand your ground—balancing male egos with your right to survive. I wanted a job, I wanted to be a good truck driver, I wanted to be able to pull my weight as a driver. So years have passed now and somehow I survived. The guys are beginning to see me as a real human, not just a broad with legs and boobs. And the dispatcher has passed to the point of seeing me as a driver, I think.

One of the hardest parts of this job to learn is that you're in charge at the job site, which is difficult as a female. You have to have a certain amount of confidence about what the truck can do, what you can do, and what's the easiest, most efficient way to get this heavy, obnoxious stuff out of the truck so the guys aren't killing themselves. And the things that people ask you to do are just insane. You know, they want you to go upside down and turn around. Also you have to be able to lift the chutes and lug one-hundred-pound sacks of cement. That's basically what the job is. It's kind of fun now when I go to job sites. They don't expect a girl to know what she's doing, and I will put them on like it's my second day on the job, and then do it *just right*. It's fun to feel some confidence—experience is a great teacher. But there will always be that "dumb broad" syndrome. It seems they will always think women aren't quite as capable.

The drivers and I are all pretty good friends now, but I don't know if they will ever think I know how to drive a truck. It's like they're always surprised if I can do a certain job. It's like you will always be a little slow, a little less than up to snuff. On this one job I was on recently, I had to go back into a kind of tight place. Another driver came up while I was pouring and said, "Oh Marge, you're doing real good." Boy, what a surprise. I mean, where has he been? What have I *been* doing all this time?

It's a normal, working-class job, and so, yes, there is racial prejudice. The men are very—not really—narrow-minded. They've seen a lot of different things and people in the course of their job. They've been around some black people. The cement finishers are often black and there's one black guy down where I work. He's one of the more together guys, as far as knowing what's bullshit and what's not bullshit. And he's fairly respected, and they don't mess with him much. But most of the guys are from the south end and grew up in real white working-class neighborhoods—it's gross, the things that they say. One minute they'll be talking about some black guy—"This so-and-so is great, really knows his stuff!" But then five minutes later they'll be telling some joke about a nigger. I think it's just the world they live in. So where they may tell these terrible jokes about black people or women, they are not as bad as they seem. They just live in a world with that kind of thinking. Construction , in most trades, is really very white, and of course very male.

You've got to take the situation of construction. Sex, money, and macho toughness are major topics of conversation. Guys tend to want to be better or best in such categories. Having been a waitress, the come-ons and standard bullshit are not so new. But still it takes a lot of energy figuring out the best way to react—when to be rude and when to laugh it off.

I don't think I've ever sat down and talked with any of the guys about the sex stuff, because guys don't understand how harassing that can be or how it gets you down—that it seems the only thing a high majority of men think about is sex and what you might be like in bed. You want to be thought of as more than that. The thought process is so different in men and women. It's opposite ends. I think it's going to be real interesting in the years to come as women go into the workplace. There's going to be a crossing of very different norms. Just being friends with a woman is a whole new world for most men. 'Cause usually they are just married to their one woman and most of the others they look at are bodies—possible escapades, or at least flirtations.

I really think most men feel they're complimenting women when they come on to them. Maybe they are—I try to be as straightforward as possible and get to know the guy for who he really is (usually married). Not always that simple, but it's nice when the sexual energy fades enough so you can be friends and

Marge Kirk, concrete-truck driver

fellow workers. There's still plenty of flirting and teasing at work now—but we're friends, having fun, helping the day pass. It took me a long time to know who to trust. I think women in general tend to trust men too quickly—something about that confident male manner. Some of my scariest moments driving have been doing something some guy told me to do. Even though my instincts maybe questioned things, I figured the guy knew more than me and certainly must know what he's doing. *Not always so.* I've learned to use my own head, put some confidence in my instincts, and keep my eyes and ears open. Ask lots of questions and pretty soon you figure out who knows what they're talking about and who's honest to you.

I've paid some pretty heavy dues in this job. As I look back on having done this for three-and-a-half years, I think I must have been crazy. When I was new, I just kept on wanting to learn how to do it. Now that I'm somewhat experienced, I realize you sacrifice a lot—your sensitivity, for one. You end up being real hardcore about some things and you have a very realistic viewpoint about the world that is a little one-sided, because you are in this position of being a woman in an all-men's field. So you get cynical about men in a lot of ways. But you also get to appreciate men in what they do on the job.

Construction is often hard work, dangerous; it takes a lot out of their bodies. Their humor and stories have kept me in stitches more than once. The camaraderie they have—it's different from the kind women have. They can be so cool to each other and yet they understand and seem to know what's going on with each other. Men seem to judge each other pretty harshly; they're terrible gossips, and yet everyone's part of this working machine. I remember the main thing they told me when I went down there was, "Just cover your own ass"— meaning you never know who will really stand by you. And it's true, they play a tough game. Yet I've learned a lot from the guys I work with. They've helped me out a lot and most of them are pretty good people. You just got to know you're going to run into some jerky attitudes and a few real jerks.

Probably during the strike was the main time of everybody coming together. The guys had gotten pretty much screwed on the contract before this one. It had a bad cost of living and the increase in health and welfare benefits came out of the wages, so sometimes our wages actually went down. This time everybody was pretty hot to get a good contract, and there was an organization that got started with the shop stewards. The stewards held meetings at every company to find out what the guys thought should be in the contract and then got together and made a list, which went back to the guys again. There was really good communication. Nobody had been through a strike. There hadn't been one in sand and gravel for thirty years. But we thought it was a prime time. It was September and everybody was finishing their work before the really rainy season and how can you do it without concrete? But it didn't work out that way. The construction companies started getting nervous and brought in concrete from out of the county—from Vashon, or they'd pay a hundred dollars a yard just to get it out of Monroe or something! They bought old rollers so they could haul their own concrete. They had all kinds of trouble with it, and it wasn't effective in replacing us. But their main deal was to not let the workers think they were winning. Then the press started coming down on us, and our union pulled out all the stops to get us back to work. They mistrusted the fact that we drivers had organized ourselves. It seemed like everything was crumbling and we all got pretty scared. Finally we went back to work with an offer that'd we'd voted down earlier. It was a real bad ending, but at the same time we *did* win some important things that we wouldn't have gotten without striking. Most important, we had stood together.

It took a long time to think of myself as a woman *and* as a truck driver. The two did not combine for a long time. At home you want to be able to do beautiful things, you want to look pretty, and to have clean nails. You want to be able to sew beautiful things and have pretty flowers in your house. You want to feel like a woman. You want to feel like you can be in a relationships and be a normal woman in a relationship. The job makes you feel sort of hardened. You gotta have your guts up to par, you've gotta go for it, you gotta go fast. It's a real grind-it-out type of thing. At home I want just the opposite type of thing—things that have always been part of my life. But they've kinda slid away. I feel like this job takes away my creativity, zaps it away. I need a week off before I can even think of making something pretty.

The job just takes so much out of you physically. I screwed up my back, had to go to a chiropractor, from lifting sacks of gravel. They weigh around a hundred pounds each. And the pounding of the trucks is bad. You're always in a rush. And the bumps on the roads, it really shakes you up. I've gotten so I wear supportive bras. Just going down the Alaskan Way viaduct is murder on some trucks.

I used to be really conscious of whether getting muscles was going to show. Yeah, I used to be afraid I was going to look like this big-shouldered broad. I didn't want to look like a broad. I wanted to look pretty. Now it's fun having more muscles. I like to get stronger. But you have to balance it out. Like some parts of your body get used a lot and other parts not very much. Also it's hard on kidneys and bladders, because on a lot of jobs, like, there aren't places for women to go to the bathroom. What do you do? You just wait.

And tired—for a long time I really cut back on social things because I was going to bed at nine or nine-thirty just so I could manage to get up the next day. In the summer you work a lot of overtime, so the main people you get to know are from work. It was real hard to get a balance where I was knowing and seeing other people. I need a social life away from work. You meet

162

people on jobs and I used to go out with men from jobs and that usually ended up in disaster. There was too much conflict trying to put two different worlds together. You don't have enough time in the middle of pouring cement to get a decent perception of a person. I don't know. Still if I meet somebody really interesting on the job, maybe I would go out with him, but almost never. There were a few that I met that were just neat, neat guys, but if you get into socializing it's awful hard when you go back on those jobs and work. I mean, the way guys do rumors is just incredible!

I think I'm finally back to having some decent relationships—where I could really feel that I was a woman, that I could really care about somebody. I screwed up a number of relationships when I first started driving truck. I was just too involved with the job, or else I would look for somebody to take me away from all of this. I don't know what I was doing. I wasn't myself. I would be confused about why somebody would like me, especially being around men on the job—you get so cynical 'bout whether somebody likes you for your body or what.

One of the hardest things for me was that there was no place for me to look to see role models. There's other women driving trucks but they're all experimenting with the same thing. I find that all women have different ways of doing it. Some go into it hustling the men. Some of them are going into it being tough machos. You just have to figure it out yourself. In some ways I have taken the easy way out, because I like to get along with the people I work with. I don't like to bring on conflict constantly, but at the same time I take a pretty hard position on what's important—how people relate to each other. A lot is past history, part of the scenario, so you don't say, "Hey, you're being a male chauvinist pig." You're working with that. It's just getting to have some kind of working relationship and then, with luck, you find you have a human relationship.

Marge Kirk, concrete-truck driver

I still ask myself if it's worth it. The hard times, the changes you go through. Some days it seems perfectly normal for me to have such a job—I like driving, being outdoors, being physical, meeting the different people on the job sites. I like the never-boring challenge of the new situations you're constantly put in. The job itself has a lot of good points. But on some days it seems like such a male world—why would a woman bother with such nonsense? I still think we can do without the nonsense, but I also think there's much we as women can learn from working with men, and there certainly is a lot men can learn from women. It's very encouraging to see more and more competent women out there working alongside the men.

The major thing I would say to a woman going into this work is try not to bullshit yourself into this kind of romantic idea. The romantic side is just not there. It's hard work. Period.

Outside Machinist

BARBARA SHAMAN

Thirty-five-year-old Barbara Shaman has a degree in business administration and spent two years as a Peace Corps volunteer in the Philippines before turning to shipyard work.

I remember my father used to always come home from work and fall asleep in the chair by the television after eating dinner, and I really never could understand it or appreciate why he was doing that—except that, "Gosh! Why did he always fall asleep?" You know, "Why isn't he more awake—have more energy?" But I can understand it now. It's exhausting! It's absolutely exhausting!

I started work as a shipscaler in nineteen seventy-six. What was it like? It was amazing. I think the first week I came home aching, feeling muscles I never knew I had. We were hauling steel, pieces of steel, out of a ship. As they were putting the ship together, they would cut off the steel supports, and we would have to lug everything out. It was heavy work—up ladders. It was physical, dirty work, very dirty. I came home very, very dirty. I remember it used to take me fifteen minutes to clean out my nose.

Exhausted! I was too tired to realize what was happening. Then I got my first paycheck, and I was just totally overwhelmed by making so much money. I remember talking to somebody and they were talking about making seven—what I thought was seven hundred and thirty-five dollars—seven thirty-five. And I thought it was seven thirty-five a month, and it turned out seven dollars and thirty-five cents an hour starting wages, and I had *never* made that much money.

I was also real naive. I know the first weeks that I was there we were following the chippers around to prepare for painting, and they didn't have any respirators, so they said, "We don't have respirators. Take a rag and wrap a rag around you." So I wrapped a rag around my mouth, the way that you see in the old movies, and worked for hours like that and would come home just barely able to breathe. But I hadn't realized there was such a thing as respirators and that they *had* to provide them. The one thing I started to learn about then was health and safety.

When I first went out there I worked repair, not new construction, so the ships were basically built. We scalers would just work on some aspect of the repair, either getting it ready for painting or cleaning up after somebody else. It meant working in confined areas like crawling in the bottom of bilges under engines. And a ship is very narrow, very small. You have to fit through small holes, which at times is a problem. You do a lot of climbing—sometimes just up ladder-type stairs, but sometimes in situations that made me feel very uncomfortable. One of the things that I think I became is more agile working down there, because I just had to get myself in places that normally I'd feel very uncomfortable about—either being too high or unprotected.

Well, there weren't many women in the shipyards. Those that were there were mostly shipscalers. The union is part of the Laborers International and has a large membership of black people and some white people. In fact most of the people of color in the shipyards were either shipscalers or painters, though over the time I was there it was noticeable to see the change in the color of people who were painters. More white men were coming in as painters. I understand that painters and shipscalers used to receive the lowest wages in the shipyard until the crafts bargained collectively as metal trades.

You see, there's all kinds of different crafts working in the yards. There's boilermakers, which weld. There's riggers, painters, shipscalers, machinists, electricians, pipefitters, carpenters, millwrights. . . .

I had noticed in the shipyards that people were coming out as trainees in the different crafts, so I tried to find out how to be a trainee. Specifically, I wanted to become an outside machinist, and I felt I was qualified to be a machinist. I had worked with machinists on the ship and quite a few times, in fact, I helped the machinist figure out what they were supposed to do—suggested how to do things—because a lot of them had absolutely no past background other then they went to the union and bullshitted and got dispatched. I tried to get dispatched to the shipyard as a machinist. When I went down to the union, they asked me for my credentials, and I said I had completed mechanical apprenticeship in Oregon for a year and a half, and they asked me if I had a state certificate. I said, "No, it was not part of a state program."

So they said, "Well, that credential is not acceptable." So I went back out to the shipyard, and I checked with personnel several times about when there would be a machinist training program and how to get in. And they said when it opened, the union and the company that run the program would accept applications. As it turned out, I went into the personnel office one day, this was back in the beginning of May, nineteen seventy-seven, or something around that time. I had been periodically going in every week and checking on it and the guy said, "Oh! Today's the last day for applications! You had better hurry on down to the union hall"—meanwhile, it's quarter after four, four-thirty; union hall closes at five o'clock—"and get your application in."

I was furious! But I got down there and got my application in. Then they were doing interviewing, and I heard they had made selections on ten people who were entering the training program. I hadn't had an interview, so I called up the union and they said they couldn't get in touch with me to tell me about an interview. I asked them, "Well, when did you call me?"

"During the day." I said, "During the day! I work down here at the shipyards. How can I be at home answering my phone?" So they said, okay, they were going to have another bunch of interviews and they were going to interview me. I waited and eventually was interviewed. In that second batch of people I was the *only* person that had any shipyard experience. I'd been working down in the shipyard for a year. One of the things they were concerned about was would you last in shipyard work. After all, it's very heavy. You have the weather. You work in very bad weather conditions—sometimes outside in the cold, wet. You work heights. And that was one of the things they were very concerned about in the interview, and I'd certainly proven that I could handle the work. In the interview they didn't ask me one question. They explained what the work was like, and I already knew what shipyard work was like. Then they asked if I had any questions, and I think I may have asked them one or two questions.

They chose eight people from this second group. I was not chosen. At that point there, I realized something's wrong. This is not right at all. Another thing that happened was that my business agent from the Shipscalers Union came up to me one day and said, "Gee, I understand that you went and applied for machinist."

And I was really surprised. I asked him, "Well, how did you know?" And somehow at the Metal Trades meeting that they had from all the trades that worked down at the shipyards, my application had somehow gotten discussed. Well, gee whiz, I figured, why did that happen? Except that perhaps the Machinists were trying to find out what exactly I had been up to in the Shipscalers Union. You see, we had been organizing a caucus and an alternative newsletter and were becoming effective in making changes in the union. So I figured that's the reason I didn't get into the training program. But it wasn't right.

Now, I'd been to a couple seminars where people had talked about the Federal Office of Contract Compliance in terms of contracts and affirmative action. I knew the company was getting favorable contracts, so I went in and asked to see their affirmative action program, and they told me, "It is the policy of the company not to allow the employees to review the affirmative action policy." Boy, I thought this was bullshit. I wanted to get in touch with agencies to find out if that was illegal, but one of the difficulties of a job is that it's hard to get in touch with agencies to find out exactly what your rights are.

Well, one day there was a bomb scare in the shipyards, and they sent us home early. On that day I was able to make some connections within the Department of Commerce, I think, Maritime Department of the Office of Federal Compliance. The agent I got ahold of was a bit disturbed about the situation and felt that, yes, in fact the company should show me their affirmative action plan. Would I not do anything, and he would speak with them and try to get them to realize that they were supposed to show me the plan? So they realized that they were supposed to show me the plan. I had to go in there after work, about ten minutes before the office closed, and read through the affirmative action plan. At that point there, I got—I started to get a reputation.

I then filed a complaint against the training committee because I was not given the job, and the man from the Office of Federal Compliance set up a meeting with the company, and they explained that they hired ten people and it turned out I was number eleven. One of the things that they used was past experience, and even though I was the only person that had any kind of shipyard experience, I'd had no training in high school shop. That was one of the points that they brought up, and I said,

Barbara Shaman, outside machinist

"Yeah, that's true. When I went to high school, you couldn't take shop."

And what came out of that meeting was that the company said, "Okay, if there is ever an opening, you'll be the next person considered." This was in September—August of nineteen seventy-seven. At the end of that month, one of the machinist trainees quit. There was a position open. Well, nothing happened in September. Nothing happened in October. In all my attempts to speak with the personnel officer, I could never get through to him. They would never return any of my calls. I wrote letters. I never got any answers. Finally, I went back to the Office of Federal Compliance. The day before Thanksgiving I got called to the telephone during work and was told that Monday after Thanksgiving, nineteen seventy-seven, I would be part of the machinist training program. So why I got in is still somewhat a mystery, but I did become part of the Machinists.

In the program they made us go to school one day a week, where a foreman taught the class. It was a terrible experience because he didn't know how to teach, and what he *did* teach quite often was incorrect and useless. We started off working at seventy percent of journeyman wages. After eight months you went up to eighty and after eight months more you went up to ninety and by the end you would make one hundred percent. It was a two-year program, and basically it was cheap labor. Since machinists were only making maybe fifteen cents an hour over shipscalers, or a quarter at the most, I took a wage cut in order to get my training. Several of the other people had experience as being outside machinists, but in other fields, so they had to get legitimate credentials by going through the training program.

Outside machinists are pretty much mechanics. On new construction you install a lot of machinery and precision fittings. In repair, you might repair, rebuild something, reinstall the line, a whole variety of work. It is outside work—not inside machining work. You use standard mechanic's tools plus drills. You may need precision fittings. You need aligning tools. On elevator work, for example, or any kind of work where you'd set up motors and pumps, you need to align couplings. You might just do honing.

At that time there was no other woman working in the shipyards in the Puget Sound area as an outside machinist. Some of the men were very supportive. And then there were some people that were outright obnoxious, rude. Some would just tell me, "You, broad, go home. You should be home. You shouldn't be in the shipyard." People wrote things on the bulkheads of ships. Just outrageous stuff about women. You'd try to find a certain area where you had to go and work, and you'd take your flashlight and all of a sudden you'd shine on this bulkhead, and there would be a comment written there, literally engraved in steel, about—really nasty, derogatory comments about women, women's bodies, and what some men would like to do.

I think, generally, a woman taking a non-traditional job is a threat, in the sense that it's taking away a job, and then there's also the myth that women don't need to work. There have also been myths that women can't do the work and that's why they haven't been there. That's also not true, because during the war women worked in all the shipyard trades. They were very capable of doing the work, but after the war, when the soldiers came home, the women were encouraged to leave the shipyards and to start families and be housewives. There's an economic reason for that, and you can talk about it with the men.

I remember one of the things that I consistently did was that I was not derogatory when I referred to a woman. I mean, I don't refer to a woman as a chick or a broad, or whatever term they use. I consistently refer to somebody as a woman, and I could see that in some people over a period of time of working with them, maybe months, they kind of changed their way of referring to a female as a woman and not as something else.

Barbara Shaman, outside machinist

I can remember once—I'll never forget this experience. We were aligning a brake in an elevator shaft, and it was a tremendous, huge piece of machinery, and I was working with this man that was very big. He was very tall, and he was very big, and they gave him this work because he could move things, and we were to align this brake, and he couldn't move it. One of the things I was learning was how you move things, how you set up different things to pry and push and pull, so I said, "Okay, Bill, give me the pry bar." This bar must have been six feet long, and we tried to pry the machinery just a li-i-ittle bit. And I said, "Okay, now I'm going to show you how to do it." Well, I got ahold of the pry bar, and I moved it so it was *just* right. I don't know why, somehow it just worked out that I did it. And that man stood there with his mouth open, and he would never, ever again in his life say anything that suggested that I couldn't do something. It's one of the things I'll never forget.

At one point between thirty and forty women filed a complaint of sexual discrimination against that shipbuilding company because of the locker-room situation. We had much lower standards of a locker room than the men did, and we were able to document and provide information that clearly showed that there was sexual discrimination on the job. Not only that, we went to the Metal Trades, which was made up of all the unions, because we felt that it was in violation of the contract, and they did not give us any support, representation, at all in this grievance. And as it turned out, not only was the company sued for discrimination, but the Metal Trades was sued as well. How that happened was that the Office of Women's Rights filed a director's complaint, which means that the director, herself, filed her own complaint against both the Metal Trades and the company for sexual discrimination on behalf of everybody who worked out there. It wasn't an individual complaint. It was a hot political issue because not only was the company being sued, so was the Metal Trades. They sat with that case for a long time and did nothing. Then there was a change in the Office of Women's Rights where the enforcement powers went to the state and, as far as I know, after three or four years, nothing came of it. Nothing was corrected.

It was an experience to realize, first of all, that the union is not going to give you any kind of support. And also realizing that agencies are not necessarily going to enforce non-discrimination or enforce affirmative action the way it should be done. A lot of people felt, what's the sense? If nothing's going to be done anyway, why waste your time and try to do something?

Well, what are your choices? What are your choices when your union is corrupt? My union, Machinists Local Number 79, is a union with a very rich and radical history. Presently it's a union that is being run by a bunch of unresponsible, unrepresentable goons that don't represent the needs of the membership, especially down in the shipyards. On a scale of zero to ten, ten being the highest, I'd say the Machinists Union—trying to be positive—deserves a score of point-seven-five, which isn't exactly the bottom, but it's far from the top—even satisfactory. Given that, what can you do? You can do nothing, or you can try to do something. How do you respond to people when they look around at the government that's in control now? Well, if they're not voted in, they're not going to have the power, and if people would vote for something else, would vote for change and to organize people so that would happen, then you'd have a choice of something different.

You need to see that the people in the union are representing the members' needs and that there's democracy within the union. I was shop steward down there for some time and filed grievances on behalf of other people and received no support whatsoever from the union. Many times the business agents would come out to the shipyards to take care of a grievance, and you never even knew they were there. They'd resolve a grievance without even contacting me or talking to me.

Barbara Shaman, outside machinist

I even had the experience, as being shop steward, of being physically attacked by the lead person, who was a member of my union. I filed a complaint the first time it happened. You have to understand that ships are *very* dangerous. There are holes to get down to different levels. A lot of times you're working around holes, and I was very lucky I wasn't in an area where I was likely to get hurt. We were on a ship and some people had come to complain that there was no ventilation. As shop steward, I went down there and had taken care of the situation, the ventilation. And on the way back up, the lead man lost his cool, grabbed hold of me and pushed me—pushed me down! I was scared. It's frightening down at the shipyards. I had heard stories when I first went out there about how years ago they handled things. I guess a lot of people in the shipyards carried guns and—that disputes were handled in not the nicest way. It also is very dangerous. It's very easy for something to fall on you. It's very easy for someone to drop something that might be light, but if it falls down three, four, five. . . .

Anyhow, the company investigated the lead man with the union's presence, but the union— This was an example of where the business agent never even spoke to me while supposedly representing my interest. They found that should this man do it again, he would face serious disciplinary action.

It happened a *second* time. A pipefitter was doing machinists' work, so I went up to the lead man to try to tell him that the work was not correct. He started yelling and hollering at me and grabbed ahold of me, and he pushed me to go back to work. I filed another complaint. Well, they did an investigation, only this investigation was a total farce. They interviewed people that weren't even there and management. As it turned out, I subsequently filed union charges against this "brother." At a pre-trial hearing it was determined that yes, in fact, the "brother" had conduct unbecoming a union member, and the charge deserved to go to trial. Several times it was scheduled to go to trial, but the member never showed up. One time there was a snowstorm and supposedly it was going to be rescheduled. It was never rescheduled. There was *never* a formal investigation of my charges. Whenever I asked, nobody knew what happened to it.

If you're a woman, your choices are to be harassed day after day to make a good living, and do it for as long as you can, and then when you can't tolerate it any more, you take a vacation. I mean I have a pattern, and I've seen it in other people, too, that work in non-traditional jobs, that you can't work there endlessly, that you need to take a break, that it just—the harassment, the daily pressures, the stresses get to be too much. You know, day after day you wake up saying, "Oh, boy! I'm gonna have to be belligerent today! What am I gonna put out today?" And you walk out of there every day after work, turn around and look in the shipyard and say, "Well, thank goodness, I'm leaving today in one piece." It gets to be too much, and it's okay to say, "All right, I've had enough!" It doesn't mean that you're not a good person, that you're not a strong person.

I've gone through stages of just totally being devastated—a mess—a wreck—physically and emotionally. I used to go dancing at least once a week to kind of try to work that stress out. For support I mostly turned to my friends. I also turned—there was a—still is—a group called Women in Trades, which offered support. Several times I needed legal advice and I got it from them. Actually, I had basically, at one point, decided that this was enough. I wasn't going to continue any more and spoke with somebody from Women in Trades and regained my strength.

I'm no longer an outside machinist. It became clear that working in a shipyard, very often you're left up to the mercy of the union, because they're the dispatcher. After I had been working at one company for some time, I had some protection through seniority, but the union and the company together

Barbara Shaman, outside machinist

were able to pull off a scam that basically said I had voluntarily quit and lost my seniority. When I couldn't get my job back, I realized I needed additional skills so that when I was blacklisted I could get a job. I took an electrical power program at the community college and now am an electrician for the city.

I think it's a good thing for women to work in non-traditional work because it breaks down the mysticism. But I also think it's devastating to someone day after day to be put through the ordeal that generally you're put through when you work non-traditional work. It's hard, though, working in any kind of job. I think even white male workers are oppressed in the sense that everybody who goes to work is making somebody else rich, and you barely get your share.

Sawyer / Bench Worker

LAURA SARVIS

She can already feel the physical effects of work on her body at twenty-four. She wonders if it is too late to get an education and a profession.

"Go get some schooling." My mother always told me that before, but I wouldn't listen. I didn't want to go to school. In high school I hung around with the skippers and quit in eleventh grade to take a job as a dishwasher. I had a little bit of a taste of money and independence, but went back to school in my senior year for my mother's sake. Then I quit again to work in a nursing home. Finally, I finished up the few credits I needed to graduate in night school.

My mother was a teacher up in Granite Falls. She is divorced and I admire her for being able to be on her own. She's educated, had her job, and we never would have made it without her. Her independence was something for me to look up to. But I should have listened to her about my going to school. Now I've really learned my lesson.

After school, I worked in any job I could get. One of them was in a wood mill in nineteen seventy-six. That was a man's job actually. A woman could do it, but at a woman's wage. I mean no man would have worked for that low wage. I was making three dollars an hour when I started and with no benefits. At first I thought my boss was a really nice person, really terrific, just partly because I gave him credit for giving me the job. That turned out to be the biggest joke.

Laura Sarvis, sawyer/bench worker

I sawed shake ridge, packed shake, and stapled shakes together. Sometimes I would pack shakes onto pallets, which would then be put into railroad cars. To do that I would throw the bundles above my head about eleven feet high. I would have to jump back six feet and run and pitch them way up in the air. I did that for about two weeks. My boss was just really happy that I was doing this. I thought I was a real toughie until I put my back out and was off work for two days. That's what comes from trying to prove yourself.

My boss was a dirty old man and got into making comments. Oh, well, maybe I brought it on myself. I had a thing around my license plate that said, "Beer Drinkers Make Better Lovers." And my boss came up to me one time and said, "Oh, is that true?" I'm sure if I had gone for it, he would have. I know for a fact he ended up shacking up with one of the girls in a motel for about two weeks. That girl was the only one getting medical. Why would she have all these benefits if the rest of us didn't? She had two kids and depended on him. There's a lot of places where a man can put a woman in a position where she has to depend on him and then take advantage of it.

Anyhow, at the mill the boss had his nailing guns illegally wired. It is supposed to be set so you hit the piece of wood and pull the trigger and you shoot about a three-inch nail with hooks into the wood. So we could work faster, he had the triggers wired back, so all you had to do was bump into it and it would shoot a nail into your hand or arm. This happened about three times down there. When it happened to one of my good girl friends, I got pissed off. She was in a state of shock and I took her to the hospital. Her car was still at work and the boss said he would pick her up from the hospital. We waited for two hours for him to show up. All the time she kept on throwing up in the waiting room. When I called down to the shop, all he said was, "Oh, I forgot. I'm sorry." Finally, I ended up driving her back to her car and my boy friend drove my car home while I drove her home.

On the way we stopped off at the pharmacy, and it just hit me. I thought, "Something's gotta be done about this place!" Two weeks later I called up the union.

Well, I started talking my ear off about the union. It was funny because a lot of the girls thought the boss was terrific. He really had them twisted around his finger, called them "Baby" and all of this stuff. They thought it was terrific to be getting three fifty an hour. What happened was that we started to get really bitter. One guy that was for the union got really mad, lost his temper, and walked out. Then he got fired. My brother, who was for the union, got another job and left. One girl left for school. And I knew we were gonna lose. I just had this feeling, because it was such a small shop. Then I got laid off, and when I came back in on the day of the vote I could see the fear in the people. Some of the girls who were afraid to say anything were afraid something would happen to them. He used me as an example and sure enough we lost the vote. That boss made me sick. He had the biggest shit-eating grin you've ever seen on his face. I couldn't face the people. How could they be so stupid to let somebody like that rule their lives?

I quit and went up to a shingle mill in Granite Falls to try and get on. When I put my application in, the secretary goes, "Well, we don't need anybody in the office."

I had on my logger boots and big burly sweater and said, "I'm not applying for the office job. I'm applying to go out in the mill." To show I could do it, I went out there and graded shingles and bundled them up and drove a forklift around. Then I ran the saw, cutting off the bad areas on the shingles to get the best parts possible. I went up to the boss, but he said they didn't need anyone right then. But I came back every other day for a good three weeks and never got hired.

There wasn't one woman out there among those four hundred guys working for him. The union rep was the same man I had tried organizing with at the other place, so I went and talked with him. He said I could go to the EEOC and make them hire a woman, but they wouldn't hire me. They'd turn around and hire another woman.

In some ways the ERA had ruined it because there's a lot of women out there that bitch and bitch that they're not getting paid as much as the guys, or they wanna do a guy's job. A lot of these women ruin it for the women who really deserve it. When they get the job, they turn around and say, "Well, I can't do this. Will you do this for me?" That infuriates the guys and I can't blame them, but everybody deserves a chance. That's all I want—if I can do the job, why not give it to me?

Finally, I gave up there and got a job at a Boeing subcontractor. I used a router a little bit in high school, so I kinda lied and said I knew how to use one. In benchwork there's different plans for different parts. We must have had thirty different parts, so you had to be careful and know what you were doing. You can't just hand a part to somebody and tell them to saw the tabs off. Chances are, if you're not watching, they might saw off the wrong tabs and ruin the whole part. You had to know which cutters to use and be able to hold tolerances within one one-hundredth or two one-hundredths of an inch sometimes.

Because of boredom I tried to learn as much as I could, and I'd do some of the weird kind of stuff. I liked getting up on top of these great big parts that were thirty feet long and drilling on them. Nobody else wanted to get that dirty and greasy and push all that heavy stuff around.

One time when I was working nights they hired a guy to work on the bench, which was pretty unusual. They usually don't start guys out on the bench because that's pretty much the girls' work. So one night we were talking while I was showing him how to do different stuff, and he said they were thinking about making him supervisor on the bench at night. I looked at him, and I go, "Have you ever worked on the bench before?"

He said, "No." And I was pissed, because if anybody's gonna

be supervisor it's gonna be my girl friend, Sue, or me, because we have seniority. Talk about a primo example of male chauvinism. They finally gave it to another guy who couldn't supervise worth shit. He handed a guy a router once with it set at fifteen thousand—way too high.

Another thing that irked me was they had an area called material prep. They were all men and would prep the material before it would go out for shipping over to Boeing. Those guys stood around with their finger up their noses half of the time, and it made me so mad. Later I found out they had a system where two guys would take ten minutes off while the other worked and then they'd switch. It bothered me because here we were getting dirty, working up a sweat, and they were so slack.

The boss was on a real ego trip. He liked the girls to kind of feather up to him, and sometimes women will do that to get up in a job. Sometimes, maybe the way the world is, we're almost put in that position. It makes me feel bad to see women working there that were forty years old and know they could be out the door at a moment's notice just because a boss got ruffled a little bit. A lot of males like to throw their authority around because they like to scare people. I don't like working for shops like that. When I quit my boss wasn't upset or nothing. He knew I wouldn't kiss his ass, so why should he keep me around?

After that I worked in a couple other mills and got on at another Boeing subcontractor. Because I was experienced I started out at four dollars and fifty cents an hour on the bench. It was a small shop with only about twelve people all together. It was really monotonous doing the same parts all day long. They were mostly just parts of the frame of the inside of the airplane. It was a lot dirtier and oilier. When I walked out of there at night, I could have slid all the way home if I wanted to. I'd rather eat a piece of wood than a piece of aluminum. That's what it was like because you'd get it in your nose and it was terrible.

The first eight months or so weren't so bad. Then I started

Laura Sarvis, sawyer/bench worker

noticing the hours were pretty long, nine a day. The boss would just as soon pay you for nine hours with shitty wages. You work that hour of overtime and everybody thought it was the world. You get to depend on the overtime.

A lot of things started building up for people. Like a guy who worked there for two years was making six bucks an hour and they hire somebody with no experience at five fifty an hour. There was no system for raises. You had to ask for them. Then they came out with this bonus system where we got a percentage of however much we averaged out that year in January. That added up to a hundred and fifty or two hundred dollars for a lot of people, depending on how many days they put in. Then they took that away by saying we had done six percent less work. We all knew we had done as much work, but how could we prove it? About the same time they bought a window company and started buying a lot of expensive equipment for the other building. By this time we were getting pretty mad. When they cut the medical plan to a lot cheaper one, we started thinking about going to a union. The one we chose was District 751 Machinists Union. We kept all this really secret because there were people that would kiss ass in order to be in good with the company. We never told them, but there were eight of us that were pretty strong for it.

The pressure on people before the election was terrible. The company had my friend pegged as one of the union people, so when they saw me talking to him out front they started looking at me suspiciously. When I went to my car the boss would stand behind a building and watch me. He'd glare at me if I talked to anyone. Then the supervisor went around talking to people during working hours trying to find out how they would vote. They gave one guy a raise and said, "We're not giving this to you because of the union. We want to make this very clear." They were just all of a sudden being nicey-nice. When one guy got burned and went to the hospital, they were all of a sudden going up to check on him. They promised the inspector all kinds of things.

After the election the inspector told me, "Laura, they used me. All of the promises are forgotten. They don't even talk to me." It hurt his feelings.

I said, "Well, what do you expect? You should have known all along."

When it came to the vote they came up with seventeen, not twelve people, for the bargaining unit. I was an observer and challenged three. We won the challenges and the election.

The next day I left on my vacation. I went down the Oregon coast on a motorcycle with my boy friend. It was during the hot spell and we had a really good time.

When I returned to work the boss would stand in the office glaring at me while I worked. About a month later I missed a day and called in sick. The next week I missed another day so he fired me. There were several others with worse attendance than me, so I went to the union. We filed unfair labor charges on the union. I'm going through them right now and don't know how they'll come out. It is my word against theirs. Also, of the two people I want to testify for me, one of them is the inspector, and he does need the job. It makes me feel humiliated, because I started out at the bottom and was bringing in like two hundred twenty-five dollars a week, which isn't bad for a girl. It's also hard for me because I stuck my neck out, and they're not willing to stick their neck out for me. I'm just getting sick of this kind of work. I want to go to school and get into something else.

A week after I was fired, the company laid everybody off. I feel they'll hang on by the skin of their teeth until things pick up. They say it is because of lack of work, but this last week they were working twelve-hour days to get out an order. That's something I've never seen that place do before. I feel bad for the people that hung in there. We had a strong group and everybody

Laura Sarvis, sawyer/bench worker

stuck together. I don't know the exact procedure, but I think after a year they can hire everybody back as non-union.

When I first walked into this kind of work, I was very self-confident. I thought three dollars an hour was terrific. Since then I've been beaten down. I'm unemployed now. Times are really expensive. I have four years' experience and can't get a job. Not working, being broke in a man's world, has bothered me a lot. I'm gonna have to get an education or something because I don't want to have to work under a man again. It should be *both* our worlds. Every shop I've worked in the women worked their asses off more than anybody else did because no man would work for three dollars or three fifty an hour.

The work has started to take a toll in the last year. I don't feel healthy and sometimes I find myself feeling very inferior. When I get off work I look like a rag. I want to be a lady once in a while. Also when you're working, you don't eat right a lot of times. You don't have time to maybe eat breakfast, or the night before you're too tired to pack a lunch, so you eat off the "garbage" truck. If you tell a doctor you're tired, he'll say eat right and you'll feel fine. But a lot of nights after work I would just lay right down on the couch in my dirty clothes and be lucky if I got up five hours later. It is taking a toll on me. If I knew other women thinking about doing this kind of work, I'd tell them my story first, and then send them to a psychiatrist if they still wanted to do it.

Union Organizer

LINDA LANHAM

The first woman organizer for the Machinists Union, Linda Lanham tries to cram twenty-five or twenty-six hours of work into a normal day. She combines political savvy with old-time religious fervor to sell the gospel of unionism.

I never wanted to work for Boeing because I felt that you would always be a number. I've always wanted to be an individual so I just stayed away from Boeing. Thought they'd just herd the cattle in, make 'em work so much, and herd 'em out. That kept me from getting a job there for years. Finally, because of my financial situation, I didn't have a choice any more. I was divorced with three children. In the past I had worked as a tavern manager, restaurant manager, and dental assistant—none of which paid very well. So I figured I would have to tolerate Boeing because it was probably the best way to be able to take care of the kids.

But once I entered the company, I found out it was not like that at all. As long as you follow procedures, rules in the contract, and do your job, it's a great place to work. You have ample vacation, ample sick leave. I think the things that the union has negotiated as far as benefits for you and your family are terrific.

To me it's unbelievable that people with just a high-school education get the training they have to have and work the big machines. Since I had never done any type of machine work, it was amazing how they can take a raw piece of material and make a really neat part—a wing that's huge. It's way beyond your imagination that a small bracket or a huge skin goes on a plane. At least to me it is. If you see one part at a time, it's like seeing a car disassembled. If you're not mechanically inclined, which I'm not, it's hard to see how it's put together. When I go to Renton or Everett or step into a 727 or 747 when I'm flying somewhere, I look around and think, "Oh, I did that, I carried that part," or whatever. But at Plant 2 you never saw a plane assembled, so you don't really think about it.

I hired in as a dispatcher, which is a pretty traditional job for a woman. Dispatchers check parts into or out of an area. I worked hard there and got very good work evaluations. For evaluations you're graded on a one to four; one is the highest you can get. A one or two is promotional level. My first evaluation was a two. Then I went to an even higher two. Then a grade five material position became available. I wanted the job, but they had already picked out another guy in my area for the position. I couldn't figure out why. I was better qualified, had greater working abilities, and my knowledge was greater. I could really have taken them to the bank on that discrimination, but I didn't. They gave me an offer for expeditor and him the material job. When I confronted my supervisor, he asked me why I'd rather be a material person than an expeditor. I said either one would be okay but material person was what I wanted to do. We talked for a while and I said I would take the expeditor position. Then I said, "Before I go, I want to ask you one question, and I promise you I will not take it any further. Just between you and me, is it because he's a man and I'm a woman?"

He said, "Yes."

Even though I promised not to take it any further, it still made me mad. The job itself was not that non-traditional. As far as the physical work, men used a jack or things to keep them from lifting. I could use the same jack. They weren't gonna lift any more than I did.

In the long run being an expeditor didn't hurt, because my

priorities changed. I began to get involved in the union—got on every committee imaginable, campaigned a lot for people running for office. I geared myself more to union activities and less towards expediting. Union work was one way I could help people. Now I'm not saying the union is always right, but it definitely makes people's standard of living better. And that's important to me. I've been there before.

In District 751 there are twenty-five thousand men and seven thousand women. Because of this, back in nineteen eighty, the union leadership began to think they needed a woman organizer, not just men. Nine people applied for the job. After being interviewed by the international and the president of 751, I was appointed to the position. I think my working ability and the fact that I had some college helped me get the job.

Other women in the union were very jealous about my getting the job. I've probably had more pressure than any other time in my life. There were a lot of petty stories going around about how I got my job by making love to all the business reps and my boss. The first two months were pure hell. People wouldn't talk to me and the rumors going around the plant were atrocious. It was so hurtful. In fact I got to the point of wondering if it was all worth it.

But with Reagan and national politics, it was more imperative than ever that we get organized. As far as Boeing is concerned, more and more jobs are being subcontracted to companies in the area that are unorganized. The machinists in a non-union shop get seven dollars and fifty cents an hour to thirteen dollars for our machinists. A lot of our electronics work is going to Macon, Georgia. Also with the new foreign trade and the new 767, I think we're only doing about twenty percent of the work. Something has to be done.

And then we can't forget the automation—new technology, robotics. Robotics are machines that can do the same work as a

Linda Lanham, union organizer

human. But they don't need vacations, they don't need to be paid, they don't need sick leave. Robotics aren't what people think. They're not little tin men running around. They're machines that do our work, and we'll more and more be losing our jobs to them.

If robotics goes into the aerospace industry, we'll end up like the automobile industry—without jobs. There'll be no more machinists. Only waitresses, unemployed, welfare. Then our economy will go completely downhill. That's why priority number one is to get organized and stop some of this. Otherwise we're not gonna have jobs to worry about. We have to draw the line somewhere.

I just organized a company up in Everett. Those people were making four dollars and fifty cents an hour. The highest was seven fifty an hour for machinist. How can they make it with families? They have no benefits and a medical plan that isn't worth anything. If they got sick, you might as well forget it—no sick leave. I don't have the answer about what we can do about automation and new technology, but I do know something has to be done.

Being a union organizer is probably the hardest job there is. We're always talking to people that are negative, that are against the union. With non-members at Boeing I think the bottom line is they don't want to pay the dues. They're getting the benefits anyway, so why pay the dues? They're just very greedy about themselves. People in general aren't educated about what the union does as a whole. The concept of "union goon" is overwhelming as far as the media is concerned. We only get coverage about strikes, killings, or embezzlements. We don't get publicity about all the good things we do. The Machinists Union funds apprenticeships, scholarships, and the City of Hope Hospital, where people can get medical care without paying a dime. As far as 751 goes, we have an alcoholic and drug program, a human rights program, and the women's committee to help with problems. I think there's an uneducation as far as the services we provide.

I think that's because we're ruled by the corporate business and have been for years. The blue-collar worker has never been recognized as having made great feats—only the businessman. But we in the Machinists Union are working to change that.

I work a lot of hours—many nights—because I talk to the employees after they get off work. Mainly I get involved by someone at a subcontractor calling and saying they want a union. When they get three other people together, they form an in-plant committee. It just grows from there until they have enough people for a petition. We like to have sixty percent of the people sign cards indicating an interest in the union before we call for an election.

The company can do many different things to try and stop the union. There are more and more firms that specialize in union busting. Companies can hire one of these firms to help them defeat the union. One of the ways they do that is what we call the "sweetheart" approach. They say, "Why didn't you tell me you were unhappy? I will give you this, I will give you that; all you have to do is come to me." Another way is harassment, particularly threatening the jobs. The fear of losing your job is one of the biggest union-busting tactics. People know they have to have the job for their own livelihood and their own families. Threatening them if they continue organizing is an unfair labor practice, but often it makes the people so fearful they don't even tell us what is going on. They just kind of fade out of the picture. The company can also threaten to close the plant down completely. I had that happen to me once. Someone contacted me and said if a union is ever organized in his plant, he will close down totally. They need to recognize that closing up and relocating costs a tremendous amount of money and probably isn't feasible. Further, any threat is an unfair labor practice,

Linda Lanham, union organizer

since workers have the right to organize as long as it's not done on company time.

It is crucial that a person document any unfair labor practice of the employer so we can file charges on them. Anyone who is being threatened has my complete sympathy, because I know the fear of losing your job. If they do get fired, we will file unfair labor practices, and, as far as the District 751 organizers are concerned, will do everything possible to find them a job. I think if it got down to it, we would give them complete support. Our president is very compassionate.

The first shop I organized was an experience I will never forget. It was so exciting. If I never do another one, it was worth it to see those people making four fifty and seven fifty an hour—with families—putting their jobs on the line. They stuck together from day one and no one ever faltered. We had the same amount going in as came out after voting. It was inspiring. All they wanted was a better standard of living. Now we're working on a contract, their first, which will give them that. That's what my job is all about—giving people a better life.

Electrician

ANNA BRINKLEY

Anna Brinkley appeared a master of performing many tasks at once. While talking with me, she changed dirty diapers, folded clothes, and bathed a child. Being "superwoman" has its price, however.

When I was a girl growing up in Cashmere, Washington, my hero was Annie Oakley. She was the only powerful woman figure that we had in the television of that day. I think that's significant. Generally, the male and female roles were pretty well defined. Like I was a cheerleader in high school.

I was a bit afraid of college, but tried it and ended up studying English and political science. During college and right afterwards I did restaurant work—cocktail and food waitressing. I disliked the restaurant jobs because of the pay, and ultimately it always came down to some kind of crap from the male above you. Like the maitre d' would make a pass at you, and when you wouldn't do anything with him you'd get fired.

I was married to my first husband at that time. It was real funny. Here I had credits for a college degree, but no skills to go out and do anything, and he had no college and could make eight or nine dollars an hour as an electrician. We were raising two children at that time, Andrea, a girl from his previous marriage, and our daughter, Latifa, who was born in nineteen seventy-four. My husband walked out of good jobs, like with the city of Mercer Island and with Boeing. I couldn't figure out why he wouldn't work on those jobs. I kept thinking to myself, "My

Anna Brinkley, electrician

God, if I ever could stabilize my family income at that amount of money an hour, I'd be to work every day."

That's when I began to think about non-traditional work. I didn't pick the career according to what I thought I'd like to do. The bottom line was the dollar. I mean, it was the money. Money meant independence, being able to support my family without having a man around, if I couldn't find a decent man to relate to the family. In other words, a trade meant not being financially dependent on a man.

There was also something about the eight-to-five life that appealed to me. It is a stabilizing factor in my life. It's a life-regulating thing, and some people find that boring and non-artistic, but I don't think it's necessarily so. I liked getting the kids out of bed in the morning, getting them dressed, driving my first husband to work in the early morning, and stopping off to have a doughnut. You know, there's something about the working-class thing that has always appealed to me.

So I went up to North Seattle Community College for vocational testing and picked out a training program called electromechanical technology, without even knowing what I was doing. It's a two-year program, eight hours a day. I was never able to carry the full load, because I had the kids to care for. I went three years and still haven't completed the hundred and sixty credits. I think I have thirty credits to go.

My first husband did not want me to go to trade school. He felt like maybe I was going out with somebody there. He accused me of having physical relationships with men. Probably going to school had something to do with him leaving, because I was getting myself together, and I no longer wanted an icky relationship. I wanted a good relationship or no relationship at all. So that first quarter of school ended up being real rough, because I was going through a divorce and custody battle, as well as going to classes. I didn't do well at all in school and was just devastated. I felt I had failed and slept a lot. I was real depressed and it took a lot of courage to go back out there the next quarter.

There were two core teachers in the electromechanical program. One teacher and I just had a personality clash. Since then I worked with one of his daughters. She's a jitney driver and told me that he used to go home at night and talk about me at every family dinner and rant and rave and be upset. What was happening was that the daughter was doing a lot of non-traditional, feminist-type things and he wanted to scream and jump up and down at her, but couldn't, and took it out on me. This teacher used to come into the electronics lab, which wasn't even his class, and tell me that I'd never make it through the program and I'd never amount to anything. He was just trying to discourage me. But that quarter I got A's in everybody's class but his. The other teacher made passes at me. That was real hard because at the time I was very afraid of men. I was overwhelmed. I had nothing. I mean, I'm not afraid now, because I have a skill nobody can take from me. I have a job. I own a house. I have some control over my life. I'm thirty-three. But at that time I had never felt what it was like to support your family. I had been totally dominated and controlled by men.

By the end of the program I was doing very well and enjoying math and physics a great deal. I had quit studying math as a sophomore in high school to do other more socially acceptable things and had been afraid of it in college. I really enjoyed picking it up again. The only deficiency in the program was that I didn't learn how to use tools until I was on a job. That was the only legitimate place the men could attack me on. All men, even the ones from professional families, have dinged around tools. I think I'm just now beginning to master tools.

An uncle of mine had been a supervisor at an aircraft plant for about a million years, and when he found out I was going to trade school, he told my parents that they were looking for

Anna Brinkley, electrician

women in non-traditional trades. He gave my name to the lady in charge of personnel for the maintenance department. She hired me without my even completing the electromechanical program. That was in April of nineteen seventy-seven. That was very lucky because I had gone into debt about ten thousand dollars going to trade school. If I hadn't found a job, I would have been deep in the hole, with two kids.

I remember I was excited, pleased to be making some money and able to support my children, but for at least the first two-and-a-half years I kept expecting that somehow I would get fired. As a cocktail waitress, the boss can come up and say, "You're gone," and you wouldn't even know why. I had never worked in a job where there was a strong union. I didn't realize in a union shop that, once you get past a probation period, it's very difficult for management to get rid of a union member. Having a powerful workers' organization like the Machinists Union was a totally new experience for me.

The other thing was that when I worked there I was so anti-management in my politics that I was unable to see anything good in any management people at all. I think that was probably bad, because I think that there are people that *do* go into management that still do have some good qualities and *do* try to demonstrate some fairness in their dealing with workers. Several of my supervisors were people who did not do anything *for* me, but did not do anything *against* me. They just basically left me alone. A good supervisor in that company does not have to do anything. They just have to maintain a middle ground and not rock the boat. One of my supervisors was great at that. He was a very slick, typical first-line manager, who dressed real nice and had a silver mouth. Under him we won the Crew of the Year Award, which was based on attendance and not having any accidents. What this supervisor did, if we came in late, was to plug us in on the computer instead of having us punch in late. So we got Crew of the Year because he cheated. Another supervisor gave me good evaluations until he found out I had black children. Then all of a sudden he started giving me poor evaluations.

I think race is one of the biggest issues in the shop. If you're Caucasian and align yourself with minorities at all, then you pull down your status in the shop. Being racist and sexist is one of the unwritten rules of social acceptance in the trades. There was one woman who worked in the reproduction area that I got along well with until she saw my children in the parking lot one day. Then she started a whole series of racist jokes every time I had to come into her area. It turned out that she was a member of a Klan organization and was a real redneck. The guys in the shop really liked her. She made it difficult to establish standards with the guys, because she used to hang *Playboy* pictures and, worse, *Hustler* pictures all over the walls. Anyhow, when her comments failed to irritate me, she left a supposed-joke thing called "Nigger's Application for Employment" in my tool box. You ever seen it? It's the worst piece of racist shit I've ever seen. It had, like, "What kind of things do you prefer to eat?" And then all the cliche type of soul food things, "What kind of car do you prefer—Lincoln Continental, Cadillac . . . ?" What's your favorite pastime—screwing white women?" It was just really gross, so I took it to my superintendent and he said, "Well, what's wrong with this? This has been going around for years. What do you want me to do with this?"

And I said, "This was left in my tool box and I know who left it there, and I expect you to do something about it." He got real mad about that, but took it to security. The woman got three days off and vowed to get me. But a little later on she got a golden opportunity to be a mechanic, so I think that was an indication of how her being a racist got her ahead. My superintendent's attitude toward me changed immediately after that. Personnel said that he had been calling and saying I was doing good work

Anna Brinkley, electrician

and I was getting along, but the next day after this incident he reported I was doing poorly.

Working maintenance, to date, has been one of the nicest or easiest blue-collar jobs. That's part of why I chose it. I'm not saying it's not difficult. There are safety hazards and times when you take a lot of chances, and you have to be skilled, but it's not as difficult as being a production-line worker. There's some intellectual stimulation in maintenance. I got to work a lot of different jobs while I worked there.

When I worked cranes, I was on the top of a building in a little—what we called the crane barn. They would drive the cranes into the barn there at the same level they would be at in the factory—high above everything. It was a dark, little room with no windows and a lot of machinery. There was a desk, a blueprint table, and boxes of tools. The whole effect was pretty grim. I guess if you hadn't been in a factory, in some ways it would remind you of the inside of a service station. There's the smell of grease and the noise of the factory—the bang, bang, bang, the clash, clash, clash all day long, and the fumes from welding become a kind of blue haze rising above it all. There was no air conditioning and it became very hot up there. In the summertime the temperature up there would be like ninety-nine to a hundred degrees. But I liked the work. There was something very exciting about working on the big machinery and the cranes coming in.

Sometimes I worked in the motor shop, which is on the floor. It was right outside the supervisors' office, which is kind of a pain. The supervisors used to come out and just watch me work. They had stuck me on a bench there repairing fluorescent lights, which was a very mundane, terrible job. It was like doing the same light over and over again. I was on that tacky job for seven months.

I worked the floor, which is where you take calls when something in the factory breaks down. A supervisor will have a big mill down and call dispatch. Dispatch will type up a card that they send to you. The card will give you the building number, column number, and maybe supervisor's number. It might take you forty-five minutes to find out exactly which mill is broken down. Then you try to troubleshoot the machine, which means fixing it, ordering parts, saying it needs to be junked, or sometimes just tagging it for a day or two while you think about what the problem is.

You could be sent anywhere. One job most of the other electricians wouldn't do, because it was so noisy, was go out on the wing line. The guys were riveting parts and when their jigs moved, their fluorescent lights broke. I liked fixing their fluorescent lighting. I kind of admired the guys that riveted. That was the lowest-paying and hardest production work and their working conditions were just terrible. It felt really good to go out and give them good lighting. The riveters used to call me Sparky and in general were much friendlier to me than the other maintenance workers. It was funny, because I could see them having some justified hostility because here I breezed in doing a better, higher-paying job.

I think a lot of the men were afraid of me because they thought if they screwed up I would file a sex-discrimination charge on them. Male workers really over-estimate that. They don't realize it's nearly impossible to win a case, and that there's not a chance in a thousand if they did something terribly sexist to me that they could ever lose their job. Things are very difficult to prove. This whole thing about discrimination confuses them. A lot of the nice guys are confused by it and don't know how to act around a woman in the workplace.

Mostly, I got support from older male workers. These men were really good electricians, really skilled, and felt absolutely not threatened by me on any level. I couldn't take their job. I could never attain their skill in their working lifetime, so they weren't threatened. They taught me and enjoyed me. A lot of them saw me as a daughter and that was fine with me. Sometimes their level of paternalism was annoying, but it was a lot more acceptable than working with someone who was a member of the Klan.

I left there in nineteen eighty because I thought it would be going down and laying off. My current husband works there, and I thought we might have a better chance of maintaining two jobs in the family if I went to work somewhere else. As it turned out, that's what is happening. They are laying off and the economy is down. It was basically a question of money and security. When I left I was making almost ten dollars an hour and I started out on my next job earning thirteen an hour. Now I am up to fifteen or sixteen dollars an hour, give or take a few cents here and there.

I'm a maintenance electrician again, which means I maintain everything electrical there with the exception of the refrigeration units. Another union has jurisdiction over that. During an event like a football or baseball game, one electrician is in charge of the entire building. You have to handle any emergency like a failure of arena lighting or the power to television and press people. In the case of power going down to television, you can imagine the amount of dollars you're talking about. Some of the men don't have any confidence in my ability to handle an emergency when I'm the only electrician there. I've worked there two-and-a-half years, and there has never been an emergency that I haven't handled, but, like I told the director, "To tell the truth, there could be some emergencies that *no one* could handle, and the best thing to do is to do good preventive maintenance and do your best to prevent an emergency."

My lead man does not put enough energy into avoiding an emergency during an event by having a really tight ship, as far as panels and connections being clean and tight. You have a situation where sixty-five thousand people are in there during a football game, and we should be thinking real preventive maintenance. My lead man sees it in terms of dollars and cents for overtime. I see that as more of a wide thing of, we may pay four electricians thirty thousand dollars a year, but if we're doing our jobs, somewhere down the road we're gonna save half a million dollars in one night.

It seems like the sex discrimination is always there, minor things like twisting my name around; it's like he was trying to make a joke out of my being there. There's other biases which are more serious. Like we work a rotating shift and sometimes work turnbacks, which means that we work events at night and have to be back at seven the next morning. Usually they try to avoid that, but with me they didn't. I think they were hoping I would fail to show up and get a poor attendance record. Just the fact that people don't have confidence in your ability to do the work, and so they don't give you the hard jobs, is a form of discrimination. They give you the things that they think you can handle, which means that you fall into that and don't learn. You will be reduced to being a "gofer." "Go get this. Go get me that," which is fine while you learn parts, but becomes limiting. Deciding when to accept this and when to fight it is real difficult.

I got pregnant with my daughter, Jamillah, while working there. They didn't know I was pregnant for a while, but when they found out they just freaked. At one point my supervisor gave me a job that he knew I couldn't handle. I had to walk around on a false roof in an attic, and I was too bulky to do it, so I just walked into his office and said, "Okay, I'm gone. It's time for me to go on my pregnancy leave. I can't handle this any more."

When I took my maternity leave, my lead man swore up and down that, if they made me a permanent employee when I came back, that he was going to file a reverse discrimination suit against me. He felt I was not qualified to be a journeyperson electrician and he based that on working with me once. That was the time I just stood and watched him try to find the breakers. He had a line of, like, six individual circuits hooked up to individual duplex receptacles, and he just started pulling them out in handfuls and letting them pop and crack and smoke, with the idea that the breakers would break, and then he would go around to the different panels and find out which breakers were off. This method of finding breakers really *appalled* me, and after watching him do that, I didn't think *he* was a journeyperson electrician, but I was nice enough not to file suit against *him*. The guy's crazy. I'll never know how he's lived so long in the trade. He's the kind of guy who will do anything for management. You know, if they want a light ninety feet up and don't want to spend the money to put in the right equipment, he'll hang by a rope with one arm to do the job.

When I came back from my maternity leave, I was real tired. I had to come back when the baby was two months old or forfeit my job. This lead man approached me right away, and he was more friendly than when I left. He told me that he thought they were gonna use him to get rid of me, and that he wasn't gonna be used. Then he proceeded to show me the building—where the panels were, and where the different circuits were. I appreciated this until he started making comments like, "You sure are thin for having a two-month-old baby," or "You sure are nice looking."

One of the things you're not supposed to do is go up a ladder until another person is, like, all the way to the top. That's because if the person ahead of you falls, then both of you go. Well one of the lead's little tricks was to follow me up a ladder just as close as he could. Get it? It's the kind of thing, if you told anybody about, would sound really petty. What do you do? Go to management and say, "This guy follows me up a ladder really close"? They would look at you like, "You're really crazy, lady." But he did that often enough, and then the little brush of his hand in the wrong place when you're in confined quarters. Call him on it, and shit, it would be an accident. But it begins to happen enough to where you know this guy has a real problem. Then he began the old "My wife doesn't understand me" stories. Finally, one time we were working in the attic, and he got bold enough to come out and ask me, "Would it be sex discrimination if I told you that I wanted to sleep with you?"

I said, "Well, it wouldn't be sex discrimination if you asked, or said that you were attracted to me, because people are attracted to people, but what would be sex discrimination is if when I turned you down, because I am going to, is how you act about that, if you retaliate."

And he said, "Oh," but basically he had a real hard time working with me from then on. It was real embarrassing. He would get a hard-on whenever he worked around me. It was a real difficult time for me, because I was very tired and sad about having to leave the baby. I dealt with it by just hanging in there the best I could. I didn't feel like I could talk with the other workers there, because he had been there five years and I had been there for only one. And my husband doesn't like hearing about what happens to me at work.

Part of the problem I've had, and I've come to realize this in the last couple months, is that I get involved with the other workers, even the jerks, in the sense of I can always see something good, if they're not management. That's where I can draw the line. I can see behind the Archie Bunker sick person to the scared little boy. I wish I wasn't sensitive to that. I wish that all I could relate to is this vicious, ugly man who is trying to get my job. I kept hoping that maybe he was going to be my friend. I think our sensitivity hangs a lot of women up.

At the same time the lead man started this sexual harassment trip, he began playing a real anti-union role in the shop. He began being a snitch and aiding the supervisor in writing people up. Then he started helping the supervisor in trying to get rid of

me. He'd tell me that the supervisor was going to upper management saying he didn't need all four electricians, and I was going
to get laid off during the football strike. I don't know if that was
really true, or if it was something to upset me. That's how they
function. They can't get rid of you unless you blow your cool, so
they shake you. My supervisor will follow me to the bathroom
and wait outside until I come out, and then just look me up and
down with really evil eyes. It's not real life-threatening stuff,
but it eats on you and scares you. I saw this same supervisor grab
a guy around the neck and choke him because he didn't like
him. Another electrician wore black turtlenecks, and the superintendent backed him into the corner with intimidating body
language and said, "Why do you always wear that black tur-
tleneck? Don't you know that black is an omen of death?" To
anyone with any brains that is a threat. It frightens me. The
word that comes to my mind when I think of him is mentally
deranged. The guys on the crew call him a cancerous growth on
us. Right now, I'm formalizing charges of sex discrimination
against this supervisor, and I'm having a real hard time deciding
whether to include the lead man. I don't want him to take the
rap, but I do have to be honest about some things that he has
done.

Two years ago I just assumed I would always be in a trade.
Now I'm thinking about what point I'm going to get out, because it's so draining. I'm maintaining the job and the kids are
okay. They're being well taken care of and reaping the benefits
of my salary. Latifa has piano lessons, horseback-riding lessons,
and is in a private school. The others are too young for those
things, but all of them have a reasonable life. But Mama's real
tired at night and I complain a lot. I think my influence on them
is not as deep as I would like. Basically, I feel that my husband
and I don't have too much of a relationship at all. We love each
other, but we don't have time for anything except for taking care

of the kids. He cooks one week and I cook the next. The week you cook, you don't get too much else done because you also clean the kitchen. The person who isn't cooking interacts a bit more with the kids and does the clothes. On the weekends we clean the house. There is no time to go any place. My husband and I don't communicate. There's no time for movies or shows or walks in the park.

Family

For a woman breaking into non-traditional work, a supportive family can spell the difference between success or failure. Families can also provide role models and teach necessary skills. For Amy Kelley, an aunt in the printing trade served as a strong female role model. As several of the women point out, boys are routinely taught the rudiments of a trade or at least gain familiarity with tools by working with their fathers. Because of sex role stereotyping, girls are usually denied this opportunity. Sylvia Lange is a gillnetter today because her family ignored that general rule. For other women, however, vocational education programs are the route to learning entry level skills required by trade jobs.

The question of whether family break-ups lead to nontraditional work or non-traditional work leads to family break-ups is touched on in several stories. Both probably occur. With divorce rates at over 40 percent nationally, it is reassuring to find that both Amy Kelley and Arlene Tupper have very supportive husbands. This helps to make their difficult times more bearable. Kathy Baerney, on the other hand, found that she had to choose between her family and the trade that she loved.

Women such as Anna Brinkley and Michelle Sanborn are in the process of developing new patterns with their traditional husbands.

The added stresses of pregnancy and interracial marriage are also discussed. Beverly Brown poignantly describes her efforts, as a divorced mother, to provide her son with a strong sense of family and home. Geraldine Walker talks about coping with shipyard work, divorce, and raising five children.

Transit Supervisor

ARLENE TUPPER

Arlene Tupper's upbeat attitude carries her through almost all situations.

I think I was fourteen when I got a job at a men's clothing store. It lasted a week and a half. One of the people who had been there for many years made a pass at me. I didn't have any idea what was going on, and I just went numb. The man told the boss that *I* had made passes at *him*, so I was fired. That was a real shock at my young age. Of course, now I can see it from his point of view. He had been there so long and had made, maybe, his first mistake. He couldn't lose his job over something like that, and I was just a punk kid.

After that I worked in a doughnut factory, in a candy store, and at the post office over Christmas. My first non-traditional job was as a draftsman. I had no skills at all, nothing to do, and out of work, when a neighbor told me they were hiring draftsmen where he worked. I had taken a lot of math in high school, so I got hired and sent to a six-week training program. When I walked into the class the first day, I didn't know what a draftsman was. That was in January of nineteen fifty-seven. My husband is a draftsman. I nailed him at work. I met him in July of nineteen fifty-seven, and we were married in July of nineteen fifty-eight. I worked there a total of three years. I had leaves of absence in between working, to have babies. After three babies, it got to where I couldn't handle the job and so many babies and quit.

I went back to work when my youngest girl was in the third grade. It was during that big layoff, and I knew my husband was going to get laid off. The money would help, but mostly I didn't want to be at home and listening to him moan and groan for the next ten months. I went to work at a department store, which was the only job available at the time. I stayed there for three years and quit when I couldn't stand it any more. I used to come home and scream at night. You worked as hard as you could work, and when they saw that you could do the job, then they would give you more responsibility with no more pay and no more hope of advancement. And I don't know if it was working with women or what, but there was so much picking. If something went wrong, there was always somebody running to the boss and telling these tales. It seemed like there was so much stress all the time in the job. They didn't even let you sit down for eight hours. After awhile the women that worked there were kind of beaten down. They had decided this was the best they could ever do.

Well, I decided that I could do better, and then they passed the law that women and minorities had to be hired everywhere in Washington. I had never thought of doing anything exciting, because in that day and age there wasn't anything a woman without an education could do. When they passed that law, I began thinking about getting a job where I could make some money. Then one of the gals I worked with—a black lady named Lula—told me her husband, a bus driver, said they were hiring women to drive bus. I told her to talk to him and find out the details. So the next day she came back and told me, "I don't think you want to hear this."

"What is it? Tell me."

She said, "He said for you to keep your big butt out of there." I went down the next day and put my application in. That was in nineteen seventy-three, when they first started hiring women. I might not have jumped so quick, but when I got that answer back, I saw it as a challenge. When I went in and applied, they just almost kissed me and dragged me in the door. They were so happy to see me. They had to hire women, and no women were applying. It just amazed me. On most jobs when you go in to apply, you feel like, "Well, shoot, I'm not getting that one." But they almost dragged me in the door. I had never had that experience before. I was the fourth woman hired.

I had a lot of misgivings about lasting as a bus driver. I had never driven anything larger than a small truck and the buses were so big. But my husband, Dean, was very supportive. He kept saying, "You are the kind of person who should be a bus driver. You'll love it, and quit this negative thinking."

During my twenty-four-day training period I was petrified. I didn't do so well. I wasn't aggressive. I was scared to death and the instructor we had was unusual. There were three women in our class and five men. This instructor had apparently been in the service and felt that, in order to train somebody, first you had to break them down. He picked on the women, of course, and had all three of us crying, and then he was our friend. He just bullied and yelled at you all the time you were driving. He wanted to fluster you, but it wasn't to get you to make mistakes. His theory was this will happen to you out on the road, so you had better get used to it. He did fire one man. The man had been a good driver, but the instructor stood up next to him and yelled in his ear all the time, "You're a lousy driver! How come you're driving so bad?" The guy got flustered and almost hit a pole and the instructor fired him. But I did make it through training, and then when I got out on the road, I could drive. But I spent all my breaks pouring over maps with this other lady who felt the same way I did; we spent at least four hours a day getting ready for our next run. We did that for the first two weeks. Then things started falling into place, but I really didn't get to like the job for three months. Through it all, my husband was very supportive. When I'd go home and cry, he'd listen and then tell me, "Well, by God, you can do it! You can do it." He just was really good at it.

At first, quite a few passengers would not ride my bus. They had never seen women drivers. The first time that happened it was a bit of a shock. After that, I just said, "Fine," and closed the door. You had your revenge by thinking, "They're gonna probably have to wait another hour because they're so stubborn."

Some of the other drivers were pretty hostile, too. When I was still in the training period, I went out with other drivers during their regular run. One driver refused to take me. He said that he didn't want students, especially women students, and then he went home sick. I found out later this guy became "Operator of the Year" and I felt bitter for a while. But it turned out that he had heart problems, and I figured that, if it upset him that much to have a woman on his bus, then he shouldn't do it. At first, when I went to the bases, the men were very macho. They swore a lot and were full of dirty stories. They were trying to scare us off, but they ran out of dirty stories. I don't think it lasted more than two weeks. Once they found out that we were there to make a living and to do a job, and we weren't taking their jobs, then they were just real helpful. It just took them awhile. Their masculinity was being threatened.

Things really started changing when the first driver got pregnant. She was one of the second or third women they hired. They had never had a pregnant bus driver and didn't know what to do with her. She was very outspoken and insisted that they do things. She was a beautiful woman, just beautiful! And very well built, and she found that being pregnant, her breasts just got so large that she couldn't drive because they bounced and got extremely sore. They had never come up with these problems at the transit company before, so they didn't know what to do with her. They put her in the office, finally, and let her work at driver's pay up until the baby was born. But she insisted that things change. She'd say, "I'm not going to go to the bathroom in

Arlene Tupper, transit supervisor

that men's bathroom." She did a lot of good and got things changed.

The first day in training our instructor said, "Now you can become a bus driver, but someday you might want to be a supervisor." Well, right that day I decided I was going to be a supervisor. I thought, "Gee, why not?" Actually when I became supervisor, it was quite a fluke. When I had been there two years, there was only one woman left that had been hired in ahead of me. Management didn't want her to be a supervisor, and they told me that. They also said they were waiting to give the supervisor's test until I had two years in and could take it. The reason they had to have me was because the government said that they had to have so many women supervisors and they had none. There were about a hundred of us that took the written exam, and then only some of us got to go before an oral review board. They had no real criteria at the time for choosing supervisors. I think they picked eight of us to be trained.

Since I've been in supervision, every department that I have gone into has been a new challenge, because they don't want women. When I first walked into a base to be trained, they said, "Oh, good! Now we have somebody to type." You know, earlier, when I kept changing jobs, I had thought, "Oh, how I wish I could type." And this was one time I thought, "Thank God! I can't type." But that was the attitude. They had never had a woman around. It took quite a bit of time.

I had learned to deal with the drivers as a fellow driver, but now I was their boss. That was another challenge. It took quite a few of them a long time to get used to me as a boss. It was a blow to their ego to have a woman tell them what to do. Some wouldn't talk to me, or if you told them to do something, they would not respond at all, and there was no way you could make them do it. At that time, there was nothing I could do. If you told 'em, "You have to work this piece of work," well, some of them would argue and say, "Why?" Now the report people must take the work. At the time, they didn't have to, so each day you'd have to go down the list and talk one into doing the piece of work. If nobody would do it, then you'd get angry and finally somebody would do it, but it was a real problem at the time.

Then, when I got out on the streets as a street supervisor, it started all over again. I can remember one man who got downtown five minutes early every day. I told him about it, but we had no real way of disciplining back then. I could write a "greenie," which was just a memo. It didn't mean diddley-shit. You wrote it, the boss looked at it, talked to the guy, and that was the end of it. That was all we could do. So I talked to this guy who was early, and he said, "Yes." He kept doing it, so I told him that I was going to have to write a greenie because he was always early. He said, "Fine, just write all the greenies that you want, and I will continue being early. There is nothing you can do about it. No woman is going to tell me what to do." So I wrote the greenie and he continued to be early, and he was right; there was nothing I could do about it.

When I first went into supervision I couldn't work in the instruction department. The boss wouldn't let me. He told me that as long as he was the head of instruction, he would never have a woman in there. And as long as he was there, I never got in. That only changed when he retired.

I think the worst challenge was going into the coordinator's office. That is dispatch, where you have control of all the buses on the road. You're actually a troubleshooter. Each person up there has from two to five hundred buses to control during the day. It is quite a job, and I had to fight to get in there. They had never had a woman dispatcher, and they were not about to have a woman dispatcher. The head supervisor in dispatch was a friend of mine and I told him I wanted to break in. He said, "Well, there's so much opposition. I just don't know." But he worked on it and I kept calling him up to ask when I would get to go in. The thing was that you only got into dispatch by invita-

Arlene Tupper, transit supervisor

tion. There was no other way in. But I kept after the head, until one day he called and said, "Well, do you want to break in up here?" I was just elated. I knew all the people that worked up there to talk to on the phone, but I didn't know them. They had all decided before I came up that they would not help me at all; they would just go by the book and tell me what they had to, and that would be the end of it. The coordinator's office was the last male stronghold, and they made more money, and they decided to keep it all male. But after the first week, when they found out I could do the job and was not threatening, we all became good friends. A lot of the drivers tell me now that they are glad I'm not in coordination any more. They couldn't handle a woman telling 'em what to do on the road.

In the coordinator's office, you make snap decisions constantly, and at first I felt uncomfortable with some of my decisions. There were so many choices you can make, but you haven't got the time. But after I made a few mistakes, I relaxed. We had a very supportive boss. He would never bawl you out for what you did. He would just tell you that maybe you shouldn't have done this. And if you did something wrong and the higher-ups came down on you for it, he would back you up all the way and say, "Hey, you weren't there. You don't know what happened. This was the best decision that the person could make." But when it was all over, he'd come by and say, "You dumb shit." You knew he knew you'd screwed up, but he'd back you up one hundred percent, and then he'd come down and say, "Why?" You have to realize that when you're making snap decisions, you're bound to make mistakes. Of course you'll make mistakes.

Another place that I finally worked in was instruction. Believe it or not, I actually got bored with it. Saturdays and Sundays were "up" days because I was teaching new people to drive, but the rest of the week was extremely boring. You didn't have much to do except ride check, which is when you gotta ride on somebody's bus, and you have a list of things you have to check off to make sure that they are doing everything properly. You check that they are driving in a safe manner, signing their bus properly, and treating their passengers right. The reason I left there was because eventually I wanted to become a chief in the base, and I thought in order to do that I'm gonna have to become more familiar with base work again. So that's what I'm doing now.

I found that I really liked working in the bases better, because as an instructor you can't really relate to the people you're teaching. You always have to keep up a facade. If they do something wrong, you can't say, "You dumb shit." You have to say, "Well, maybe you should have done it this way." You can't really get to know the people. In the bases, you can get to know the people.

Figuring out where the different drivers are coming from and how they think can be a real challenge. You can't treat everybody the same. Some people when you greet them in the morning, you say, "Good morning. Nice to see you." Other people you say, "Well, how the hell are you today?" It's a real challenge to know how they want to be treated.

At the bases I make sure that every bus has a driver, that they all get out of the base on time, that everybody signs in, that they're all paid properly, dressed in their uniforms, and all the paperwork is done. There's a lot of paperwork, but most of it revolves around making sure that every bus has a driver. Sometimes it gets very hectic, like when three people don't show up and you have nobody standing around looking for work. Then it gets tense, but it's fun.

I love to hug people, but at one base I got in trouble for it once. When my friends came to the window at the base, I would give them a hug, and I'd usually pick out two or three older drivers that had been there thirty years—they were the drivers that would come to work, sign in, not talk to anybody, and they'd go to work, and then all of a sudden they retired, and nobody knew who they were. It was sad to me, so I started hugging them every day. I just felt that they probably needed it, and then they would start talking to people. They'd come in the morning and smile. I just felt they needed physical contact. It doesn't have to be sexual. It can be just a "I'm glad you're here today," and a big hug. Anyway, my boss told me I had to stop hugging people. I quit for a week and everybody thought something was wrong with me, so I thought, "Piss on him. That's not me." I started hugging again, and told my boss, "I'm sorry, I tried it, but I don't think it's influencing my work. I just can't go around not hugging people." He never said anything again. He realized that was just the way I was.

My husband, Dean, has never been upset by my being around all these men. In fact, one time he came into work right when this one guy had grabbed me over backwards and was giving me a big kiss, right? So when Dean walked in the door, I said, "Hey, Dean, I want you to meet so-and-so."

The guy said, "Oh, that's your husband. Hi," and gave me another big kiss. He was just that way. I asked Dean if that bothered him.

He said, "Shoot, no, you guys looked like you were having a good time." And we just started laughing about it.

Oh, I'm sure that Dean has had some doubts in his own mind, but he has never said anything to me. He knows how much I love him. In fact, after I went to work there he said that he was really glad that I did, because I became a more interesting person and wasn't shut up in my own little world. Dean doesn't like to go out with me and the guys from work for drinks because all we talk about is work, and he finds it extremely boring. He knows I always come home. If we get carried away in our conversation, and I get home late, Dean doesn't say anything. One time he did say I was doing it too often, and I was. You know, two or three times a week was too much, so he did mention that. But he has never worried about me going out with men from work.

I've never had too much of a problem of men coming onto me. Sometimes a guy has too much to drink, and then they're kind of sloppy, but you don't worry about those. When I talked with other women who started about the same time as I did, I found out that my being married made a big difference. I didn't believe it at first, because all the men were friends to me. We would go out for breakfast, eat lunch together, go out and have drinks, and nobody ever made a pass at me. But the single women found that the men were very overt in their advances. One gal that I got to know really well told me they would wait for her getting off the bus, and the men would not just say, "Do you want to go have a drink?" She said they said, "Do you wanna fuck?" When she told me this, I thought, "Well, maybe it's just her." You really don't know because it had never happened to me. But she married a driver, and all these people quit doing it and became her friends. Then I believed her, because it immediately changed when she got married.

My kids have always thought it was a great lark that I was a bus driver. They're all grown and gone now, but they were still home when I made supervisor, and one of my kids said, "Mom, do we have to tell anybody you're a supervisor?"

And I said, "It doesn't matter to me, but why are you asking?"

She said, "Well, people ask what does you mother do, and you tell people she's a supervisor, nobody cares, But if you say, 'My mother is a bus driver,' they're impressed with that. I don't have to tell 'em you're a supervisor, do I?"

I said, "No."

My life with Dean has changed a great deal, too. We don't live in a house any more. We live in a sailboat. I think the way it has changed is that the kids are all gone, and they used to cook

Arlene Tupper, transit supervisor

dinner for Dean. He hates to cook, and now he has to fix his own dinner, because I work such odd hours. That means he doesn't eat very well. One night I asked him what he had for dinner, and he said, "Peanut butter."

And I said, "What do you mean, peanut butter? Didn't you have anything with it?"

"Oh, yes. I dipped it in butter," he said. After that he bought a microwave because he didn't have time to cook his own dinner on the wood stove. So that is different. I still do the laundry and housecleaning and what-not.

The other big change in my life is that I am not afraid to go anywhere or to do anything by myself. Before, I used to have a friend go with me. Now I think I would do almost anything by myself. I think that came from having my free time during such odd hours that nobody else has the same time off, and from working on the street as a supervisor. Shoot, I'd go down First Avenue now at night and wouldn't think anything of it. You learn that there are really not very many places that you can't go. It's just that people have always told you, "That's a bad place to go," so you wouldn't go there. In Seattle, there's only a few places I wouldn't walk at night. One's at Fourteenth and Jefferson. I would never walk there at night, but I don't know of a lot more.

Telephone Frameman

KATHY BAERNEY

Kathy Baerney left a trade that she loved in order to keep her family together. Now she dreams of visiting Venice and worries about saving the whales.

I started working for the phone company in nineteen sixty-five as an operator. I was still in high school. My mother used to work for the phone company and my father is in management with the company. As for me working there, it's not that I chose it. It's just that it was there.

I was an operator for a year and a half, a thankless job, not a fun job. Back then you didn't vary from speech patterns. If somebody said something that was not on a card that had already been written down somewhere, the response did not come, because there was no response. I mean, you had these statements that you could make and you could not vary. You know, not one word. Your best friend could be making a long-distance call and you could not say, "Hi."

From there I went to the plant service center, where they make sure orders are run though smoothly. I was on the order desk and when the installers finished a job, they'd check in with me. It was a fun job 'cause you got to talk to the guys all day long. I stayed there for three years. It was during that time I started thinking about non-traditional work. There was a couple installers, I don't know whether they know this was coming or not, but they let me ride with them on Saturdays. Not ride in the truck, 'cause that's a no-no, but follow them from house to

Kathy Baerney, telephone frameman

house, because I wanted to install bad. I'd go in with them and hook up the wiring inside, adjust the set, do all the stuff. And that kind of got me into the idea where—if something hadn't happened, I probably would have said, "Hey, why not? I don't understand this." Because I never did understand—I never felt held back until it occurred to me and by the time it occurred to me, I wasn't.

It wasn't because the phone company *had* been hit by the federal government [but to prevent it]. The government wanted the company to achieve parity, which is where you have equal amounts of minorities. And then in order to reach parity, you have to employ—parity was a lousy word for a long time. They did not do it right as far as I'm concerned. They didn't just open up the gates and say, you know, "This job is now ready for women; if you're qualified, go for it." What they did was, they held back some men that should have been promoted, should have been rewarded for services done, before these people, no matter whether they were man, woman, or child. These people should have had the jobs first. But they said, "No, it's gotta be a white woman or it's gotta be a black woman or it's gotta be a black man who's in this position." So it was not nice.

To get a jump on the government, the company went around and asked all the females if they wanted to do other things. And I said I wanted to install. I wanted to go outside. They said I was too short. I could not get the ladder down from on top of the truck. But I fooled them. You can climb on the bumper and get the ladder down. But climbing on the bumper, however, was against company practice. So they pushed me, persuaded me, they did everything they could to get me to go down to the central office. They really needed a woman in the central office to reach parity. The woman level there was too low, so they pushed me into it. I really wanted to go outside.

At the central office you have relays that will make or break a dial tone, place a call, bill you correctly, and let you receive calls—according to what type of an impulse is received. So I went down there as a frameman. I worked on the main distributing frame, a long structure where they have all the cable that is run out so the surrounding areas come up into the terminals. There are two terminal lugs per cable, and that makes a loop back to the central office and you get your dial tone. So what I did at first was run jumpers from your office equipment and laid down cable inside to make sure your dial tone was going right. Then I'd hook it up and you've got your phone service.

I was pretty young when I worked as a frameman. I'm a good worker and I busted my buns. They were all telling me not to bust my buns, but I did. And that, I think, made the difference. I really worked hard down there. Not as far as thinking, because you know, you gotta think, but it's not that taxing. But as far as physical labor goes, I was really good.

In the morning I'd get there early and sort out all the orders of the day, and then the next two hours are spent in frantic activity running in all the jumpers, scuffing up your little hands, scuffing them up a lot. A lot of scars from stripping wire and soldering. The rest of the day, depending on the work load for the next day, was either advancing them in, straightening out problems from the people who assign the office equipment— I'm talking of things that you know nothing about. I mean, it's hard to explain to someone exactly what it is, because it's your own language and it doesn't mean anything. What it comes down to is running up and down the wires. They have three hundred pairs that are vertical and you run up and down the ladders. You were fit and had to like heights on that job.

My supervisor there was very supportive, very condescending, very "Gosh, I hope she makes it 'cause I like her," very nice, very easy to work with. Men, for women, are easier to work for—this is not coming out right. Okay, women have a tendency to know men well enough to know how to play them. This sounds really cold and calculating, but you could really do

Kathy Baerney, telephone frameman

whatever you wanted to, as long as—this is not coming out well at all. This particular man was used to being a boss of men and didn't quite know how to deal with a woman because he had daughters of the same age, and yet he couldn't treat her like a daughter because she was an employee. And he was very easy to manipulate.

For example, at the telephone company when you're working around equipment, it's required that you wear safety glasses. These safety glasses have been given no change of style since the early-safety-glasses period. I mean, you can still drop a lead ball on them from eight feet and they will not break. I mean these are terribly uncomfortable, unattractive, un-everything glasses. I did not want to wear these glasses and I told him that. And he said that he didn't think we could get around it. And I just told him that I was gonna get some frames that had the same safety glass in there, but the frames, although they were made similar, were not the exact frame. I got a note from the doctor saying these frames were as good or better than the ones given by the phone company. And I said, you know, "Wouldn't that work? Come on."—Is that whining?— Just, "Come on," you know, until he finally gave in. Whereas a guy can't do that. A guy can't whine. You know, there's troubles for guys that whine down there.

After two to three years as a frameman, I became a switchman. Switchmen take care of the equipment. They man the offices on the weekends. If we have a snow or John Wayne dies, you know—I mean, the coiling of relays go crazy. People can dump the central office by everybody picking up the phone at once. You have huge generators, you have a turbine—I mean, this is big stuff and they can go and die. That is scary; that is the part I did not like. On Mother's Day, here I am, a mother, stuck in a central office in Renton that has three floors, and people are calling in saying, "I'm gonna jump, I've had it." Usually the fire department will call and say, "She says she's gonna jump, we can't find her." And I'm going, "Ohhh!"—and naturally the phone company won't let you work in an office with which you're familiar. They will send you from Auburn to Renton to man the operation. So there you are, not really knowing the place, and the responsibility on the weekends is large. I do not feel I was trained well enough to handle that.

My first race was a man who'd called up, who'd had a heart attack. And they'd put on a speakerphone and you could hear him gasping for breath and I was going, "Oh, God! Hold on!" To try and find his location, I used something we called a channel. It's like a large-headed pin, sometimes not even as big as that, and they are made in a row of six. You try to find the ones that are closed, rather than open. Now these are teeny, tiny things we're talking about. And from there that will send you to another row of switches and relays that will have the same thing, but you've got to find all of this. You have to follow these through and find out which one is made and which one is closed. And it will eventually bring you to a line location, which you can use to go back to the main distributing frame and that connects directly to his cable and pair, so that is where his is. Then you can call the police and pull the line card and give the police the address. Then they're off. Sometimes you can do it in four minutes, sometimes in fifteen minutes. It just depends on where they are. You know, when somebody's gasping for breath it's not fun, not fun. It's harrowing because you know you've got somebody who's, like, who's not gonna make it, if you don't hurry; you know, that's real. . . .

It's terrible! and the worst part was, towards the end of my stint in the central office, I would think, why do they have to call somebody and tell them this? Why don't they just do it? And that was the worst part, because I'm thinking, these people out there need help and I don't want to go through the hassle, so I'm saying, "Do it, but don't call anybody and tell them." I felt really guilty about it for a long time.

Kathy Baerney, telephone frameman

I liked working with the guys in the central office. Men can be just as picky as women can, but it's more of a broad-type, let-'em-be thing. I find that in an office, it's more of a gang-up-and-get-'em thing. In an office dominated by females, it's more of a revenge thing, where working with all guys it's more of a laugh and joke, it-doesn't-really-matter-type thing. They were just as picky and just as gossipy, they're just people. But I've seen women take revenge and be nasty and vicious. I mean vicious. Whereas in the central office with the guys, they were wonderful. To me, they were not hateful and hurting.

When I first went to work there, the men saw me as really innocent. I wasn't as innocent as all that. In all honesty, I did a lot of role-playing there, you bet. Men like to be so big and wonderful and protective and I let them. I was more or less what they wanted me to be. More or less what they wanted. I didn't even know, then, what *I* wanted. So I was more or less what *they* wanted. First of all they wanted somebody who was gonna be some kind of token down there. And then they found out I could do the work and I could do it better than most of them. Not because of mental things, but because of determination and because, being a woman, I was easily adapted to doing mundane chores and doing them well. I *do* think there is a certain amount of conditioning there. I think women have more of an ability to do that. I hate saying that, but I think it's true. But they started to accept me then, and when I got married we started joking about things that I never joked about before.

The first day back from my honeymoon, in the central office—when you're working with twenty guys it's not a fun day for the light of stomach. I mean, there were all these comments like, "How's your walking?" You know, right out there. It's funny to see the change over the period of time I worked there. When I first came down there, a gal that was large of bust was walking down the street and I was standing there soldering some terminal lugs. And the guys were looking out the window and they said, "Will ya look at those?"—and they knew I was there—and they said, "Big little *eyes.*" You know, the gal had on dark glasses. You couldn't see her eyes. But that was the way they treated me. And after awhile, I don't know whether it was because of things that I had said or what, but it got to be more of a familiar, less-careful-of-standard-conversation-type stuff to each other. We could joke about things that I would think were funny, too. Shoot, then I got married and I knew it all. Maybe it was my getting married, but afterwards we were all really close.

We joked about things that I never joked about before and talked about sex a lot. We had it all figured out down there. And the things they did to me, oh my God! They would make these foam rubber articles—male genitals—yes, a complete set—and hang them out over a piece of equipment. Then they'd ask me if I'd check it. What can I tell ya?

When I was pregnant I was terribly embarrassed to be pregnant, especially down there. I've never been very good at things like that anyway. It was my first time and I was really embarrassed. Not because of everybody knowing what I'd done—that was no biggie; we'd already talked it out beforehand—but because I was gonna get fat. I didn't wanna get fat, and it was a whole new thing. Things back up on you when you're pregnant, and you're not quite right all the time if this is the first time you've done this. And evidently I've got more hormones than most people or something, but it took me very badly. I was totally embarrassed but they were so good about it. They gave me a cake. They gave me a shower. They put smelt in my tool pouch. I threw up. I showed them! I didn't clean it up either. They had a good time laughing that morning. I came in bright and sunny, and I'd been putting my tool pouch on a little lower, and I could feel something, rather than see 'em. And I was trying to put this tool in my pouch, poking away, and I looked down, and there were scales and guts and crud all over. Scales! Do you know how hard it is to get scales out of your . . . ? And I looked at that and there was this eye laying on my foot and I just got sick, real bad. I loved it.

I don't think mothers and fathers have the same feelings. I don't think biologically it's possible. I think a man may love his kids, but with a woman it is more physical. I mean, I didn't want to get pregnant the first time. When I got pregnant I was in total shock. I'm one of those people that never took any precautions and I get married and I'm surprised. I'm what? I did not want to be pregnant or fat. I did not want to have a baby. I was devoid of all those feelings. And consequently when we lost the first baby, I went through a lot of guilt and a lot of bad things. I wanted a puppy after we lost the baby. It was a real physical need for something to love, to hold, to mother. So I got pregnant again about four months later, and from then on with me you love your kids, you need 'em.

When I was down at the central office, we had a wonderful union president. I love him. I mean, I love him. He's a wonderful person. I was the first case in the valley where a woman was pregnant and was paid while I was off. Before, you had to hide your condition, which is hard in a tool belt. You know, people know. You had to hide until they said quit and then you didn't get paid or anything. But thanks to the union, I was one of the first cases of a woman being able to go home in my eighth month and do my nesting thing and have the baby and get paid for six more weeks. It was good.

The telephone company did something really wonderful for me, though, and for which I'll be forever grateful. When I had Matt, my first baby, I told them I didn't know whether I wanted to come back or not. This was all bluff on my part because Russ, my husband, was at that time out of work again. They told me that because I was such a good worker (and I had a feeling it had something to do with parity) that they would bring me back at four hours a day. This was at top pay, vacation, and benefits. And it was wonderful. I asked them for it after my second child,

Maggie, was born and I could have had it for six months, but then I would have had to go back to working days. I should have taken it. I regret that, but I wanted to stay in Auburn and work evenings.

My husband worked days and I worked evenings after Maggie was born. I would be home during the day with Matt and Maggie and it was really nice. I don't regret the time at all. I worked four to midnight and we had a girl come and stay for forty-five minutes in the transition period when I had to leave for work and Russ was coming home. Then Russ had the kids at night. I should have realized, but I didn't—maybe it's 'cause I didn't want to, maybe I wasn't as caring as I should have been—but he felt trapped. And then on the weekends—he's got this great love for fishing. I mean, he loves it. The man is a born fisherman. He should be guiding a boat somewhere. On the weekends he would want to escape and I would resent it because I had been home all during the week. I had cleaned and I felt on the weekends we should do things with the family or something should be different, rather than him going off fishing. I didn't realize that he felt trapped. He worked during the day, had to be there, came home at night, and could not go out with his friends, could not go watch the fights at somebody's house without taking two little kids along. You can't enjoy a fight with a two-year-old girl and a six-year-old boy. It was hard for him, and we didn't talk about it. He ended up resenting the kids. I ended up resenting him. It just didn't work well.

I think if you stand back and look at a situation objectively, you've got to decide your priorities. That's why I went back to a clerk's job. I decided I felt better giving my time and energy to my kids and my husband, instead of a career which I really would have liked to pursue. I've made my decisions. Now why can't I cook? I feel a loss though. I really do. I feel bad that I'm not working with my hands 'cause I enjoyed that and was good at it.

Kathy Baerney, telephone frameman

I made some of the prettiest solders you ever saw. That's what impressed them a good deal when I went down there, that I wasn't clumsy with soldering. I miss the physical part of it. The job I have now is more stressful in terms of being stuck in one place and having thirty-seven people wanting an answer. But I miss that physical part of it, the working with tools.

Label Printer

MICHELLE SANBORN

In Michelle Sanborn's living room stands a massive oak china cabinet. It is full of expensive china and crystal. Michelle has come a long way from the projects in Oakland. The ink stains under her fingernails are only part of the price she has paid.

I never knew my father, and my mother died when I was a baby. My grandmother raised my brother and I. Would you believe we lived off public assistance? Grandma never worked. She just stayed home and took care of us. For three or four years we lived in public housing. The rest of the time we lived in different apartment houses—all in Oakland, California.

Grandma drank a lot. I could never have anybody home from school 'cause I never knew if my grandmother was drunk or not. So I ended up pretty lonely and very non-social with other people. I tried to get school officials and welfare officers to do something about Grandma. They'd come to the house, but it never changed. She still drank. So I just went to school and misbehaved. My brother was the same way. Neither of us had any desire to do anything at all. I hated school and probably had a D average. I kind of got into running the streets—not really getting into trouble. You know, not getting picked up by the police, but hanging out with older people.

The first job I got was when I was in tenth grade working in a restaurant. Then I went to work in a nursing home in the kitchen. I made a dollar fifty an hour. That was under minimum

Michelle Sanborn, label printer

wage. Because I was not considered full-time help, they could pay me less. After I finished high school, I got married. Then in nineteen seventy-one I went back to work in a nursing home as a nurse's aide. I made a dollar thirty-five an hour for cleaning up shitty bottoms, getting beat up by old people, and just basically taking care of them. There was some satisfaction in helping someone who couldn't help themself.

Then I went to work for a doctor as a receptionist. I started out at two twenty-five an hour and when I left I was making four dollars an hour. I left there for a job as a receptionist and book-keeper at another clinic. Working for a doctor was good for me. It taught me a lot. I learned that I could do things I hadn't thought I could. I mean, working for a doctor is high class. I learned to get along with people and found out about a whole 'nother world—what it is like to be around people who have money, the things they do with that money, and how cheap they are. Eventually I got tired of it. I saw myself going nowhere—financially or mentally. It was the same thing every day. I wanted to do something else.

I went out looking for a job and got on in a factory that made plastic bags. The pay was good, five fifty an hour. I was fascinated with the way the label printers put a roll of paper on the press, ran it through, and came out with a finished product. Things that we see every day in the store are all printed. Anyplace you look there is something printed. My first job was rewinding, which meant taking the rolls that are done off the press and rewinding and fixing them so we could send them to the customer. It didn't take any skill to be a rewinder. The rewinders and packers were girls and all the printers were males. Printers made nine-something an hour, so I decided that was something I wanted to learn. I wanted a trade to fall back on if something ever happened.

I don't remember any fears about becoming a printer. I knew in myself I could do it. It was just a matter of time to learn how.

So when the company needed another printer, I went and asked the bosses for the job. I thought I knew what printing was like 'cause I had seen the guys do it, but it turned out to be more difficult. It took a lot of patience and I don't have a lot of patience. You have to learn how to mount a plate on a cylinder so that it is straight and that can be very difficult. Dies are pieces of metal that are set in rollers. You have to learn just how much to tighten the die down, make it straight, and set it to cut through the paper, but not all the way through. It is pretty complicated. It took me three months to just learn all the different kinds of paper there were.

Working conditions for the printers were pretty lousy. It was very noisy and the ventilation was poor. You had trouble breathing because of all the fumes. All your solvents were alcohol-based and smelled. You would get really high off the fumes. It's like you'd smoked a joint or something. If you're a woman, you have two choices—either you go find yourself another profession which pays nothing, or you try not to inhale—as much as possible.

Besides the printing, I had to do all the shit work around the place. I had to do inventory, slit paper, and run the forklift. There were times when I felt like I was being treated really shitty. Like once a bunch of material came in on a pallet that was busted and my boss told me that I had to go and move all of these rolls by myself. There were thirty or forty rolls of paper on this pallet, and the rolls weighed from fifty to seventy-five pounds each. So I went back into the warehouse and moved them manually with no help. But I feel like you sometimes have to do things like that on a job, so I did it and kept my mouth shut.

My foreman was in charge of the whole company. He was a super person, always chit-chatting with the workers. You never felt like you were any less than he was. If you made a mistake, he told you how much it cost, but never really got down on you.

He was not on my side, though, when one guy made some crude comments about me. This one guy and I had gone 'round about something. I don't even remember why, but I had gone into the bathroom. The man came and stood outside of the bathroom calling me "a fucking bitch," as loud as he could so everybody in the whole company could hear it.

When I went to the supervisor and said, "I don't appreciate being called a fucking bitch," he told me, "Well, that's your problem. We can't do anything about it." Seemed to me that no matter what I had done, there was still no reason to be called that.

It was unfair. The reason I say that is later on I got really mad at my supervisor and said, "You know, you guys are all male chauvinist pigs." And the big boss had the balls to call me into his office and tell me that I was wrong. They wrote it up against me on my record. It wasn't right. The guys I worked with could call me anything they wanted, but if I said anything it went against me on my evaluation.

Every once in awhile they would try and intimidate me. After one of the girls got her hair caught in the bag machine, we all had to wear hair nets. Even the little old men who were sixty years old and bald. Everybody had to wear a hair net and all our hair had to be in the net. Well, the men started to wear baseball caps and some of the women started to let their bangs hang out of their nets. But one day the boss from another department said I had to have all my hair inside the net. I told him my whole head of hair wouldn't fit inside the net and that I was leaving to go buy myself another hair net. I left and didn't even go back that day.

I called the Human Rights Commission to complain. I was pissed the old men wore baseball caps and the young guys let their hair hang out in the back, and the girls in the bagging department had their bangs hanging out, but *I* had to put my whole head of hair in the net. I felt like I was being picked on.

The commission told me that I could put a suit against the company, and it would cost them oodles and oodles of dollars whether I won or lost, or they could call and tell them someone had complained. I said to just call up. I needed the job because we had just bought a new house and it was a good-paying job for a woman. I didn't want to screw up and lose it, but felt it was important to do something. My husband was the one who told me to call up the Human Rights Commission, but I don't know exactly how he felt because he never said. Anyhow the Human Rights Commission called the company up. They didn't tell the company that I was the one who had called, but it was obvious. After that they kind of relaxed about the hair nets. There were still problems, but I felt you could only push so much. As long as they left me alone, I didn't care. And they left me alone.

Not too long after that the company was sold, and I was told they probably wouldn't keep me. A salesman told me that the company I now work for needed a printer. I went down to apply and started work about two or three days later. They were willing to pay me what I was making at the other job, so I started out at seven dollars and fifty cents an hour. They said I would get a raise in three months. It's six months now, and they say I *don't* get a raise in three months; they say I don't get a raise until a year is up. In fact my salary has brought on hostility from the first day I started work. What I heard is, the company went bankrupt, was rebought, and then opened up again last September. The new company decided to cut everybody's wages. A lot of the production workers had been making five and six dollars an hour and were cut down to three eighty-five an hour. Here they were all taking pay cuts, and I came in making more money than my supervisor. Nobody would associate with me or talk with me. I ate my lunch in my car by myself until I told the boss I preferred working a straight eight hours and then just go home.

A bunch of the people decided they weren't going to stand for the pay cuts and voted in the Steelworkers Union the week that

Michelle Sanborn, label printer

I went to work there. They hired me as a "lead" printer so I couldn't join the union. The company's very against unions and told me so. At one point it looked like the leads were going to be involved in the union so I was told to go to a meeting. They had to hold a vote for shop steward because one of the girls was leaving, and I said, "Sure, I'll be steward." I figured I would get only one vote, my own. It shocked the hell out of me when I got elected. All I can figure is that they now like me more than at first.

The company had me in the office for three hours after the election. They told me if I wanted to be shop steward that they would drop all my benefits and drop my wages, and drop my title of lead. Basically they put the screws to me. At home I called the union to find out for sure if leads were going to be in the union or not. They weren't sure, and I said, "You had better find out." Finally, they decided that leads, supervisors, and all personnel upstairs were not going to be in the union. So I couldn't be the shop steward.

This is a very male-oriented company. Even the girls in the office have said the same thing. My boss is a male chauvinist pig. He doesn't accept my word for anything. When I tell him something, he calls up his buddy in Redmond to find out if I'm right or wrong. Like, I told him the dies needed to be sharpened. They hadn't been sharpened for three or four years. He wouldn't do it on my say-so, but after he called that other guy, all of a sudden the dies were being sharpened. That makes me feel about one inch tall. And I know it's because I'm a woman. We have a new maintenance man and whatever he says goes.

I just keep telling myself that I am a good printer. Sometimes I'll compliment myself by saying to one of the guys there, a salesman, "Don't you think that looks really good today?"

And he'll go, "Oh, yeah." I need to do something because I get no appreciation.

I want to quit but we need the money. We have two children,

both boys. One is eleven and the other is eight. And my husband is not working right now, so we don't have enough money coming in. He is disabled. In fact, he didn't work the first seven years that we were married. But I figure as soon as he goes back to work, I am going to quit. I don't care what my husband says or how he feels about that. I've had it up to the top of my head. I hate working for that company.

Having a good-paying job has made me a lot more independent. I was driving my husband's reject cars and they would break down at six in the morning in back of the woods, and I would have to hitchhike to the babysitters's and call my job and say I couldn't come in because I had no transportation. And finally I got to the point one day that I told my husband that I was going to buy a new car. And that's the way it was, because I made enough money that I felt that I could afford to buy a new car in my name. It's my car. My husband was very angry. We went round and round about it, and he knew that I wasn't going to back down. He still gets very angry when I say it's my car. He says it's our car. It's not, as far as I'm concerned. It's my car and he should ask permission to drive my car. He has his cars and I have one of my own. It's mine.

Last year my husband was on a four-day work week so I made only eight hundred dollars less than he did for the whole year. I wish I had made more, for my own ego. One paycheck I made over seven hundred dollars for a two-week period. That's more than he ever made in a two-week period. I was in seventh heaven. I was equal to him. I wasn't below him. It took a lot of skill when I worked as a bookkeeper for a doctor, and I worked as many hours as my husband did, but got less than half what he made. Now I made damn near as much as he does. And I work just as hard as he does, and he knows how hard I work. I think that's been hard for him. Traditional people have been brought up that a woman isn't in the same classification as her husband. Now I feel like I'm just as good as he is. Maybe I'm even better.

Tugboat Mate

BETH GEDNEY

At twenty-four, Beth Gedney feels she has done pretty well for herself. She has a house, a career, a husband, and children on the way.

My father is a sea captain. I don't know if I was just pig-headed or what, but all I ever wanted to do was go to sea. We were always taking trips with Dad. I remember talking once to my sister, who is several years older than I am, and saying I wanted to go to sea, but at that time it wasn't a viable option, so I didn't know what I was going to do. Then, when I was a sophomore in high school, California Maritime Academy accepted their first women. I applied about a year later.

My mother thought it was terrific, but it took my father awhile to get warmed up to the idea. At first he said it was over his dead body. Then about six months later he decided it was okay and took me down and introduced me to all his buddies at the Academy. Later he helped me with my studies.

I started at the Academy in August of nineteen seventy-five. The school used to be a technical program. I was in the second class to get an accredited bachelor's out of it. My B.S. is in nautical industrial technology. The school was divided into deck and engineering programs. I chose deck because I'm more of a thinking person than a hands-on person. And, you know, engineering is a hot, dirty, uncomfortable job most of the time. So I studied navigation, cargo handling, ship stability, and enough general education to round it out for the degree.

Once I decided to go to the Academy, I pretty much forged ahead. I do remember the first morning I had to report to the Academy driving across the bridge and looking down on the campus, and going, "Oh, my God, what have I done?" And it got worse when I walked in and realized there were only three other women out of a class of two hundred. We lost one girl the first day and that just gave everybody tremors. They broke us up into divisions, so the first couple of weeks you were so busy with your division that you didn't even see the rest of the gals except as we passed each other while brushing our teeth. It was pretty intimidating.

We went to school eleven months out of the year. But one semester we took a ship to sea and that helped us get through the rest. We had classes from eight to five on weekdays. As freshmen we weren't allowed to leave campus except from five to midnight on Wednesdays and from five o'clock on Friday to five o'clock on Sunday. Actually it was pretty good, because you didn't have anything else to do so you got really good study habits.

I feel like I got a good, usable education. Didn't have any trouble finding employment, unlike a lot of college graduates these days. And just the living conditions were very educational. I feel like at this point I could handle just about anything. You were in such close contact with so many people and so many were male. Like when we were on ship we girls had our own little area, but it was only separated from the men by a canvas sheet. If I had been a very private person I would have quit the first day.

And learning to deal with men's attitudes was a whole other education. I mean some of those men we went to school with were so pig-headed. Even after four years, when you were doing a pretty good job and were obviously going to make it, some of them were still terribly unaccepting. We had a demerit system at the school and some of them would try to find little things. I don't know if they were trying to get you to quit or just ruin your day, but for four years they did their bit to make your life impossible. God, they'd give you demerits for anything—wearing earrings, having hair under your collar, not making your bed, being late for class, not having your car parked in the right spot. . . . I learned in school that a woman had to do twice as much as a man. You had to paint twice as much as some guy did just to prove that you were equal.

But when I graduated from school I had the choice of three different well-paying jobs, which is something everybody should have. I chose a tugboat line.

I would say there's around three hundred employees that actually work on the boats. We have sixty-four boats all together, but there's only eleven of what we call outside boats. Those are boats that run from Seattle to California, Mexico, Alaska. The rest of them are the harbor boats that you see all the time working in the harbor, and then we have a lot of little one- or two-man boats that work logs in Everett. This is a kind of a catch-all phrase, but it's pretty much the oldtimers that have the inside jobs. Fellows with seniority like those jobs because you only work fifteen days a month and are guaranteed wages for that fifteen days. Whereas the outside work is catch-as-catch-can. A lot of times in the summer you'll think, "I haven't had a day off in so long I think I'll die," and then in the winter you think, "I want to go back to work or I'm gonna starve to death."

When I went down to start work it was real funny, because my folks were teasing me because I would have to have a roommate. Tugboats are real small and there was only a grand total of three or four women working on the boats. So my folks kept teasing me that my roommate would be bald, not have any teeth, and suck on a whiskey bottle all night. When I got down to the boat the first day, the skipper was there and I was the first one to arrive, and he said, "Well, you're in the forward cabin."

And I go in there and think, "I'm done." Hard bunks; not only am I going to have one bald-headed guy that sucks on a whiskey bottle, there's going to be three bald-headed guys, so I was really nervous. Since I was the first one there, I took the bunk I wanted, the bottom one. I was tucking a sheet in and bending way over reaching into the back corner of the bunk when I hear this voice behind me go, "It's gonna be a long trip." And I just went, "Oh, no! What have I gotten myself into?" But he ended up being a real character and we got along well.

There were three able-bodieds [seaman], myself being one, and an oiler who worked in the engine room in the cabin. The AB's, as able-bodieds are called, turned out to be terrific, but the oiler did not say one word to me for the entire twelve days we were out on the trip.

I was pretty nervous about being the only woman doing the work. Aside from doing my watch in the wheelhouse, I went down on deck when we were handling lines or hooking up the tug, which involves a lot of heavy work like dragging this chain around. I didn't want to make a fool out of myself doing the physical work.

Just the nature of the job can be pretty dangerous. You got a barge moving down a river alongside the boat and you have to get from the boat to the barge, so you're jumping over a distance greater than you actually feel comfortable with. I don't know if it would be classed as dangerous, but one of the worst habits you get into involves something which is known as a tow shackle. It is a big steel shackle which weighs ninety-five pounds and is used to shackle two chains together. Of course, one of the points of merit to being a deck hand is whether you can pick up one of these tow shackles. Everybody had to prove they could pick one up. I mean, really for somebody my size picking up ninety-five pounds of steel is ridiculous, but of course you had to do it to prove you were just as good as the rest of those jerks. The fellows shouldn't be lifting the ninety-five pounds either, but they do.

Beth Gedney, tugboat mate

But I think some of that wears off after awhile. You see too many people get hurt or almost get hurt by sheer stupidity. Just standing in the wrong place is the biggest problem we run into. It's especially dangerous working up north where you have two or three inches of ice on deck and the snow is blowing and things are extremely slippery. Then it's pretty hairy.

A lot of times I have to take somebody aside that works for me and say, "You're not going to do that any more because it's dangerous. I don't care what anybody says. You're not going to do that." Proving yourself is something that everybody, not just women, do. It's something about being a macho tugboater.

Let me describe what the boat is like. The last one I was on for a year and a half is pretty typical. I had a cabin that was about seven foot long and about five foot wide and contained a bed, desk, drawers, and a locker to hang my gear in. When you were out of bed there was about two square feet to move around in. I shared a bathroom with the skipper and chief mate. I was the second mate. We were up on one deck, and the rest—the engineering and cook and deck hands—were all down on the next deck and had their own head [bathroom]. Then the wheelhouse was up a couple decks. It has a big console with windows all the way around, throttles, your two radars, all your gauges for your engine, and two big chairs, which we sit in. That is real unusual. On most ships you literally stand up for your four-hour watch. It's real nice on tugs because you get to sit down, and most skippers don't mind if you play the radio on deck so you stay informed about the news, which is really good. On watch you're basically looking out the window to make sure that you don't run into anybody. You keep a watch on your radar and once an hour, sometimes every half hour if you have a lot of current, you get a position off the radar or off the navigation equipment to make sure you're going the right way.

We haul just about everything imaginable. On the last job we hauled bulk cement, eleven thousand five hundred tons of it.

On top of that, when we went to Anchorage and Kodiak we'd take thirty-four house trailers along on racks. As I said, I was pretty constant on this run. We'd go to San Francisco, pick up the cement there, and take it to foundries in California, Seattle, Anchorage, or sometimes Canada.

One of the joys of tugboating was the work schedule. When you came home, sometimes you knew you were only home overnight or twelve hours or whatever. Other times you were supposed to be home overnight and it turned into a week, or into three weeks, and you just never knew when you got off a trip when they were going to call you back. If you weren't steady on one boat then, Lord, anything could happen. You could come and go. They might call you at midnight and ask you when you could be there. They do that a lot. It's just the condition of the business. Things happen at all hours of the day and night. But the pay helps make up for that. I earn ninety-five dollars a day. On top of that we get five extra hours off for every eight we work, so it's around a hundred and ten dollars. You can't throw stones at that.

I've served with seven, eight different skippers. I would say fifty percent of them were terrific and easy to get along with and compliment you on a job well done. The other fifty percent were impossible. I mean, they weren't going to accept you if you carried that barge on your back. Part of it's being a young kid. Anybody under forty years old to those guys was just a whippersnapper, but I would say most of it was being female.

Surprisingly enough, I had trouble with skippers' wives as much as with skippers. One skipper's wife said that he didn't work on a floating bordello and she wasn't going to allow females on his boat. Luckily I didn't have to do anything. The company told him, "You take women." I ended up refusing to take another trip with him. He made my life impossible. Oh, he was on my case about everything right down to how clean I kept my cabin, whether my bed was made every day.

But I was in a better position than some of the other gals that work as deck hands. They can be shit on a lot easier than I can. You know, there's a dividing line between officers and crew, so they couldn't mess with me as much.

The last skipper was the one I worked with most, and it's funny, he was one of the most outspoken ones about not having me on the boat. When he went into the office and they told him he would have to take me, he thought the roof was going to come down. But after two days, he actually called me into the wheelhouse and said, "You do the best job of any second mate I've ever had. You can come back any time." That was the nicest thing that happened in the three years I've been at sea.

The most subtle way they show appreciation that you're doing a good job is the fact that they leave you alone instead of, when you're navigating, being up there every fifteen minutes to make sure you're doing a good job. Not seeing the skipper is the best vote of confidence, especially on the Inside Passage up to Alaska. It's a real narrow channel, and if they let you take the way through it by yourself, it's a real pat on the back. With one skipper I ran into a fishing boat fleet of about two thousand boats, and he was up there every time I changed course, whether it was two or three degrees or a lot. Every time he came up to see why. By the end of four hours of that, you don't even trust yourself.

The men I worked with either had the attitude that "In spite of that fact that she's a woman she does a good job, so she's okay," or "I don't care what she does, she's a woman and she's never gonna do the job." What can you do? You can't change these guys. And actually I ran into more trouble with people who were trying to be helpful. You know, "She's such a frail, little thing, she can't lift that so I'll do it for her." I swear I spent more time telling somebody to get out of the way and let me do it myself. That, as far as I was concerned, was worse than the guy who said, "I'll be damned if I'm gonna help her. I'll just leave her alone."

You keep eight people at sea without any companionship of

the opposite sex, the topic of sex is gonna come up once in awhile. It's pretty hard to avoid. But as far as anything directed at me, I shut 'em down right from the gate, so I never had any trouble. After living with all those guys at school, you just kind of learn how to deal with them. You make it clear that you're acceptable to some fooling around, but that's as far as it goes. That phrase, "fooling around," gets interpreted wrong. What I mean is statements and joking are acceptable, but no farther. And something that always amazed me is a lot of the men were very intimidated by my husband. He's a fairly large fellow, but I never thought of him as physically violent or anything. A lot of times he would carry my bag down for me on the first morning and talk to the fellows. If he didn't like one of their attitudes, he would say, "Don't let him get away with anything as far as pushing you around." He's very protective.

I've had men tell me, "Jeez, I'd ask you to fool around, but that big husband of yours would probably beat the bejeezus out of me." Having a husband made it a lot different than if I were single, which intelligently doesn't make a lot of sense, but that's the way they saw it.

I did have trouble getting the AB's I was supervising to do what I told them. Part of it was I had AB's forty years older than me, and they're going, "Well, this is just a stupid kid and can't possibly know as much as I do. I'm not going to do what she tells me." Some of the time I handled it on my own.

A lot of times I had the captain step in and say, "Look, you jerk, she's in charge and what she says goes." The worst instance I had was actually with a young black fellow that had a chip on his shoulder and was not going to do anything that I asked him. Luckily one day he started badmouthing me and didn't realize the captain was standing on the deck above him. The captain had him pack his bags when we got back. That was the end of that. The captains don't always back me up. It just depended on whether the captain wanted me there or not.

Beth Gedney, tugboat mate

There are certain runs that this company has never assigned women to. One run in particular is from Sitka to Adak, which is in the Aleutians. It is very strenuous, but it shouldn't be the office's position to tell you that you can't handle it. You should be able to say, either "I don't feel I can handle it" or "Let me try it and see if I can handle it." But the office never gave us gals the opportunity, and we didn't realize it until we got to talking together. Then we women found out none of us had gone on some of the runs. Most of the runs they haven't sent us on are the higher-paying runs, because you get paid more in Alaska and the North Strait, and just because those runs consistently have more overtime, which is a big thing for us. And a lot of times it came down to working that run or not working for a month. I guess in a way it is subtle discrimination as far as pay. I'd never thought about that before.

I know that I did go on our cargo-van run, which goes to Sitka, Juneau, the southeast towns, and when I came back from the run, the gal in the office said, "That's such a hard trip. How did you do it?"

I said, "That was the easiest run I've ever been on." Physically it was the least demanding, but she couldn't believe it, because everyone had convinced her it was too much for a woman.

I've never learned how to handle that. You can't go in and beat on their desk and scream and yell at them, because that's not going to get you anywhere. One of the gals that works with us filed a class action suit against them. Consequently she's usually on the bottom of some kind of list and has a bad reputation. All that because she has the nerve to speak out for her own rights. The men feel we should be happy and shut up because we have a job.

My being gone has been hard on my home life. Much as I try and deny it, I didn't want my husband to be doing anything enjoyable when I wasn't there. I'd call home after a lousy trip, and he'd be telling me about all these parties he went to. I didn't want to hear about it. Also, it's hard getting used to not being home for deaths in the family, illnesses, birthdays, Christmas, graduations. My in-laws just can't understand why I'm not there at Christmas.

My husband's pretty good about doing housework. A lot of times I can tell that he ran around for two hours and did three weeks' worth of work before I got home. That's okay. But I know a couple times I came home and had two or three days off and really resented the fact that I walked into a house that was a wreck and spent one of my two days off cleaning. That didn't sit too well. The last thing you want to do is come home and clean, so he has tried to do more at home.

It would be really hard to go back to tugboating when the babies are born. I know how it felt when I was a kid to have one parent gone all the time. There's some jobs available that are eight to five, like Washington state ferries, cruise boats, and tour boats. I'd like to keep my hand in, but be home at night. The other possibility is working shoreside in the office. A master's in business administration or a degree in maritime law would fit into that very nicely.

Gillnetter

SYLVIA LANGE

Like many people, Sylvia Lange leads a dual life. Hers is split between an apartment in Seattle and salmon fishing in Alaska. She calls it a lifestyle, especially for native people, but is watching smaller runs and limited entry destroy it.

One of my grandmothers was Aleut. The other was Tlingit. My grandfathers were Swedish and German. That is the way Cordoba is—a real mixture. There's Norwegians, Swedes, Germans, Aleuts, Greeks. When the Alaska Native Land Claim Act was passed in nineteen seventy-one it cleaned up the prior treaties— and it worked, so in Cordoba we don't have the same kind of hostility towards natives that you find down here in Seattle. There has always been discrimination in Alaska toward natives. It's something you don't see on the whole, but twenty years ago it was real apparent. In my adult life we've had some discrimination, but nothing serious and now, with ANCSA [Alaska Native Land Claim Act], the natives have real economic power, so the relationship is more on a business level than anything else.

I've never done anything but fish, so I just don't have any kind of employment history at all. I worked in a cannery one year when our boat broke down and as a waitress for seven hours out of an eight-hour shift.

When I was fishing, I didn't think I was doing it for a living. You know, I did it because it was a lifestyle. Cordoba's a town that everyone fishes. That is, except for the women. But my mother did, and we're a real close family, so it was just something I did. The fishing grounds were a ways from town, so as a girl I either stayed in town with a babysitter or went fishing. I wasn't interested in hanging out in town so I went out with my folks.

You had to be licensed to have a net. Fourteen was the earliest you could get a license. As soon as I turned fourteen I got my license and went out in a twenty-two-foot-long open boat, a skiff with an outboard motor on it. The skiff was as old as I was, because my mom and dad had found it on the beach and salvaged it about fourteen years earlier. It was low-sided and wide, probably about six foot wide and made out of plywood. There was a rattly, old, twenty-five-horsepower outboard motor on it. The roller with the net came up over the transom, over the stern of the boat. I had to put a plastic bucket over the propeller of the outboard motor so it wouldn't catch the net as it came up. It was a pretty rinky-dink set-up.

I remember being in a complete tizzy about setting my net in the water for the first time. I didn't know where to put it or what to do or anything. And my father's not somebody who would tell me either. He'd say, "Do it, even if it's wrong, just do it." That's something I still do. You can't learn anything unless you do something. You can fail, but big deal. So there I was without any real distinct ideas of what it was going to be like. You have a net with floats on the top and leads on the bottom so it lies vertically in the water. The fish swim into it and tangle up in it. It's a real fine nylon net. Aboard the boat, you have a drum to reel it in and that's called the reel. As the net is reeled in, you take the fish out and then set it back out.

I put my net in the water and didn't know when I was supposed to bring it in. I hadn't been paying attention. I saw what my mother did when I'd gone out with her, but I didn't know how long the net should be in the water, and I didn't know what the tides were doing, and it was getting dark and I'd have to bring it in pretty soon. So I started reeling it in, and I had a lot of

Sylvia Lange, gillnetter

fish—ninety-seven red salmon and seven king salmon. I was little when I was fourteen and the king salmon were practically as big as I was. Some of them weighed eighty pounds. I didn't know how to pick the fish out of the net, which is something you have to learn. They come in a great, tangled glob and you don't really know what to do with it. All I could do was sit there and cry. I'd untangle them and cry. It was getting dark and I had no idea where I was, couldn't see what I was doing, and my boat was getting full of fish. I thought I was going to sink.

Finally my mother caught up with me, and she was really mad, because I was quite a ways inside the marker, which was illegal. I had drifted with the tide a mile up river where you're not allowed to fish. You know, I was just sobbing by the time she reached me. I told her I didn't know how to get the fish out of the net, so she tied her skiff up to mine and hopped aboard and helped me take 'em out and showed me the way back down. I remember that real distinctly, but I don't remember much beyond that.

Let me explain in more detail what it was like getting a big king salmon out of the net. They were huge fish. One was so gigantic it fit between the ribs of the boat, just fit there tight. The salmon would come up over the roller, and I didn't know what to do with them; they'd be thrashing about and they'd plop right down on the deck of the skiff, and all I could do was sit there and pound on them with my gaffhook. A gaffhook is a real menacing-looking thing. The modern ones look like baseball bats with a big stainless steel hook on the end. The hook is just like a meat hook. If a king salmon is just barely tangled in your net as you see it coming out of the water, you gaff it on the head and haul it in. But as a girl, I couldn't have hauled one aboard if I tried. What I usually did if I saw it just hanging there, I'd try to roll it up in the net and then let the reel haul it in. But then I'm faced with trying to get it out of the net and they're too big for me to move. So all I'd do was slam it in the head with the gaffhook until it was stunned and then I could unroll it. They were still too heavy for me to move, so when I continued picking my net I'd have king salmon in the way. I'd just drag 'em around until I was done.

That first year I made about six hundred dollars, enough for all my school clothes and things. I think my mom and dad absorbed all my costs so every fish I caught generated income for me. Later I kept my own books and got a social security number.

The fishing season runs from May until the end of September. Actually, there are three seasons. The first season is king salmon and red salmon. Then the summer season is mixed— king salmon, red salmon, and chum salmon. Later on you get the silver salmon—coho. Each species has their own value. King salmon can run up to eighty pounds apiece and sockeye salmon is usually only six pounds, but their values are pretty close—per pound. The pink and chum salmon are a lower-value fish, and the cohos are a high-value fish.

In nineteen seventy-one the legislature passed a law that limited the entry to fishing. It said anyone that fished prior to nineteen seventy-one could get a permit to fish if they accumulated a certain number of points. I think it was twenty-one or twenty-two points. The number of permits allowed was based on the maximum amount of people that had fished in the past. Because I had gotten my first license in nineteen sixty-seven, I was one of these individuals, but I had to prove that I had attained those points. When the state sent out their pre-printed form showing how many points they thought you should have, I got two points. And everybody else who had fished since nineteen sixty-seven was immediately given their permit.

So I had to go back and get all my old fish tickets and I hadn't kept good records. That was from the time I was fourteen to eighteen when fishing was just a lark to me. Suddenly it was business, and I had to go about proving I was a fisherman. In my

Sylvia Lange, gillnetter

mind's eye I was, but I still had to prove it to the state, so I went about finding all the fish tickets and what-not.

One of the heavy point things was economic need, and since I was a minor I couldn't prove economic need. Another of the points was how much you invested in fishing, and since everything had been given to me by my parents, I hadn't invested anything.

I was a real special case, so they sent out a state commissioner to interview me. And he said, "You can just tell me, on the level, what you're really doing here, you want this permit so that you can sell it, right?"

You see the licenses have a financial value to them. They're just like a liquor license or any other license. There's a finite number of them and it's an open market system on them. A couple years ago they were worth fifty thousand dollars. Then we had a couple bad years and they went down to twenty thousand. Now they're back up to forty to forty-five thousand. Anyhow, I asked the commissioner where he got off saying something like that. Even if I *did* want to sell the permit, it's certainly my right to do that since I've had it since sixty-seven. On the other hand, it was quite possible I might want to fish for the rest of my life.

The commissioner got real nasty about it. He couldn't believe I was serious about fishing. A lot of wives in the past had licenses so they could go out on the boats with their husbands. To even cut up fish you had to have a license. People who hadn't really fished in the past, but had fishing licenses, wanted to get permits because they had value. So I could understand to a degree why he was saying these things, but *I wasn't* somebody's wife. I was there by myself, and all the fish tickets had been made out to me personally, and I had my own gear, which saved me. Finally they gave me an interim permit which I fished on for three or four years.

Limited entry really affected the native lifestyle, especially in the Cordoba area. In the villages natives lived a subsistence life and knew nothing but fishing. When limited entry came along, only the heads of households were given permits. Consequently the children of these permit holders weren't given permits, and the lifestyle was deeply affected. That's the thing about fishing. It's a lifestyle. It's something that you just do.

During the fishing season, we have different regulated hours. They're regulated by the State Department of Fish and Game or biologists, depending on where the fish are. In the spring season, the first period runs from Monday morning at six to six Wednesday morning, and then it's closed period. It opens again on Thursday morning at six to six Saturday morning. It's called a split week. You have forty-eight on, twenty-four off, and thirty-six on, or something like that. You spend that entire time out on your boat. The boats have all the amenities—bunk, sink, stove. During the off time you repair your net or fix your engine or whatever. The split week usually gives you just enough time to do some repairs on board. You leave town on Sunday evening and don't get back until Saturday, so your boats have to be set up to live on. Your net's in the water just as much as you can keep it there. The fishing grounds are anywhere from twenty to eighty miles away from town, so the canneries send out tenders that pick up the fish and bring us groceries and fuel.

I make a comfortable living from fishing, but I couldn't support a family on what I make. Fishing is strictly a question of motivation. You can do whatever you set your mind to. You get out of it a lot of what you put into it and, because I just have myself to support, I don't take some of the chances that other people do. Sometimes with your equipment and weather, you don't have a choice and you do what you have to do. But I know a lot of fishermen who are very motivated, and they wanna be out there twenty-four hours a day giving it one hundred percent, and

Sylvia Lange, gillnetter

I don't allow myself to do that. Life isn't long enough to be spending so much energy all at once. Every year somebody dies on the flats. It's a river delta right on the Gulf of Alaska, so it's unprotected. There's a bar line, and you either fish inside or outside the bars. But whichever you choose, you have to go over the bars to do it. On nice days that's no problem, but if you're out there fishing and the weather comes up, you have to go back into that bar through breakers. How long you wanna stay out there, and if you wanna go through at night or at the edge of the tides, where the conditions are very poor for crossing the bar, depends strictly on what kind of gamble you want to take. And I just don't want to take too many gambles because it's scary enough. All of this, then, is weighed against eventually how many fish you're gonna catch. I generally just keep myself alive and compete to where I feel respectable about it.

I really started competing with the other fishermen in nineteen seventy-six. I got my first good boat that year. It was an older skiff with a little cabin on it. For the first time I started going out by myself and staying out the whole week. Previous to that I had the open skiff and would go back to my parent's bigger boat at night. My mother would be on board and have dinner made. It was just like going home for the night.

That was a really good season, and I was able to get a bank loan for really good equipment over the winter. I had a boat shop build a boat just the way I wanted it. That boat changed my whole way of fishing. I didn't just putz around making do. I worked about a third as hard as I had in the past and caught three times as many fish. It was a real revelation the way people started treating me differently. Up until that time I was not exactly a mascot, but I think that's how I viewed myself. I was cute and unique—but when I got the bowpicker I had equipment that other people actually envied. I had better equipment than some of my brothers who had been fishing for years. It was fun, it was different; I discovered in myself that I could do things I didn't know I could do, and I became one of the boys, genuinely.

Some people weren't really hostile, but were bewildered as to why I would want to fish in a serious manner. One fellow in particular thought I had no business doing it. One day I was mending my net when he came by and said I wasn't doing it right and got into a conversation with me about why in the world was I doing this and didn't I realize it was dangerous, and that I had no business fishing, because I was making other people concerned about my safety. It struck me very odd, and I laughed.

No one had ever said these kinds of things to me before. My dad had always encouraged me. In fact, when he saw my bow-picker, he ordered one just like it. But I do think it bothered him some that it looked like I was going to be a fisherman for the rest of my life. He really did want me to be a professional of some sort. Now I think he's just as proud of me, even though I didn't turn out to be a lawyer like he'd envisioned. One aunt of mine, who raised several boys, told my mother, not me, that if she had it to do all over again, she'd do it just like I've done. That was one of the nicest things I've heard. All of her life she'd fished some, but had to give up a lot of things.

I'm a true colleague with the other fishermen. They respect my opinions and know that when I talk about something, it's because I know about it; I've lived it, and it's not like I'm faking it. Generally I don't have troubles, but I don't think I will ever have another boy friend who's a fisherman. It's just too close. The fishing community is so small. Your livelihood is your life and it's all intertwined and it's really nice to get away from it—and not to be talking fishermen, fishing, and boats. Out of the five hundred and twenty permit holders in the Cordoba area, only two or three women actively compete. There's no doubt

Sylvia Lange, gillnetter

about it being male dominated. And I would like to have the companionship of more women. Like I said, then you wouldn't be talking boats and fishing all the time.

But I guess I am pretty well accepted by the other fishermen. This last year I was elected to the board of directors of the marketing association. As independent businessmen, we're not allowed to collectively bargain, so we do our price negotiation through the marketing association. It's an old-fashioned system. The processors call up to talk price and the negotiating committee will meet with them. Prior to that we will have come up with what we think is fair price and will compare their offer to that. We'll kick the offer around a bit and then present it to the membership with a recommendation to accept or reject it. If the membership doesn't want it, then we will go back and forth. If by May fifteenth, our opening day, we don't have a price, it's considered a strike.

To circumvent this process last year, I was part of the getting together of a fishermen's co-op to market our own fish. We don't have processing capabilities, so we had to subcontract all of that. Our costs were astronomical and we didn't meet the ground price which the other processors were paying, but this next year I think we will. This year we're gonna probably lease a floating processor. Theoretically, with a co-op we should do really well because the profit will go back to the producers, but the six land-based processors are throwing chinks into the machinery, so to speak. They have the marketing areas all sewn up. We're trying to develop new markets domestically, but mostly we have to rely on the Japanese. Japanese are the biggest buyers of salmon. Their whole culture is practically built around seafood. It is starting to come together.

I guess I'm just an activist at heart. It's the politics of it, I think; I like to have a hand in the decision-making process of things which affect my life. I can't turn a deaf ear to politics.

Papermaker

BEVERLY BROWN

She was described to me as neither very articulate nor overly bright. I think my middle-class informant was grievously mistaken.

I've always done a lot of needlework. Needlework and bead-work, any kind of real intricate work with your hands, I liked. In fact, I still embroider a lot. But I don't tell too many people about that or that I spent fifteen months living in Israel and have traveled throughout Europe. When you work in a mill like I do, with people who are lucky if they make it up to Bellingham and back, you don't say much about anything else. A paper mill is like being in a very tight family. It's the only place I know of where a job is like family. It's a clique. It's very tight and no one just comes in there thinking they're going to be a papermaker. I never went in there with that attitude. I went out there because it paid good and if I had to work I might as well work for the money.

I had done warehouse work for a small company down in Seattle. They sold out to some California people and we were all laid off. So I came back to Everett and I go, "Four dollars and eleven cents an hour! Wow!" That was in nineteen seventy-three. I'm on my second time around down there. I started in seventy-three and quit in seventy-five to have my little boy. I stayed home with him until he started walking. They rehired me in nineteen seventy-six, and that's when I decided to change areas where I worked.

Beverly Brown, *papermaker*

Before, I'd been real happy hand packing, roll inspecting—just standing there for eight hours. But when I came back and I was in the same place, I just couldn't take it. I don't know why. It seemed like I wasn't going anyplace, and I knew they were going to automate finishing and that would do away with me. The wrapping and packing of the finished paper products like toilet paper would all be done by machines, so I put in my bid for the paper mill and all the other things that would open up, like material handling and shipping.

The paper mill bid came up first, and the men below me in seniority just hit the ceiling. "Oh," they said, "that's no place to go. That's no place for a woman. The last woman that was out there, she got hurt." And she *did* get hurt. That was her, it's not me. And there was a reason why she got hurt and, I mean, everybody knows it. She was careless around machinery. She didn't think before she did things and got caught in one of the rewinds. They said, "That's gonna happen to you. Every woman that's been out there has been hurt. It's no place for a woman."

And I said, "Well, there has to be a reason why they got hurt. Did you teach them the right way the first time?"

They said, "Well, we tell 'em."

"Yeah," I said, "but telling them is different than showing them. How about—do you show the men?"

"Well, we *work* with the men, too."

"But," I said, "you work with *women*, too."

"Women just don't understand machinery." I heard this over and over again as they tried to talk me out of going.

And the different people I worked with, the men *and* women, who knew me from before and then knew me when I hired back in, wanted to let me know that they were going to pray that I should change my mind. Oh, but I was really upset about it, and I said, "Let me try, let me try! I want to try!"

Then the men higher up in the company that are over everybody in the paper mill decided they had to interview me. I'm not going to give names because these men know who they are and they just know for a fact. They finally decided to let me try for ninety days and, if I didn't like it, I could go back to the other side without losing my position.

No matter what I do there I get the fringe benefits, like your medical, your dental, and everything else. When you hire in you get this as a package, but out in the paper mill the *money* was there. When you moved up from a position you didn't move up for pennies like in finishing. You moved up for dollars out there. From one position to another there's sometimes a dollar, two dollars difference in pay. When I went out there as a roll handler, I got eight-something an hour. Now as a junior fourth hand I get eleven dollars fifty-and-a-half cents an hour. The highest paid man, a machine tender, runs the machine. He makes sixteen dollars an hour.

I started out in the paper mill throwing rolls. They call it bouncing rolls. You throw thirty-five-pound rolls—twenty-three to a shaft—onto a pallet. You pick them off a conveyor belt and stack them four or five high onto the pallet. All day long— all day long. And they're a nice size—they're hefty. I had to build myself up a lot to do that job.

After that I went into broke handling, making beaters. That consists of taking paper that they can't use as a finished product and repulping it and sending it back to the machines again. You put one-and-a-half tons of finished broke, which is the paper that is being reprocessed, into a beater and you add water, steam, and bleach and pulp it up, and you turn it white and send it back to be used on the machines again. To get an idea what it is like, imagine you're talking to a housewife. It's just like you had a beater and a bowl and you keep adding to it. And you have this big agitator, like an airplane engine, to beat all this up while you're cooking it and adding the different acids and the bleach to it.

Beverly Brown, papermaker

You dump these carts full of paper into this big beater. These carts are, oh, about five feet long, maybe three feet wide—full of paper, clear high. You can imagine how heavy they are. The carts are dumped by hand. They have a door in the front. You hit the paper out this door into the beater. I kick it. You're not supposed to kick it out, but you have to wear a safety line to do it because you're around this beater. If you ever went down in that beater, the only thing they'd ever find of you is what's metal—your teeth fillings and your belt buckle is about all they'd find. No one has gone down in *this* plant, but I've heard of people *nearly* falling in. If it wasn't for their safety line, they would have fallen in. We've had scares that someone did, but I've heard that up north they *have* fallen in.

After that I moved up to train as a fourth hand. That's where you work in what they call pulp. They work more or less with the paper mill, but they aren't considered a machine crew. Being on a crew has a lot more status.

As a fourth hand you help the third hand change the blades, rewind, help core up, and if the machine hays out you're right there with her. Let me explain what that all means. Haying out is where they have a hard time keeping the paper on the reel, and the best way to explain that to a fella who doesn't know is—it's just like rolling a big piece, a big roll of toilet paper on a cylinder. This is what it does. Paper follows smooth surfaces, so when your pulp first comes out it goes over a wire that more or less shapes it to the uniform-size paper they need. Then it goes over these different felts, a fabric material. Your paper isn't dry or anything. It's lying just like cookie dough, not baked, on this felt and at the same time pressure is applied on different rolls to flatten out the pulp into paper. Then it goes through drying, and how much crepe they want determines how dry they want it to get.

After reaching a certain dryness it hits the blade that crepes it, and then it goes through a dryer to get the dryness needed to make a certain weight of paper. Your different weights would depend on if you want paper towels, toilet tissue, or other paper products. Then it is either made two-ply or decorated and is ready to go to packaging. It's a big process.

Changing the blades that crepe the paper is a little scary. They're really big blades, right? They're very long and a little thicker than a razor blade and probably four inches wide, and you go the whole length of the machine putting the blade in. You see, when the blades get worn sharp they start causing problems with the paper coming off the dryer, so you have to change them. I wear gloves. It would be real easy to cut yourself. I wouldn't want to get in the way of a blade for anyone. You don't stand around when they take it out, and you don't stand around when they put them in, because *they're sharp*. Putting one in is quite a stretch for me. Everything out there is made for about a six-foot person, I swear, and I'm only five-five. I'm second to the shortest of all the crews.

When I went out into the mill they told me, no matter how long I'm going to be out there—it could be twenty-five, thirty years—every day I have to prove myself. I had to follow a bad path because of the women who'd been hurt and who couldn't handle the job and had given up. I wasn't that way. There was something in me that said, you know, "What's so bad about this?" And I just carried through. I wasn't out there for any big women's rights thing or any ERA thing. I wasn't out for that. I was out there because all I could think of was, "I have a house to support and a child to support and I'm not going to *ever* depend on welfare." I'm just stubborn. I was going to make it. I wanted it that bad. So I carried through. And every day I make it part of my work to learn something new, because there's so much on those machines to learn.

It has not been easy though. The men harassed me a lot. I've had a few guys shove and push me and pull me around—push me out of the way. I didn't care for it, and it upset me. I told the

Beverly Brown, papermaker

supervisor about it, but you would have to be down there to understand what it was like. I came unglued a couple times. I just excused myself from the job, which you really don't do, but I did, and I went in the women's room, and I cried, because a man pushed me under a machine. And I don't want to be pushed around a machine, and then I'd tell the supervisor about it and nothing would ever take place, you know, because they don't come up against this man because he's so mean. They don't *ever* say anything against him. They just say, "He's *known* for that. He's *known* to push people around. He's *known* to throw a punch. He's *known* to do this. I mean, he's done it with *everybody*. What makes *you* so different?"

Aside from the physical, I've heard stuff about women doing a man's job from all the angles. The men admit they think it's a man's job and a woman has no right out there. I always ask them back, "You get the book and you show me where it's written in black and white that this is a man's job and then I'll think about it." They've never been able to provide me with that book, but everybody's told me that.

Everybody in management, from the head guy on down, said, "It's always been a man's job." I've even gone to personnel and asked for their help and they've said, "Hey, it's just like the blacks had to fight down South about sitting in the back of the bus. You take the back seat."

. . . I've had supervisors try—it's always a big joke. "Let's get Beaver"—that's my nickname—"behind the machine." Because see there's a big aisleway behind the machine that no one can see anything that goes on. I mean, there's a lot of places in that mill—there's a lot of nooks and crannies that no one would ever find you. I've had a lot of men try to corner me—just thinking it was fun and jokes. *I* didn't think it was fun and jokes, and I let them know now.

Men! I swear their whole life is sex anyway. They come out with some really weird things that women wouldn't even think about, much less talk about. Like for example—"You aren't going to get your tit caught in the winder, are you? The other lady did. We don't want you to do that." "Gee, you could show a little bit more cleavage there." "Boy, we sure like the way you bounce when you bend over." And they make fun of the way I walk, or "Boy, Bev, you're putting weight on. Look at that ass on you."

"Well, shoot, I know it," I said. "I just have to get back to this manual labor again just like you guys."

They also make a lot of fun of me bending over. They always tell me, they've warned me—"Don't bend over like that in front of me, you know better." If I do, they get a broom handle, a air hose, or whatever and—you get some really weird people out there. I'm not kidding. We get some real weirdos.

I've had to put emotion aside—just say there's no such thing as having feelings. But I still will get hurt if someone comes up and says, "What a dumb broad," if they aren't kidding. But you don't let them know it. If they're kidding and I know it, I just kid them back. I've learned how to come back with some pretty smart remarks.

When men touch me, the first time I accept it as an accident. The second time I just tell them right out, "Watch it, Buster. If you really want your front teeth, you really like to look nice— just watch where you put your hands." I really do. I have to now. That's the way it is.

Other times I'll decide if you want to be that way I can be the same way. I say, "You grab me there and so help me, I'll tear your balls off." And I do—you think it's funny, but it really puts them in their place more so than you would think. And when you start talking about messing around with their male physique, you know, it's a no-no. Females, it's fine, but the men— they can get sensitive about it. I've learned how to hit home really fast.

Beverly Brown, papermaker

Another thing that really ticks the men off is to have you give them the finger. Boy, they come unglued. It's okay for a man to flip another man off—give them the finger. Fine. Have a woman do it to a man sometime. They come unglued. "Don't you ever do that to me!" It's just the worst disgust. "It's just disgusting to us, just downright intolerable!"

But a lot of the times they will do it to me, and I'll look at them and I'll go, "God, I only wish. I'd rather be doing that now than what I'm doing here at the time." Because usually it's a bad job when guys lose their tempers bad enough to give the finger to somebody or flip somebody off. It has to be a really grungy day, so a lot of times I just look back at them and say, "Oh, you only wish," or "Wishful thinking on your part." And it stops them in their tracks three-fourths of the time.

When I first started working out there, I was very embarrassed by things like that. I was very upset about it. I didn't like it. I wasn't used to it. I'm still not used to it, but now I expect it to happen—being around men. I'm still not used to it. How does it make me feel? Nothing—I don't have any feeling towards it any more. I really don't. Not any more. I've gotten hard to my feelings. Let's put it this way. If I went home from work and had an old man sitting there, I would probably beat him up. You know, that's how I feel towards men sometimes when I come home from work. It's lucky that I don't have anybody sitting here at the house. I come home and take my frustrations out. On my boy I never have and never will, because he's so much a part of me. But if I had someone, a boy friend—I don't. I don't have any boy friends, you know as boy friend boy friends or lover boy friends. I just don't. I just haven't. I don't have any girl friends. I stay with my son and myself here. If something really bothers me, I come home and I have a good cry about it. That'll make me feel better and I'll go to bed and forget about it. And something, if it really, really bothers me, I'll write it down. But then it's shut up, shut away, and nothing's ever brought up about it again, because I guess I've just, you just get numb to it, more or less, because a lot of times it happens over and over again.

I was married for two, two-and-a-half years. My husband—ex-husband now—worked for the same company. We both worked different shifts. He knows that outfit. My ex, he's been down there now for sixteen years, something like that. He was really against my going out into the mill, but he didn't come out and say, "No"—not to do it, not to try it. He just was against it because of how men are set against women being out there, and the work it consists of, and of the paper mill being a very tight family.

I get child support from my ex-husband. And he's good on it—sometimes not. I don't force it. I make more than he does, so I don't force it—never have. He's very self-centered so he comes first, and Aaron, our son, comes maybe third or fourth in line, after he gets through with all his friends and everything else, but he still has made quite a bit of time for Aaron. And a lot of times I'm real grateful that he doesn't spend a tremendous amount of time with the family and make it harder on me.

I mean, I make a home life just for my son and me, and nobody else. I make our home as cozy as I can. I try to make it a nice place for both of us to come home to. It's our isolation from the world. Both my son and I, if he has a bad day at school or at the babysitter's, or I have a bad day at work, this is our place to come to. We're very close, maybe too close, like they say. It's just that we don't find that much time together, so when we're together, we're *together*. I've never made a thing of going anyplace without him. On my vacation, like I'm home now—this whole week is *his* week. He had his birthday party this week at his cousin's place. After school we go places he wants to go. This is our week to be together. And everything I do, any time I have off, is our time together. Aaron comes first, no matter what.

Spending time with Aaron is much more important to me

than some other things like vacuuming; things like that—just to me—come last, later. When things really buckle under and I feel like I'm just swimming, I get help. I go out and have a lady come in and do the work. She more or less knows what has to be done. I'm not a Supermother. I keep my boy clean and keep his clothes clean, but when it comes to the house—yes, you will see needles from the trees outside on the floor here and there. You will see dust on my tables. I'm just not going to let that bother me.

I keep in touch with what my boy does in school and go to the pancake dinners, or any festival things he has, or circus things he participates in. I like to make sure he gets his end of the social aspect of growing up. But me? I just don't think of myself. I don't know how to think of myself.

I have a hard time participating in social things. I feel like I'm so different than the people around me. They've made me feel that way. I don't associate with a lot of women. I work with nothing but men. I see the women come through the paper mills, but they aren't working there with me side by side for eight hours a day, seven days a week. So I get out of touch with women's talk. I get out of "Well, what's in *Better Homes and Gardens* today?" or what's going on in this or that, what are good buys, how to make meaals, who we're entertaining, where I'm going out to have a good time. The men just aren't into that. Three-fourths of the men you talk to, their main thing is sports, and I haven't learned that much about sports, so I'm in a limbo. I can hear what the men are saying, I can hear what the women are saying, but I'm just right there in limbo. I'm in a real twilight area. I can't say I have a bad relationship with women, but I can't say it's really good either, because I don't associate with them. I can't say I have a bad relationship with men. I don't know. I really don't associate with them. I'm right in that limbo.

I'm not a macho person but I don't really lean too far to the left because I'm not a real feminine person. You know, I'm not a really frilly, squeaky, high-voice, "Oooo, poor little me," and I'm not a real "Boy, let's get out there and cut another cord of wood." I'm right in the gap. I mean, I do go out and cut my own wood, because I have my own stove, but yet I could go out there and bake a dozen cookies better than most women. It's hard. I haven't found anybody that fits into that area that I can talk with, you know, intimately, yet be accepted for what I do. Men don't want a woman that goes out there, cleans her sledgehammer, and hits a plastic wedge to break wood apart. And a lot of women don't see me as being feminine. They can't talk to me because of the work I do.

I don't even know what to think of myself. I can say that I'm proud I've come as far as I have, being twenty-nine, having my own home, not that it's paid for, but it's my own home. It's nothing extravagant, but it's a home for my son and me, and I've taken on my own responsibilities. I am a responsible person. Oh, I'd like to have a big house some day. My boy and I both are that way, and we keep saying to each other, "Aaron, boy it would be nice to have a new house," and Aaron'll go, "Yes, Mom, I'd like a new house." We'd like to better ourselves—not just material possessions, but I'm putting away for Aaron's education. I want him to have an education. I don't want to see him go into papermaking like me. I don't want him to even touch it. To me, it doesn't take any brains to be—I like to hear me say that, it doesn't take many brains to go into a factory. It's not what I'd want for my boy.

Index

266

INDEX

Metal Trades Council, 165, 167, 171
Mexican-Americans, 99, 101, 108, 109. *See also* Race
Minorities, 8, 10, 81, 83, 99–100, 119, 125, 206, 217. *See also* Race
Moral Majority, 45
Mormons, 59. *See also* Religion
Murray, Katie, 99, 100, 132–139

National Labor Union, 141. *See also* Unions
National Youth Administration, 41, 42
Native Americans, 99, 243. *See also* Race
NiCarthy, Ginny, xi, xvii
Nineteenth Amendment, 4. *See also* Legal equality
Nursing, 143–144

Occupational safety and health, xiv, 51–52, 228. *See also* Accidents; Dangers; Disability; Physical strain
Office of Women's Rights, xiii, 171–172
Office work, 7, 13
Olsen, Tillie, xiii
Oral history, xi, xiii
Outside machinist, 164–175

Pacific Northwest, xii, xiii
Painter, 143–149
Papermaker, 252–262
Paternalism, 59, 197
Pay, 9, 19, 20, 43, 47, 49, 99, 101, 102, 103, 104, 111, 120, 124, 133, 134, 145, 152, 164–165, 180, 186–187, 197, 227, 252, 254
Pfandler, Laura, 5, 19–24, 51
Physical strain, 14, 16, 51, 83, 94, 106–107, 109, 110, 145, 157, 161, 164, 183, 246, 254. *See also* Accidents; Dangers; Disability; Occupational safety and health
Pipefitter, 19–24
Plumber, 53–63
Plumbers Union, 141. *See also* Unions
Political education, 44
Pornography, 20, 60–61, 126, 194
Pregnancy, 7, 16–17, 42, 65, 123, 132, 198–199, 204, 208–209, 222–223
Printer, 226–232
Protective legislation, 142

Quealey, Nora, 6, 52, 91–97
Quotas, 10, 217. *See also* Court decisions

Race, xiv, 10, 99–100, 101, 194. *See also* Alaska Native Land Claim Act; Black Muslims; Blacks; Fair Employment Practices Act; Interracial families; Japanese; Mexican-Americans; Minorities; Native Americans; Racism
Racism, 44, 95, 105–106, 109, 110, 116, 129, 132, 133, 134–139, 157–158, 194–195, 243. *See also* Race
Rathke, Mary, 5, 7–18
Religion, 44, 66, 67, 70, 101, 132, 138–139. *See also* Black